AF371542

*Astonishing
Things*
The Drawings
of Victor Hugo

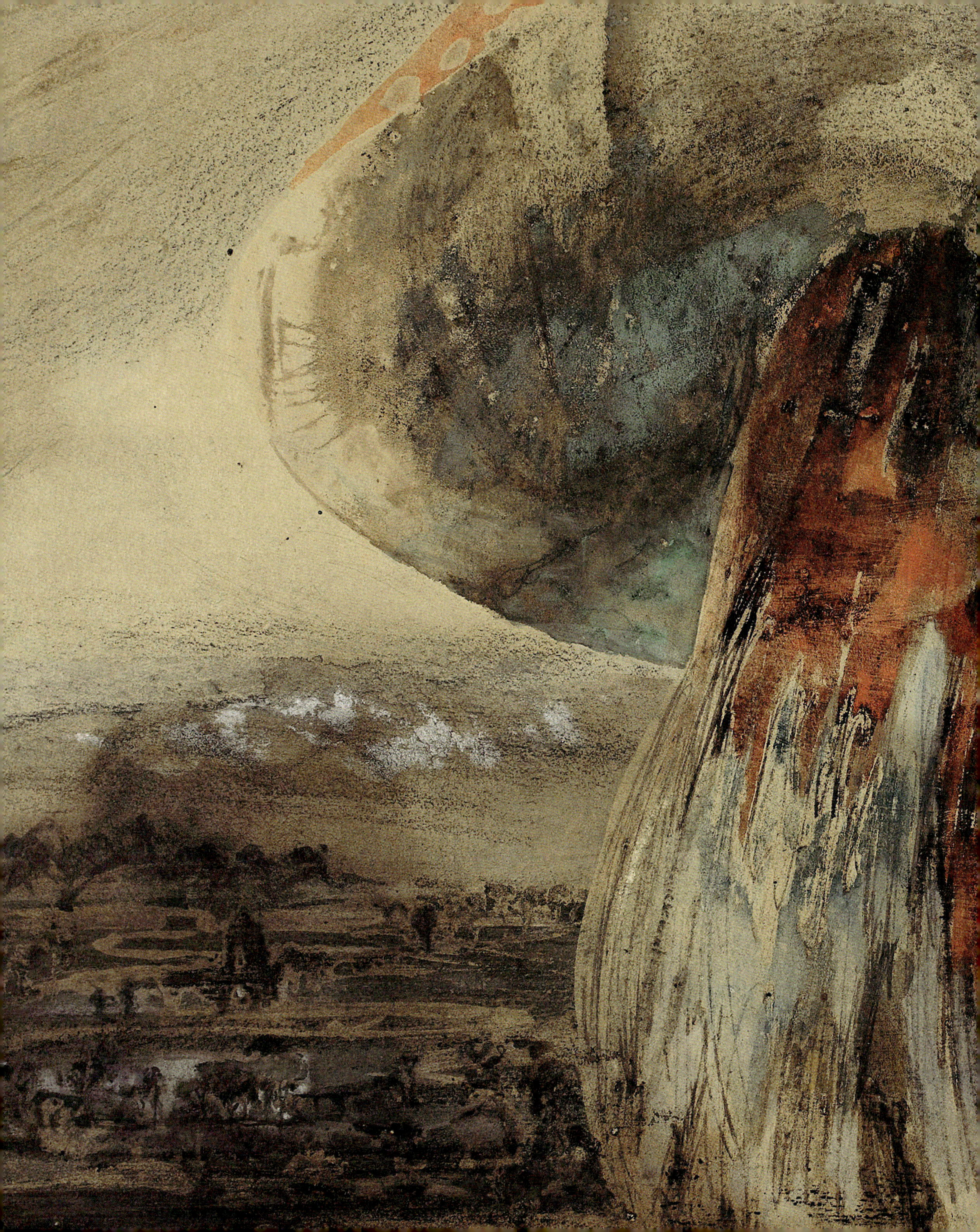

Astonishing Things
The Drawings of Victor Hugo

ROYAL ACADEMY OF ARTS

First published on the occasion of the exhibition

Astonishing Things
The Drawings of Victor Hugo

Royal Academy of Arts, London
21 March – 29 June 2025

Exhibition organised by the
Royal Academy of Arts in collaboration
with Paris Musées – Maisons de Victor Hugo
and the Bibliothèque nationale de France

Supported by

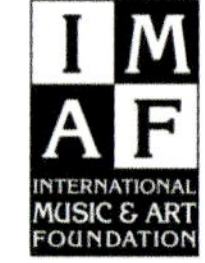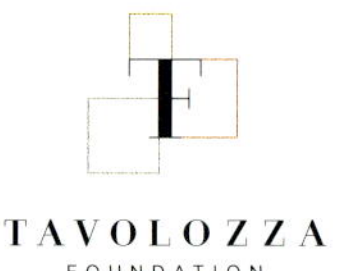

Catalogue supported by

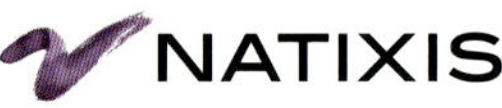

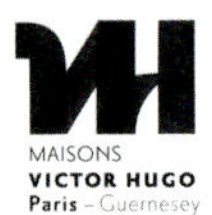

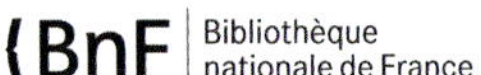

With additional support from

The ISLANDS of
GUERNSEY

Colin McCorquodale
The Dr. Lee MacCormick Edwards Foundation.

This exhibition has been made possible
as a result of the Government Indemnity
Scheme. The Royal Academy of Arts would
like to thank HM Government for providing
indemnity and the Department for Digital,
Culture, Media & Sport and Arts Council
England for arranging the indemnity.

Department
for Culture,
Media & Sport

DIRECTOR OF EXHIBITIONS
Andrea Tarsia

EXHIBITION CURATORS
Sarah Lea
with Rose Thompson

EXHIBITION ORGANISATION
Abbie Latham and Rebecca Bailey

PHOTOGRAPHIC AND
COPYRIGHT CO-ORDINATION
Caroline Arno

EXHIBITION CATALOGUE
Royal Academy Publications
Florence Dassonville, Production
and Distribution Co-ordinator
Carola Krueger, Production
and Distribution Manager
Peter Sawbridge, Head of Publishing
and Editorial Director

Translation from the French
(texts by Thomas Cazentre and
Gérard Audinet): Caroline Beamish
Copy-editing and proofreading:
Linda Schofield
Design: Kathrin Jacobsen
Colour origination and print:
Gomer Press, Wales

Copyright © 2025 Royal Academy
of Arts, London

Royal Academy of Arts
Burlington House
Piccadilly
London W1J 0BD
www.royalacademy.org.uk

EU Authorised Representative
EAS Europe, Mustamäe tee 50, 10621 Tallinn,
Estonia
gpsr.requests@easproject.com

British Library Cataloguing-
in-Publication Data
A catalogue record for this book
is available from the British Library

ISBN: 978-1-915815-11-8

Distributed outside the United States
and Canada by ACC Art Books Ltd, Riverside
House, Dock Lane, Melton, Woodbridge,
IP12 1PE

Distributed in the United States and Canada
by ARTBOOK | D.A.P., 75 Broad Street, Suite 630,
New York, NY 10004

EDITORIAL NOTE
- All works illustrated are by Victor Hugo
  (1802–1885) unless otherwise stated.
- Dimensions of all works of art are given
  in centimetres, height before width.

ILLUSTRATIONS
Front cover: *Octopus*, 1864–66 (cat. 70)
Frontispiece: detail of cat. 8
Page 6: detail of cat. 56
Page 9: detail of cat. 10
Pages 10–11: detail of cat. 35
Pages 50–1: detail of cat. 7
Pages 66–7: detail of cat. 37
Pages 102–3: detail of cat. 38
Pages 128–9: detail of cat. 72

Contents

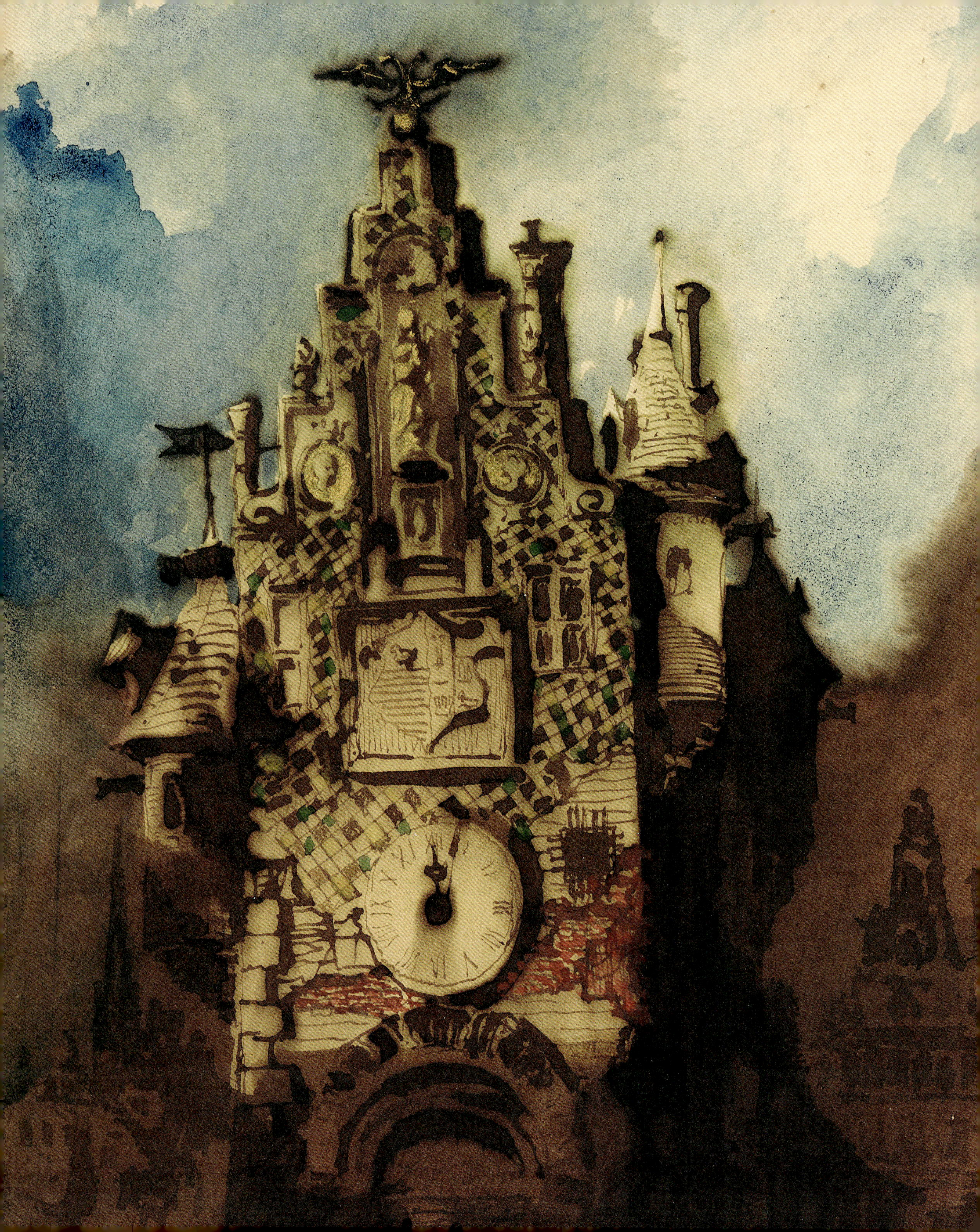

President's Foreword

In a letter to his brother Theo in 1890, Vincent van Gogh compared Victor Hugo's works to 'astonishing things'. We cannot be certain if he was thinking of Hugo's drawings, or passages from his voluminous writings, but his admiration is clear. Like many artists of his generation, for Van Gogh, Hugo was a towering public figure, whose characters and themes became embedded in people's minds as cultural references; Vincent's close study of Hugo's novels coincided with his burgeoning artistic career. As avid print connoisseurs, the Van Gogh brothers would probably have known some of Hugo's drawings from the prints made after them, although at the time of the first exhibition of Hugo's drawings, in Paris, in 1888, Vincent was in Arles. Despite this, a strong link remains between the two artists, for whom both drawing and writing were important activities, dual imagistic processes that bled into, fed and enriched one another. Subsequent generations of artists and writers have admired Hugo's innovations with language, literary form, visual imagery and 'automatic' processes, among them André Breton, who owned two drawings by Hugo, now in the collection of the Centre Pompidou in Paris; Max Ernst, whose artistic techniques frequently resemble Hugo's; and such contemporary figures as Raymond Pettibon and Antony Gormley.

Building on the scholarly foundations laid by Pierre Georgel, who curated the last UK exhibition of Hugo's drawings, at the Victoria and Albert Museum in 1974, the present show sets out to see Hugo's drawings from the vantage point of his own time, considering the different contexts that led him to create these 'astonishing things', but necessarily viewing them also through the lens of our own era, in which the debates around freedom, sovereignty and equality that concerned Hugo remain highly relevant. The curatorial approach puts forward the processes of drawing as a means to explore and express different ways of thinking and knowing.

The exhibition has been curated by Sarah Lea, with Rose Thompson. The selection was made in close collaboration with Gérard Audinet and Thomas Cazentre, specialists responsible for the two most significant holdings of Hugo's work. We thank them both for their constant support, insightful expertise and generous spirit of partnership.

The exhibition has been organised by the Royal Academy of Arts in collaboration with the Maisons de Victor Hugo and the Bibliothèque nationale de France. We thank the late Delphine Levy and Anne-Sophie de Gasquet of Paris Musées, and at BnF, Gilles Pécout, Marie de Laubier, Guillaume Fau and Sylvie Aubenas for their leadership and support; both institutions have granted truly exceptional loans to enable us to present a selection of Hugo's most remarkable drawings from throughout his long life. We thank Claire Lecourt-Aubry and Fabienne Besnard respectively for working closely with Rebecca Bailey and Abbie Latham at the Royal Academy on the complex requirements of exhibiting these fragile works safely. We thank the Musée du Louvre, Paris, for lending an important drawing, and the British Museum, London, and the John Rylands Research Institute and Library at the University of Manchester for lending the few drawings by Hugo in British public holdings.

Special thanks are due to Jean-Baptiste Hugo, Victor's great-great-grandson, for his advocacy of this project, and to the Victor Hugo Society in Guernsey, whose work continues to gather and renew the scholarship surrounding Hugo's legacy. Sarah Lea would especially like to thank Bradley Stephens, University of Bristol, for his encouragement and advice, and Adrian Locke, Chief Curator, and Anna Ferrari, former curator at the Royal Academy, for their instrumental roles in developing the project, which was programmed under the leadership of Axel Rüger, former Secretary and Chief Executive, and Andrea Tarsia, Director of Exhibitions.

The exhibition has been designed by Fieldwork Facility, and we thank Robin Howie and Tilia Bertrand-Shelton for the creativity and sensitivity they have brought to the display, working closely with Satu Streatfield on the lighting design, The White Wall Company and the RA's Sigrid Muller on realising the build and the RA's expert Art Handling team to hang the exhibition. We thank Kathrin Jacobsen for designing this elegant catalogue for RA Publications, and Caroline Arno at the Royal Academy for managing the image rights associated with the exhibition.

We extend our deepest gratitude to our exhibition supporters Natixis, with additional support from VisitGuernsey and the Dr Lee MacCormick Edwards Foundation. The catalogue has been generously supported by the International Music & Arts Foundation and the Tavolozza Foundation.

Rebecca Salter PRA
President, Royal Academy of Arts

Acknowledgements

The Royal Academy would like to thank the following individuals for their assistance in the making of this exhibition and its catalogue: Dawn Adès, Timothy Adès, Cedric Bail, Patrick Belaubre, Roy Bisson, Odile Blanchette, Caroline Bruyant, Hugo Chapman, Emmanuel Coquery, Doireann Cott, Fiona Cox, Ellie Dawkins, Marie de Laubier, Stéphanie Duluc, Nadège Duqueyroix, Ashley Elliot, Guillaume Fau, Mark Furness, Fabrice Golec, Jill Holmen, Richard Howard, Adèle Hugo, Leïla Jarbouai, Laurence Le Bras, Valerie Loth, Larry Malčić, Gilles Pécout, Margarita Pirogova, Gérard Pouchain, Christopher Pressler, Karen Quandt, Marie Robert, Marie-Pierre Salé, Isabel Seligman, Jessica Smith, Bradley Stephens, Gregory Stevens Cox, Valerie Sueur, Flora Triebel, Sadie Twigger, Sarah Vowles, Maria Wehner, Henrik Yau, Michelle Young. We are also grateful to the many staff of the Royal Academy who have contributed to this project.

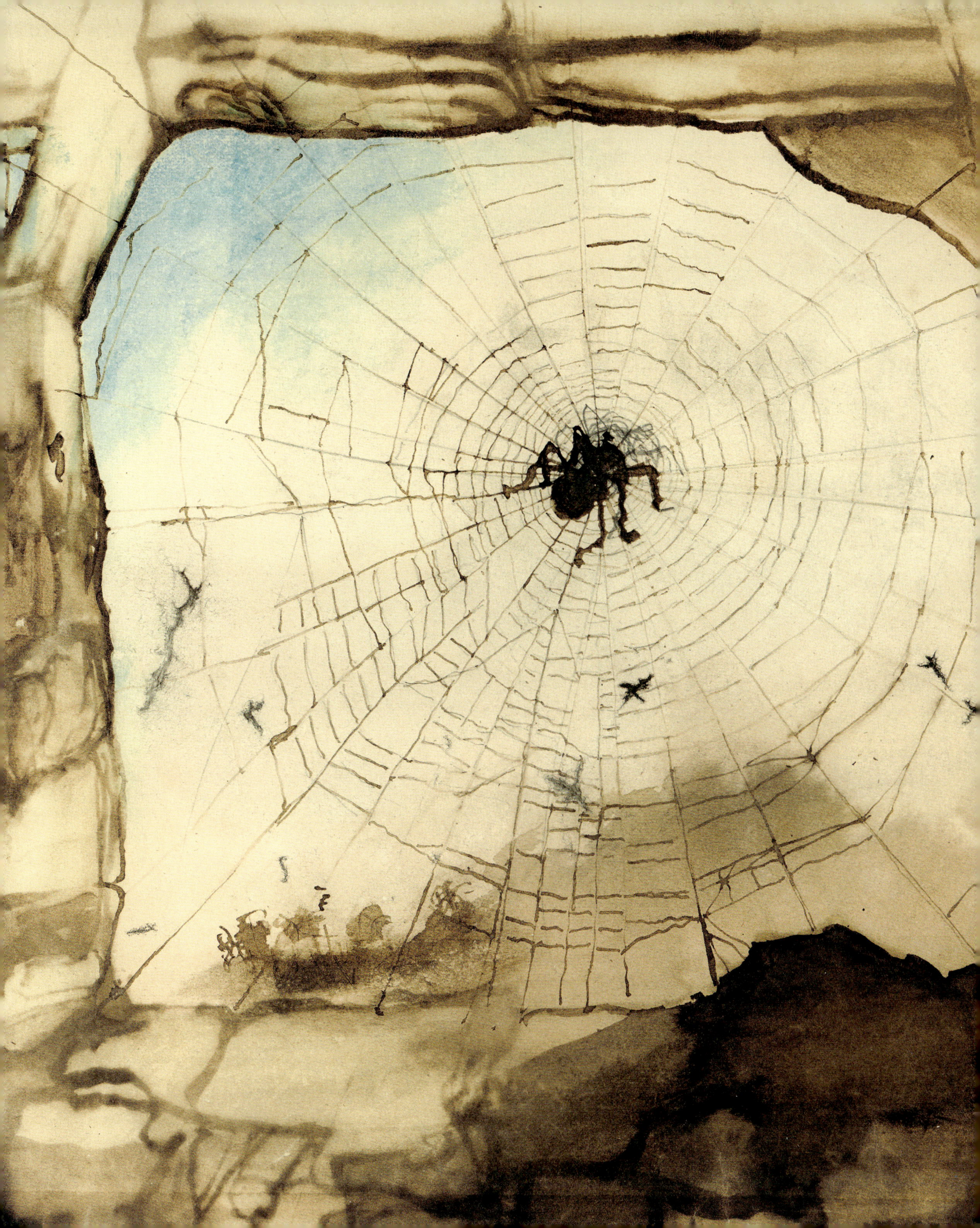

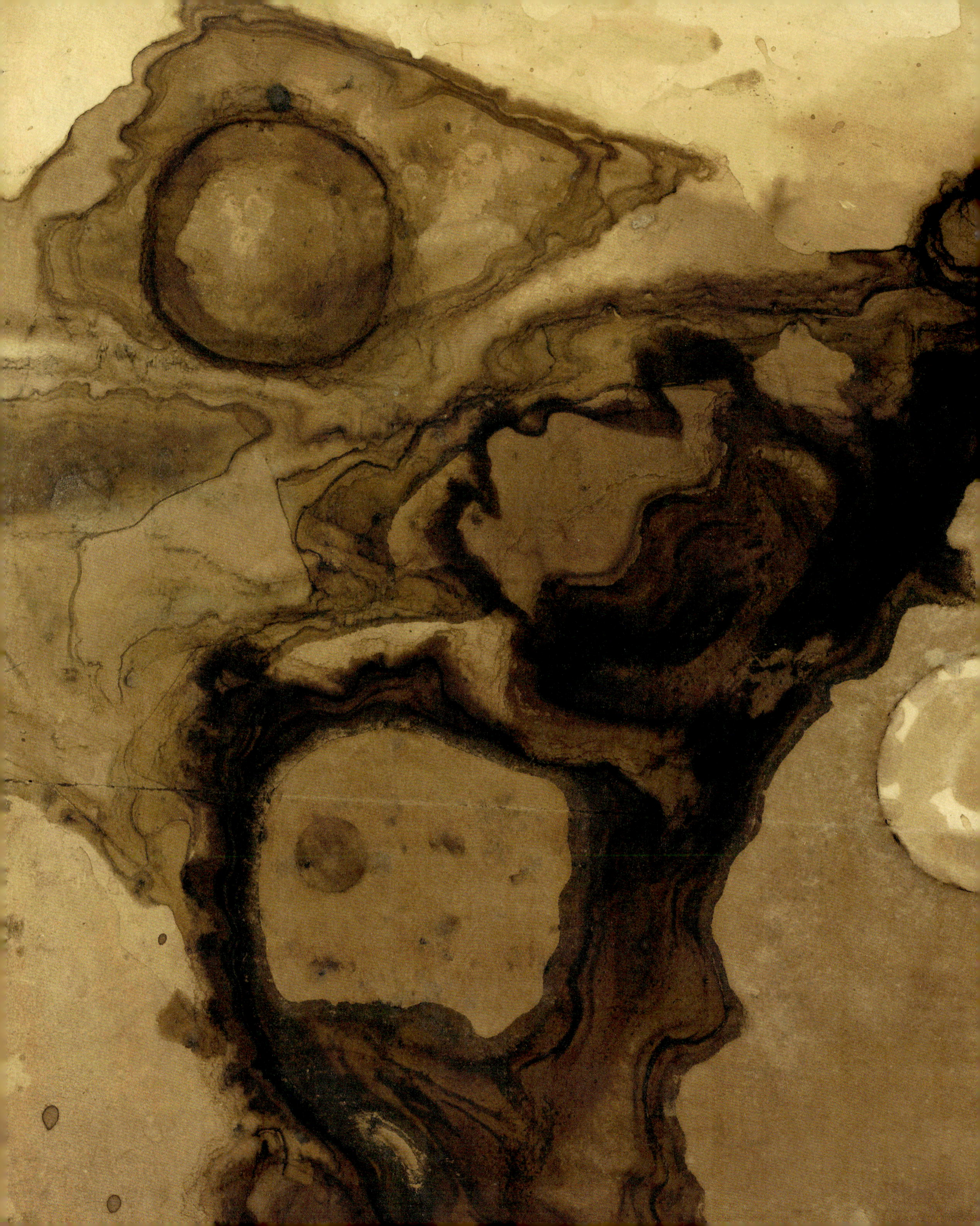

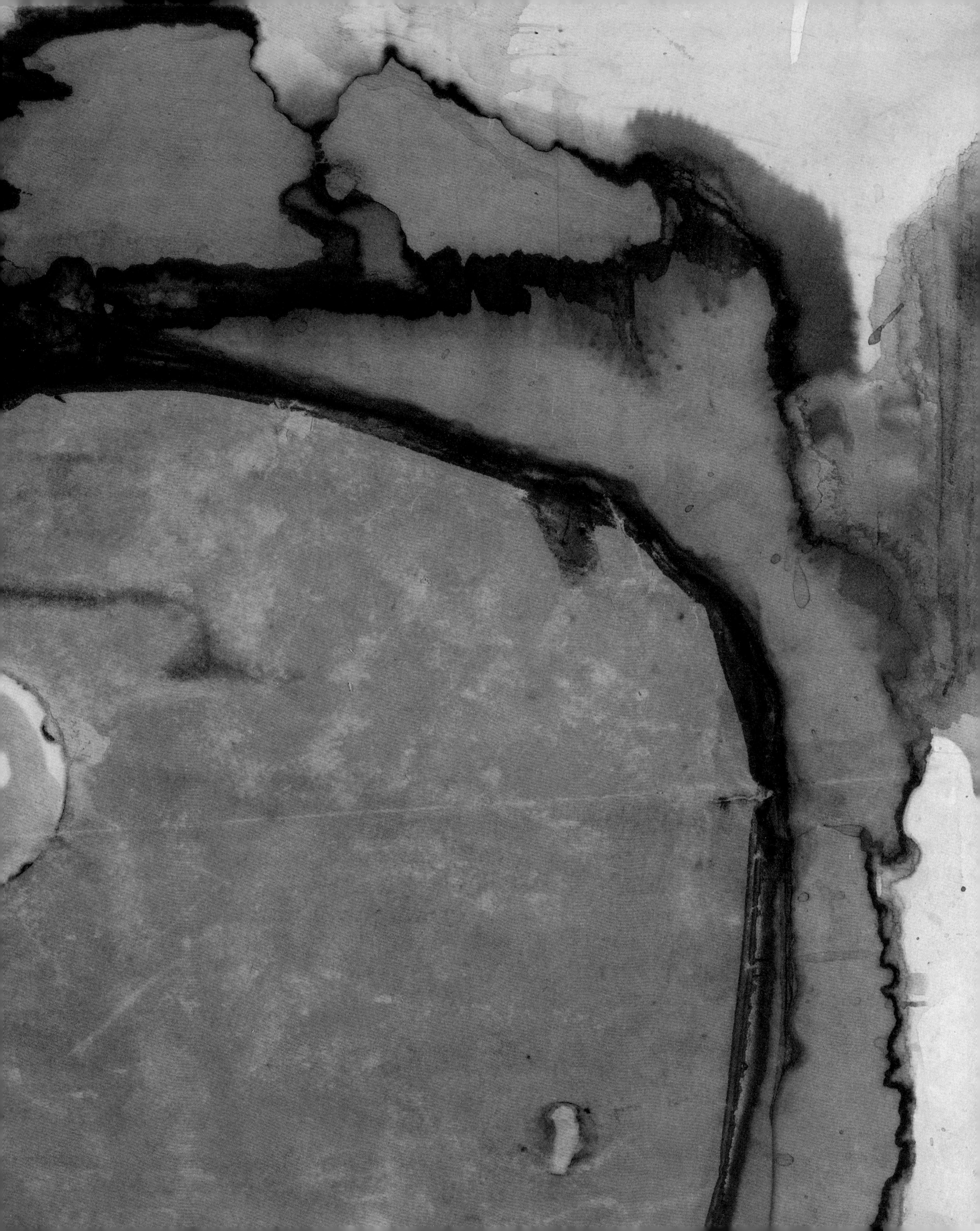

La miltière, le mardi 9 ou 10 mai.
[1825]

Je commence ici, mon cher Paul, avec l'intention de t'écrire en de
[illegible] longue lettre que j'aie encore
écrite depuis que je suis parti. Si
par hasard, elle ne répondait ni à ton
attente, ni à la mienne, n'en accuse
pas mon intention, mais bien je ne
sais quelle cause imprévue qui sera
venue me couper ma satisfaction et mon
loisir. D'ailleurs j'irai [illegible] t'envoie
bientôt à Paris, où je te raconterai
tout ce que je ne [illegible] pas t'écrire.

Je suis pour le moment dans une
salle de [illegible] attenante à la miltière,
le lieu qui m'sert le [illegible] j'écris
sur mon papier de [illegible] dans [illegible]
dont je t'envoie le dernier, puisque
tu désires que ma lettre contienne

N.B. je ne [illegible] pas [illegible] le mardi au mois
suivant. [illegible]

Double Vision: Victor Hugo's Mind's Eye

SARAH LEA

Victor Hugo's oeuvre of drawings would be an extraordinary artistic legacy for anyone to leave. The fact that it is the creation of a writer and political figure of immense fame and influence in the nineteenth century, both in France and the wider world, complicates the standing of these already remarkable works of art. The originality of these works on paper expresses a facet of a prismatic imagination that roamed freely across creative disciplines and private and public spheres. Hugo's relevance was sustained over his long life (26 February 1802 to 22 May 1885) by his near twenty-year exile in opposition to Napoléon III. His status – a symbol of the Republican cause – was used to advocate for civil rights, such as a free press, universal suffrage, secular education, penal reform, the abolition of slavery and an end to capital punishment.

The moulds of patriarchal genius in which Hugo's image were cast represent paradigms that no longer hold water. For some, the dizzying contradictions and indiscretions of his life have undermined the values he stood for; for others, they reflect the times in which he lived and the scope of the issues with which he grappled. In today's world, in which the type of populism that Hugo cultivated often serves less benign objectives, we might reflect on his commitment as a bellowing voice of conscience, in spite of the risk of 'monstrous egotism and complete hypocrisy' – the judgement of one extreme commentator at the time of his death. If, as Karl Marx's son-in-law, Paul Lafargue, pointed out, in practice Hugo's commercialism upheld bourgeois values, Hugo carefully stayed close to power and extolled genuinely held humane principles of justice and equality.[1] In public speeches, which were often reported globally, Hugo expressed total faith in future peace based on a belief in historical progress and the universal fraternity of humankind: 'In the twentieth century, war will be dead; the scaffold will be dead, animosity will be dead, royalty will be dead; but Man will live. For all there will be but one country – that country the whole earth.'[2]

Hugo's beguiling drawings were not exhibited during his lifetime – one of many factors contributing to the extreme difficulty of dating them accurately – but they were

Fig. 1

Letter from Victor Hugo to Paul Foucher, 10 May 1825. Maisons de Victor Hugo, Paris / Guernsey, inv. no. ah420 known to family, friends and less directly to the public via a small number of published prints.[3] In search of an art-historical context for Hugo's drawings, some readings have characterised them as proto-surrealist or expressionist, divorcing them from the complex sociopolitical contexts of their making and emphasising only certain aspects of Hugo's diverse practice.[4] The fact that some of Hugo's drawings might appear abstract to modern eyes should not lead us to assume any direct connection with J. M. W. Turner's experimental paintings of the 1840s, for example, nor the later works of the Impressionists, whose first exhibition, held in 1874, took place at the end of Hugo's artistic life.

Hugo began to draw amid the rise of Romanticism in French nineteenth-century painting, but the grand portraits and tableaux of the Salon have more in common with Hugo's dramatic and narrative writing than his idiosyncratic drawings. A comparable sensibility and context for Hugo's interest in atmospheric effects might be found in the earlier, tempestuous landscape paintings of Georges Michel (1763–1843), an 'artist's artist' on the fringes of professional practice influenced by the Dutch and Flemish schools, later understood as a forerunner to the Barbizon School.[5] As Richard Taws discusses, Michel was perceived in the late 1870s as belonging to a 'community of sensations' – artists unknown to one another but connected by 'a contagious air' – including the then-outsiders of the British school, John Crome and John Constable.[6] It is perhaps in similar terms that Hugo's artistic outlook might be retrospectively understood as sharing elements of Symbolist, Dadaist or Surrealist art. The notion of creative kinship across time aligns with Hugo's thought, but he expressed it primarily in relation to writers, among whom he positioned himself in a pantheon of geniuses from Homer to Shakespeare. In his own lifetime, although Hugo counted such artists as Eugène Delacroix, printmakers as Célestin Nanteuil, photographers as Félix Nadar and critics as Théophile Gautier among his circle, his lack of formal training and his indifference to the professional art world freed him from conventional modes of pictorial seeing. Not simply an amateur, as Luc Sante summarises, 'Hugo approached visual art as if he himself had made the concept up.'[7]

Hugo's primary frames of reference and inspirations for his drawings were his affinities with materials, the people he loved, the domestic spaces in which he lived, the natural environment, architecture, histories of humanity, spirituality and the worlds of his stories and poems, which are always inflected by autobiography. The connection between writing and drawing as parallel activities and confluent streams of thought is vital to an understanding of Hugo's works on paper, which are emphatically not illustrative, but generative.

Writing

Hugo's fame began when he was an adolescent, conservative royalist; in 1819, aged only seventeen, he became a prize-winning poet, and later came to be known as 'l'enfant sublime' by the Parisian literary elite.[8] On 10 May 1825, by now aged 23 – the year he was invited to the coronation of Charles X and was made a *chevalier* of the Légion d'Honneur – he wrote a letter to his brother-in-law Paul Foucher that preceded his first extant sketches by around a decade (fig. 1).[9] In it he urged Foucher to interpret the whorls drawn 'as if haphazardly' across the lines of script: 'Use your imagination. Tell yourself that the drawing was traced by the sun and the shade, and you will see something charming. This is how

Fig. 2

Charles Hugo (1826–1871), *Victor Hugo Writing, Seated at His Table*, 1853. Daguerreotype, plate 12 x 9 cm, frame 14.9 x 12.6 cm, with poem inscribed on reverse. Bibliothèque nationale de France, Paris

Fig. 3

Célestin Nanteuil (1813–1873), *Bug-Jargal*, 1832. Etching, 23.7 x 15.8 cm. The Metropolitan Museum of Art, New York, inv. no. 29.18.4(4)

Fig. 4

La blanche ouvrit de grands yeux / et la noire fit la moue (*The white one opened her eyes wide / and the black one pouted*), c. 1869. Pen and brown ink wash on wove paper, 13.9 x 13 cm. Maisons de Victor Hugo, Paris/Guernsey, inv. no. 946

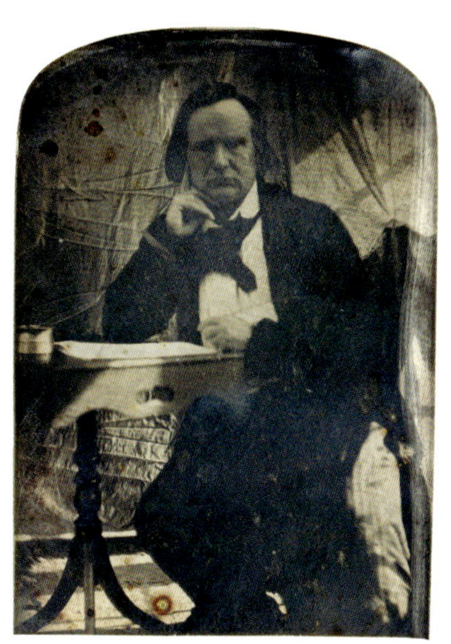

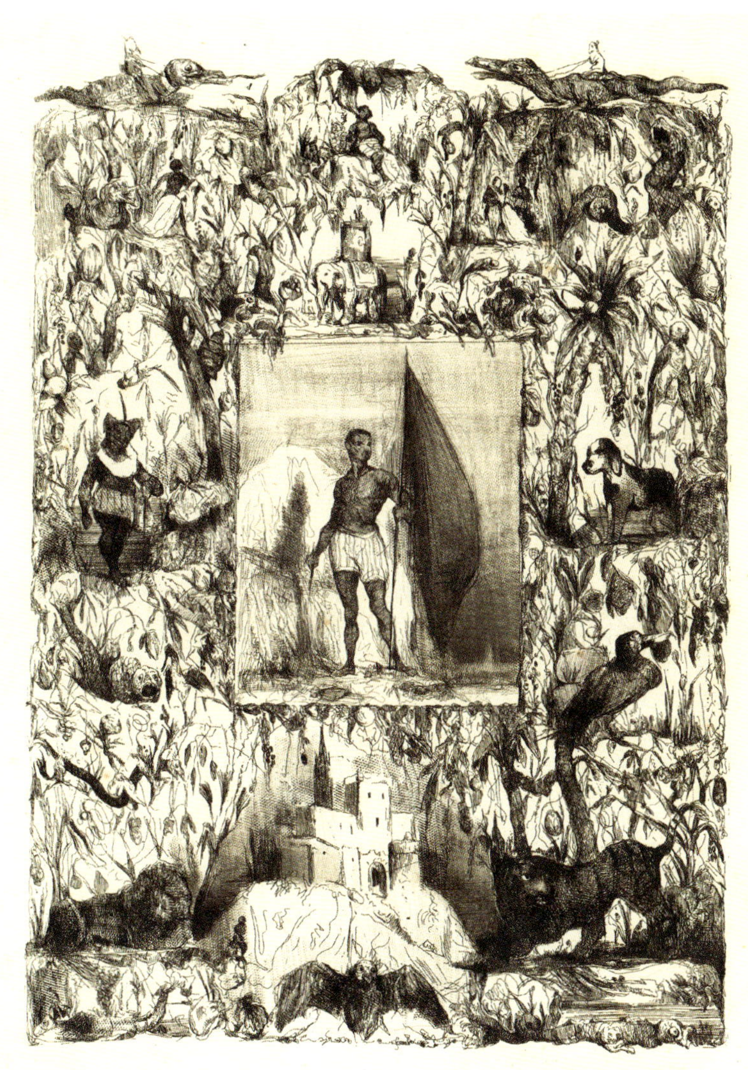

BUG-JARGAL

Publié par Eugène Renduel.

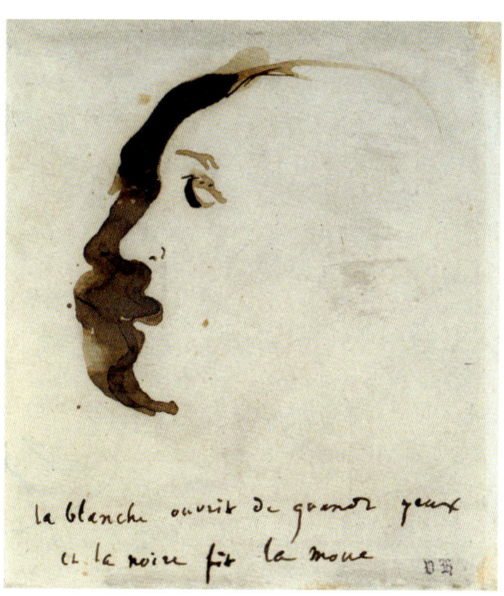

those lunatics called poets proceed.'[10] This self-conscious analogy of spontaneous creativity cast Hugo's body as a medium of nature, consonant with the ideals of romantic sensibility, and even suggestive of the embryonic technology of photography, which his son Charles was to take up in Jersey during the 1850s (fig. 2).

The image of the young poet, seated in an arbour, tracing on his page the shadow cast by strands of ivy, evokes the garden of Les Feuillantines, the Parisian home where the three Hugo brothers, Abel, Eugène and Victor, lived with their mother from 1809 to 1813. This sanctuary they shared with other children, including Victor's childhood sweetheart Adèle.[11] It was to Les Feuillantines, according to Hugo's biographer Graham Robb, that 'every path in Hugo's brain leads back eventually', a still point amid the instability of the 'constantly changing and conflicting loyalties' that characterised Hugo's youth.[12] The antagonism between his formidable parents was exacerbated by a fluctuating political landscape, intertwined with regimes and revolts in France. Hugo's father Joseph Léopold was a general in Napoléon I's army, whereas his 'ideologically progressive but politically conservative' mother Sophie allied herself with the royalists.[13] In these violent, volatile times the children lived for periods with their father near his dangerous military postings. Léopold's and Sophie's marriage broke down in 1815, the year of the Battle of Waterloo, an event termed by Hugo 'the hinge of the nineteenth century' in *Les Misérables* (1862).[14] The garden of Les Feuillantines is recalled in various guises in *Les Misérables* and the plot culminates against the backdrop of the uprising of 1832, the June Rebellion, which Hugo witnessed. In these years his celebrity grew. He scandalised the Académie française with collections of poems such as *Les Orientales* (1829), revolutionised the theatre with plays like *Hernani* (1830) and invigorated the Gothic Revival in architecture with the popular novel *Notre-Dame de Paris* (1831), better known to English speakers as *The Hunchback of Notre-Dame*, a title that Hugo hated.

A less familiar novel that sits uncomfortably in Hugo's literary and political trajectories is the obscurely titled *Bug-Jargal* (1826) (see fig. 3). One of very few European nineteenth-century novels to foreground the Haitian Revolution (1791–1804), it was adapted from a short story Hugo wrote at the age of seventeen.[15] Whether Hugo had any personal or financial connection with Saint-Domingue remains unproven; nonetheless, several characters bear adapted family names and the narrative is interwoven with echoes of Hugo's own relationships.[16] Robb's suggestion that the emblematic 'ug' of Hugo is enshrined within the title is plausible when taking into account Hugo's interest in the aural play of language in his poetry and in the visual play of his name and monogram, rearranged in various permutations in later drawings and interior designs reflecting a fascination with the 'architecture' of writing (cats 4, 9, 57).[17] The novel revolves around two central protagonists, an enslaved African king (Bug-Jargal) and a French military officer, a pairing perhaps recalled in a much later drawing (fig. 4) but which is, in the text, anything but simple. Since its publication, the novel has prompted contradictory reactions, interpreted on the one hand as a subversive, abolitionist text and on the other a reactionary, repressive colonial one. In their separate analyses of the novel, both Chris Bongie and Jennifer Yee have noted that *Bug-Jargal* is permeated by an 'obsessive doubling'.[18] As the novel unfolds, this strategy is used to investigate complex themes of hidden identity, the difficulty of communication or understanding between people, and the unreliability and corruption of language, as well as its importance as the basis of power. Bongie asserts that by refusing to allow the narrative to continue beyond 1791, Hugo problematically reinvented the Haitian Revolution as 'unfinished and potentially reversible'.[19] Yet Hugo's rewriting of this work in 1825 – at the very moment of the Franco-Haitian accord – in a manner that unmasks its own artifice, was a transitional moment for his thought, a nascent shift towards liberalism partly driven by artistic expression.[20]

The point of this digression is to introduce Hugo as an ambitious writer who sought the critical spotlight through controversial subject-matter and experimental literary styles. *Bug-Jargal* probes the vexed relationships between history and language, truth and invention, fiction and reality in ways that are self-consciously immanent in the text. The principle of antithesis would become fundamental to Hugo's thinking and literature, and yet the complexity of the temporal slippages, cycles and connections operating in his imagination required an altogether more subtle expression, layering as they do individual and collective memories. The question is: what did the act of drawing, such an instinctive extension of the travelling of ink across paper, offer to this writer?

Sketching

Hugo drew to entertain his children[21] and his friends in the milieux of literature, theatre, criticism, journalism and politics, in which caricature and satire played a key role in evading changing censorship rules. One type of drawing that emerged from the informality of amateur caricature remained throughout Hugo's life a forum for him to explore characters, be they people he observed, protagonists in his stories, nebulous visions of hybrid creatures or 'types', sometimes inflected by racialised stereotypes. Thomas Cazentre has noted of these 'figurines', as Hugo called them, both their 'challenge to the canons of classical beauty' and the sense of discomfort they arouse in us today: collectively, these grotesque forms exude a frustration or even a misanthropy that Hugo excludes from his writings out of conscience.[22]

Compressed in caricature are modes of observation, exaggeration and invention that Hugo explored in different forms of drawing. He was involved in the scenography of his plays, working with artists, among them Delacroix, who employed various materials and techniques of illusion in stage design. But travel was the catalyst that transformed Hugo into a draughtsman: his illustrated letters (cat. 2), small sketchbooks and large albums from trips during the 1830s and 1840s combine verbal and visual notes, and chart his gradual attainment of proficiency in pencil and ink. He learnt by emulating the qualities of prints by commonly admired artists such as Albrecht Dürer (to whom Hugo addressed a poem),[23] Rembrandt and Francisco de Goya, and from friends such as the artist and engraver Célestin Nanteuil (see fig. 3).[24]

Hugo's trips to the Rhine, the Alps and the Pyrenees were in part 'working journeys' during which he produced travel writings intended for publication, often letters, mostly addressed to his wife Adèle. The motivation for these trips, which re-exoticised well-known paths to appeal to an established international readership for guidebooks, was to escape, not alone, but with Juliette Drouet: muse, lover and an important supporter of Hugo's artistic practices in drawing and interior design. Their relationship, which lasted from 1833 until Juliette's death in 1883, was akin to a marriage.[25]

Parallel paths in Hugo's drawing are indicated by two works of 1837 that he gave to Drouet. In *Malines* (cat. 12) Euclidean space is defined with crisp, effortful control, whereas *Temple Oriental* (fig. 5) comprises an outline filled with decorative patterns without geographical or historical specificity; this pair represent the poles of observation and invention. *Temple Oriental* is one of a group of related drawings that amalgamate imaginary architectural features with sketches of objects of chinoiserie – a passion shared by the couple – at irrational scales.[26] The syncretic melding of disparate times and places contained in many of these drawings also found expression in Hugo's taste in interior decoration (indeed later, in Guernsey, there would be not only Hauteville, but also Drouet's residence nearby, Hauteville II).[27] In Drouet's conception, Hugo's drawings were destined for their private 'museum'; her adoring praise constituted their audience. On the other hand, the inscription on *Cursed Ruins* (fig. 6), which refers to blood spilt and God instructing nature to reclaim the cities, links this series of oriental fantasies to *Les Voix intérieures* (1837), very much a public work, especially the poem 'To the Arc de Triomphe', in which Hugo imagines the recently inaugurated monument as a ruin in the Paris of the distant future:[28]

> *When the banks where the water breaks on sonorous bridges*
> *Are covered once again with the murmuring reeds …*
> *When the Seine flows on over obstacles of stone,*
> *Eroding some old dome which has tumbled into its stream.*[29]

Thus, these drawings, created in an intimate context, are cast within the wider histories of the rise, and violent fall, of civilisations. The image of ruins recurs persistently throughout Hugo's drawings. If here it is consistent with conventional Romantic associations and serves a mythologising purpose, in 1871 a description attached to a very different drawing (cat. 11) presents the reverberation of specific personal and national histories:

> *This is the meeting room of the municipal council of Thionville in the state*
> *where the Prussian bombardment left it. The whole house is destroyed.*
> *The archives were burned. In this room, which was the great hall of the*
> *city, there was the portrait of my father. He disappeared in the fire with the*
> *freedom and nationality of Thionville. The mayor told me this with tears in*
> *his eyes. I told him: I am charmed by this ending for the portrait of my father.*
> *My father should not have been a prisoner of Prussia, even in effigy. My*
> *father left a great memory in Thionville. The women know that he defended*
> *and saved their city in 1814 and 1815. I drew this room on 30 August 1871,*
> *at four o'clock in the afternoon. Next door is the public garden. I saw*
> *a Prussian soldier on sentry, and while I was drawing I heard children*
> *singing the Marseillaise.*[30]

Picturing

During the 1840s Hugo's artistic repertoire evolved with extraordinary pace, propelled by life-changing events. In 1843, while on a trip to Spain, he learnt from a newspaper that Léopoldine, his favourite daughter, and her husband had drowned in a boating accident five days previously. No stranger to loss,[31] Hugo stopped travelling and published no major

Fig. 5

Temple Oriental, 17 January 1837. Pen and brown ink wash on wove paper, 26 x 13.3 cm. Maisons de Victor Hugo, Paris / Guernsey, inv. no. 133

Fig. 6

Cursed Ruins [December 1836 or February 1837]. Pen and brown ink wash on paper, 12.9 x 20.1 cm. Maisons de Victor Hugo, Paris / Guernsey, inv. no. 122

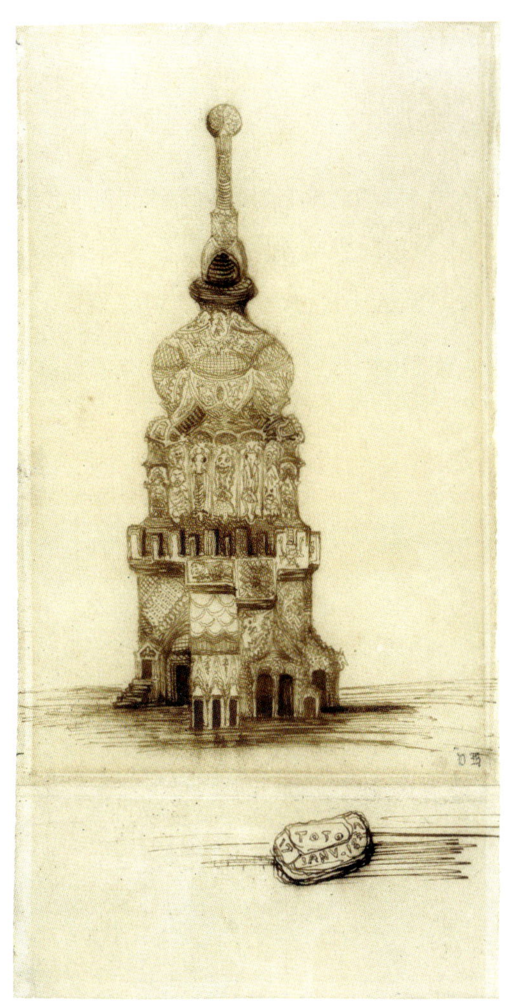

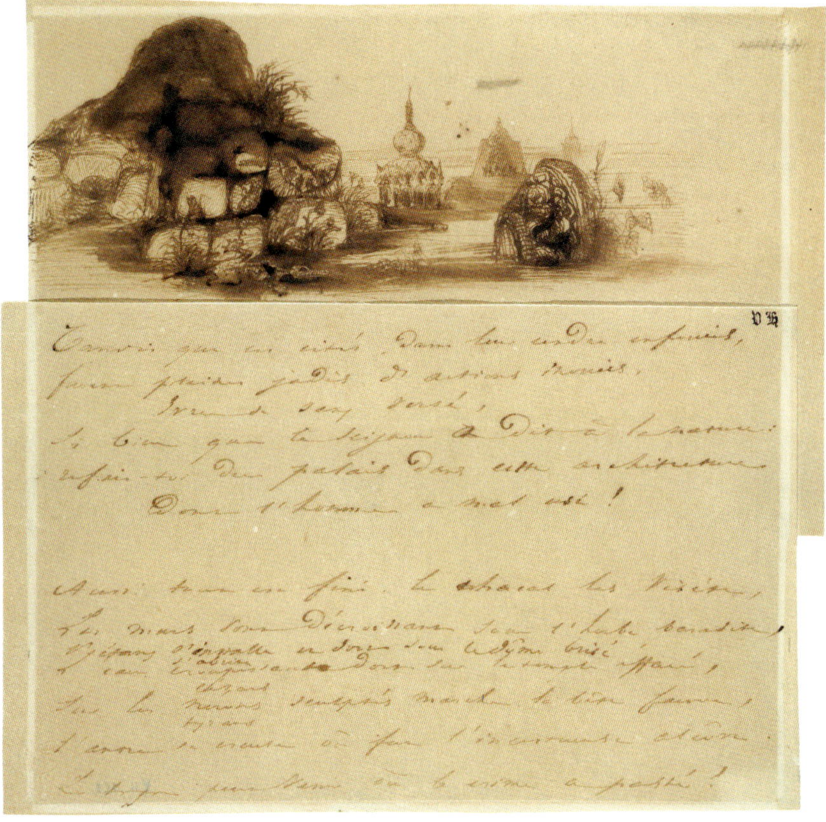

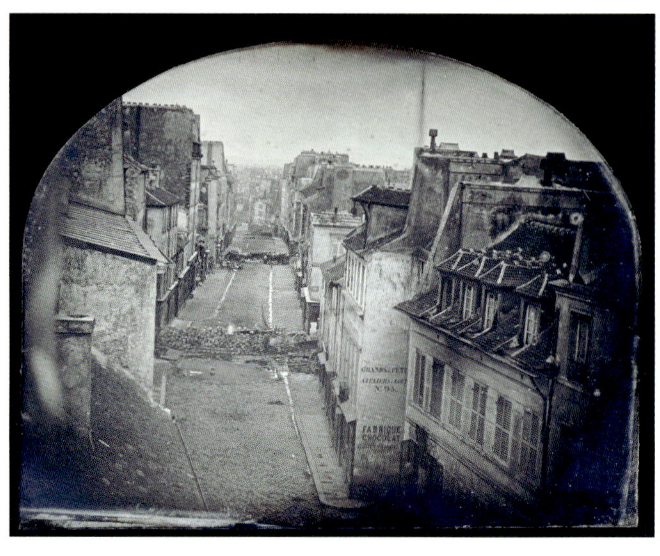

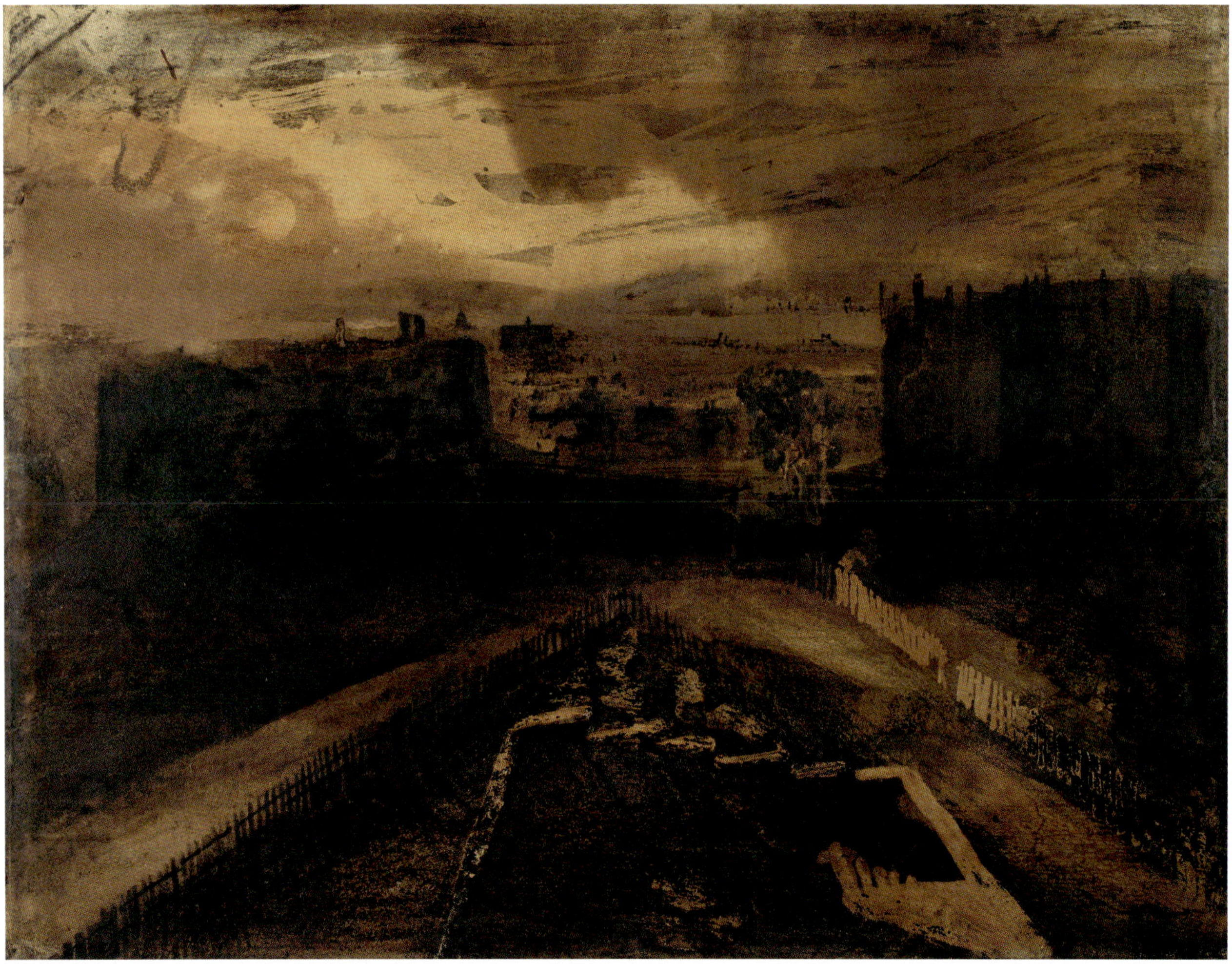

Fig. 7

Charles-François Thibault
(1801–1871). The first known
photograph of a barricade
in Paris taken on the morning
of Sunday 25 June 1848,
looking down onto what is
now the Rue du Faubourg-
du-Temple. Musée d'Orsay,
Paris, inv. no. PHO2002-4-1

work for more than six years. The depth of this personal grief, experienced in the public eye, marked his life profoundly. Outwardly, he focused his energies on politics in the lead-up to the revolutionary turmoil of 1848–51: a prominent elected member of the National Assembly, Hugo supported the new Republican government and participated (unarmed) in the brutal repression of the June Days uprising, later becoming a leader of the parliamentary opposition to Louis Napoléon Bonaparte's government.[32] Inwardly, drawing became for him a means of escape and catharsis.

Hugo's drawings of 1850 entail intense technical and aesthetic experimentation. Made in Paris on Drouet's dining table equipped with materials purchased for the purpose – chalk, pen holders, scraper, inks, colours, lithographic pencils – this comparatively large-scale group of works was envisaged as a cycle to adorn the walls of his apartment, culminating in the masterpiece *The Castle with the Cross* (*Le Burg à la Croix*) (1850; Maisons de Victor Hugo, Paris / Guernsey, inv. no. 40). The castle motif embodies both the violence of domination and defence of territory, and the beauty and romance of fairy tale; a world apart containing those with and without power, rulers and prisoners, a society in microcosm. Unpopulated by humans, other mysterious scenes invite us to inhabit an uncanny, parallel world. The low horizons of distant landscapes are rendered unsteady by a towering Gallic rooster,[33] a gigantic mushroom (cat. 8) or ancient druidic stones,[34] while the ode to the texture of rock in *Hic clavis, alias porta* (*Here the key, elsewhere the door*) (cat. 22), one of two surviving parts cut from an even larger sheet, transforms the temporally complex idea of the ruin into a grand allegory of impasse. In *The Two Castles* (cat. 44), the viewpoint takes off and the already double motif of the castle is redoubled.

Aerial views captivated Hugo ever since he had climbed the dome of the Sorbonne and the towers of Notre-Dame in his youth. The bleak, vertiginous *View of Paris* (fig. 8) employs a painted, dissolvable resist and circular stencils to retain highlights. Compositionally, it recalls daguerreotypes of the barricaded streets taken from Parisian rooftops (fig. 7), but Hugo deliberately omitted such specific markers, leaving his designs infused instead with a harrowing atmosphere hewn from dramatic tonal contrasts. Characterised by their ambitious pictoriality and theatricality, these drawings of 1850 chart Hugo's abiding interests as if each is 'cut from the mental landscape of Hugo's imagination', as Gérard Audinet puts it.[35]

Taken collectively, the notable feature of the drawings Hugo made on trips, reconstructed later from memories or imagined, is their lack of any sign of modernity. Markers of the industrialisation that was then embedding social inequality are absent: no factories, no steam trains, no telegraphs; such machineries that, in different ways, collapsed time and space, and manifested the human progress that Hugo endorsed, were evident in the landscapes he experienced but appear nowhere in his drawings.[36]

Contemplating

Forced to leave France on 11 December 1851, Hugo understood that the challenge of political exile was to remain visible. First from Brussels, then from Jersey, copies of *Napoléon le Petit* (1852) and *The Chastisements* (1853) were smuggled into France by ingenious means, amplifying their author's voice through their illicit appeal. From 1856, newly published works were allowed to appear in France, and after Hugo's refusal of the amnesty granted to

Fig. 8

View of Paris, c. 1850.
Pen and brown ink wash,
black ink, black pencil,
charcoal, graphite pencil,
dissolvable resist and
scratching on paper,
44.5 x 63 cm. Maisons
de Victor Hugo, Paris /
Guernsey, inv. no. 804

political exiles by Napoléon III in August 1859, his absence from France became a matter of principle. From this moral high ground, Hugo received letters seeking his support for various causes, and wrote open letters not only to heads of state, but also to whole countries.

On his 'garden island' of Jersey,[37] invigorated by the natural environment, Hugo revisited his earlier travels through drawing. With dramatic chiaroscuro he produced brooding compositions, as in the shafts of light that strike the mountain in *Le Mythen* (cat. 7), and expanded his repertoire of materials (cats 9, 28). Other works returned to the simplicity of ink on paper. In *The Shade of the Manchineel Tree* (*Notes from a Trip to the Pyrenees and Spain*) (cat. 6), a memory filled with the trauma of Léopoldine's death, the sanctuary of shade has become deathly; the inscription's evocation of rest sought but denied frames the drawing as a vision of death, grief and retribution.[38] A human spine and the almost cartographic contours of a skull become the shadow or root of a manchineel. Native to the Caribbean and the Gulf of Mexico, these trees are so toxic that sheltering beneath them during rain causes burns and their ingested fruits are lethal; their sap fuelled the poisoned arrows of Indigenous peoples defending themselves from European colonialists. A thick drip of ink leaks across the gutter of the original album (obscured by the current mount) like blood draining from a wound. Viewed with one's head tilted left, the shadow or skull approximates the shape of the tree's foliage, mirrored along the horizon; via this imaginary enfolding, twinning becomes double-seeing, at once cross section and perspectival view.

This multiplicity of angles and fluidity of shifting perception are hallmarks of Hugo's drawings. Examples include the improbable settlement perched atop a bridge of rock pierced by two eye-like sockets in *Landscape: Town and Towers on the Horizon* (cat. 36), sculpted by fine concentric contours produced by drying ink, like slow-growing tree rings; or the view of 'trees' (impressions of lace) reflected in a river or lake (cat. 37) seen either from within a cave or hollow overhung by vegetation or, rotated, from a high bank overlooking the water. Terrain is in constant metamorphosis, its potential for revelation perhaps linked to the new age of palaeontology and archaeological discovery. Looking closely at these apparently spontaneous drawings, it is evident that they were often the result of sophisticated stages of manipulation, some requiring quick action while the page was wet, others needing distinct layers separated by time, in a physical echo of Hugo's psychic process of re-memorialisation (see Gérard Audinet, p. 32). Drawings brimming with gestural energy and stain-like marks (*taches*) activate the power of ambivalence through the compositional placement of the 'figure' on the empty ground; *Cloud over a Field* (fig. 9), for instance, is grounded by the title it has acquired, not one given by Hugo. Untethered, possibly rotated, it could transform itself.

The extrapolation of images from 'accidental' blots or *taches* has a long tradition in art, from Leonardo da Vinci's contemplation of the patterns caused by a sponge hurled against a wall, to the published treatises of the British artist and drawing teacher Alexander Cozens (1717–1786). Cozens devised a method for inventing idealised landscapes obedient to classical rules of composition, basing them on a set of suggestive ink blots reproduced via experimental printmaking techniques (fig. 11). The series of 'blot' landscapes was only one of a set of complementary drawing aids that included his *The Shape, Skeleton and Foliage of Thirty-Two Species of Trees* (1771) and a pattern book of skies that a young John Constable copied out, influencing his oil sketches of clouds.[39] Although it was intended for amateur landscape artists, it is unlikely that Hugo was aware of Cozens's work, as he proceeded intuitively, rather than

Fig. 9

Cloud over a Field, c. 1854–56. Brush and brown ink wash on beige paper, 21.5 x 28.4 cm. Private collection

Fig. 10

Justinus Kerner (1786–1862), *Kleksographien*, 1857. Illustration 64, Deutsche Verlags-Anstalt, Stuttgart, 1890

Fig. 11

Alexander Cozens (1717–1786), Plate 12 from Plates 1–16 for *A New Method of Assisting the Invention in Drawing Original Compositions of Landscape*, c. 1785. Aquatint on paper, 24 x 31.4 cm. Tate, London, inv. no. T03180. Purchased 1980

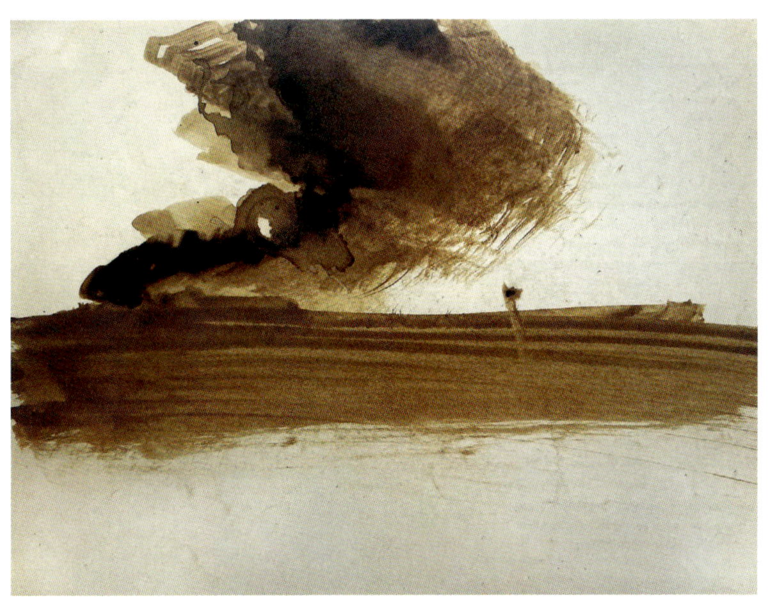

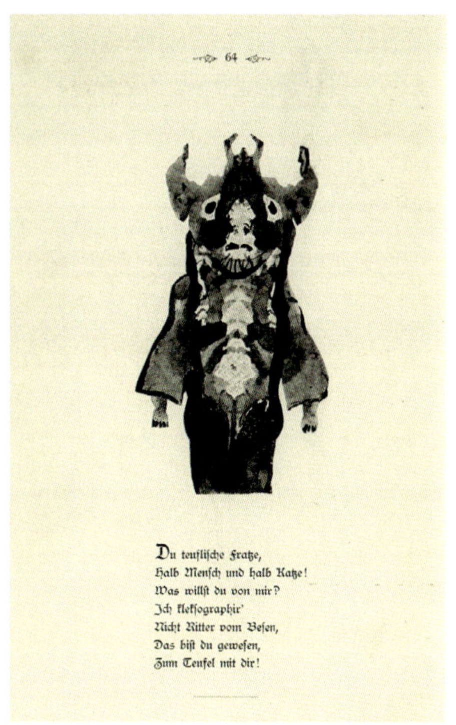

Du teuflische Fratze,
Halb Mensch und halb Katze!
Was willst du von mir?
Ich kleksographir'
Nicht Ritter vom Besen,
Das bist du gewesen,
Zum Teufel mit dir!

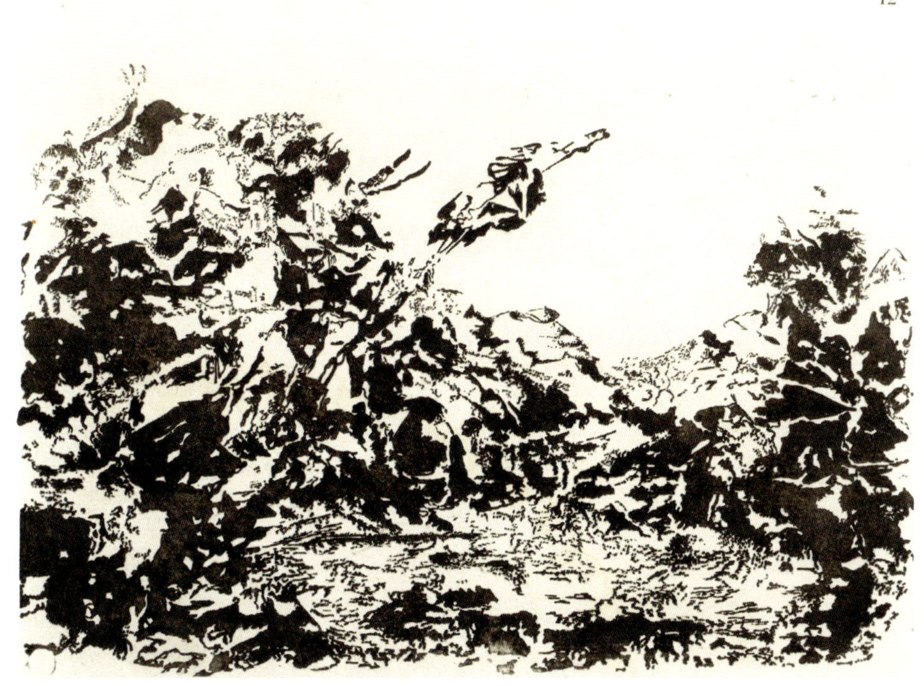

referring to drawing manuals for techniques. Closer in spirit, perhaps, are the conceptually entirely different blots of the poet, physician and mystic Justinus Kerner (1786–1862), who moved in German Romantic circles and in 1857 published *Kleksographien*: folded blots elaborated into diabolical figures presented with memento mori poems (fig. 10). These chime with Hugo's *pliages* (cat. 32) and find their popular counterparts in late nineteenth-century parlour games, anticipating the use of Rorschach tests in the practice of psychology in the early twentieth century.

Hugo's embrace of automatic processes as a driver for creating images was linked to the context of the spiritualist movement. In Jersey between 1853 and 1855, Hugo, Adèle, their son Charles and a small circle of friends participated in seances or 'table turning', a phenomenon then in vogue in the USA. Initially sceptical, Hugo found irresistible the pull of the world of spirits, including Léopoldine, and the appeal of language become animate (drawn by a pencil attached to the table, or tapped out in code); such communications then seemed less alien than they might now. In the 1830s and 1840s in France, mesmerism was popular as an alternative therapy throughout the social classes; it followed the theory posited by the Austrian physician Friedrich Anton Mesmer (1734–1815) that a non-material fluid shared by living things and throughout the universe could respond to the invisible force of magnetism.[40] Hugo's anti-clerical religiosity led him to embrace the mystical, especially when ideas aligned with his pantheistic, unifying view of nature and his notions of a timeless community of geniuses (see Rose Thompson, p. 69). Over time, Hugo developed a strong faith in a deeply personal metaphysical system that combined aspects of Western and Eastern thought; he believed that all things have souls, animate or otherwise.[41]

The perceptual-psychological play at work in both the *taches* and the conjuring of spirits can be seen in an extraordinary sketchbook that Hugo kept between 15 March and 18 April 1856 (cat. 33) at the moment *Les Contemplations* was published (the success of this volume of poetry allowed him to purchase Hauteville House on 16 May). Across the pages, Hugo's relentless, hard pencil line meanders; here, drawing offers a meditative pastime, perhaps filling the void left by the end of the seances. A sense of deliberately abandoned control pervades, as if the eyes are fixed on an object drawn without looking at the page. The fractal-like contours suggest a scopic tracing of distant views of foliage, clouds or rocks, or perhaps the edges of leaves, shadows, ink stains or maps. Or was Hugo listening to music? Trembling lines might register vibrations and rhythms, and often similar shapes are echoed at varying scales on the same or sequential pages. The random line is particularised with a free hand to invoke an orgiastic array of monsters, animals and humans. Some ivy-clad, they brandish musical scores, sing, drum, play horns, flutes and violins; fragmented faces are transmuted into seahorses or elaborate wings; a decapitated head has an animated discussion with its body; one creature squats to aim a rifle; elsewhere people converse with menageries of birds, ride flying dragons or row interstellar boats. The potential of the linear as a conjunction of positive and negative space is revealed to be as fruitful as the *tache*; the blank page becomes a theatre for four-dimensional musing, verging on animation.

This sketchbook also manifests the freedom of mind offered by drawing, an activity capacious enough to reflect upon literary outcomes, to connect ideas and imagine viewpoints. Allegra Pesenti's insightful discussion of skies and the celestial explores the influence of astronomy on Hugo's drawings and the reception of his work among the Surrealists in the early twentieth century, with a focus on Hugo's perceptual, ontological revelations while viewing the moon through a telescope.[42] On the page inscribed *La chiffonnière MORS* (fig. 12), one of his more deliberate compositions in the 1856 sketchbook, Hugo inverted this perspective, taking a 'God's-eye' view[43] of earth – a vantage point that is also evoked in the mysterious *Planet-Eye* (cat. 34). 'Mors' (Death) is also the title of a poem in his *Les Contemplations* (1856), but the view in *La chiffonnière MORS*, of earth seen from space, with the outlines of Europe clearly visible, reflects another poem in the same volume, entitled simply '?': 'Where furious peoples collide bloodily; – / And all this makes a star in the heavens!'.[44] Drawn in the wake of the Franco-British alliance during the Crimean War (1853–56), the image aligns a female personification of death with a ragpicker (a person who collects waste items for reuse or sale). Hovering amid the stars, this figure invites contemplation upon wastage and salvage. This minor sketch offers a glimpse of the vast scope within which Hugo saw terrestrial humanity and of his untenable political dreams of global unity and peace. In a speech at the Paris Peace Congress in 1849, Hugo had publicised the notion of a 'United States of Europe', but his vision – as a patriot – later expressed in *Paris Guide,* published on the occasion of the Paris Universal Exhibition of 1867, was of a Europe with Paris as its capital.[45] In 1870 Hugo planted some acorns at Hauteville to grow into 'The Oak of the United States of Europe' and envisaged an eventual worldwide republic. There is an irreconcilable gap between his ideals of equality and pacifism, and the persistence of his own imperialist attitude in the era of the Third Republic, evident in his *Discourse on Africa* (1879), which reflects widespread beliefs during the late nineteenth century in racial and cultural hierarchy and the duty of European nations to 'civilise' Africa.[46] Jordi Brahamcha-Marin has addressed complex questions surrounding the coexistence of such public speeches advocating colonialism and anti-racist discourse embedded in Hugo's literary works, and the connections between Hugo's position on colonialism and his wider ideology encompassing internationalism and progressivism.[47]

Hugo both condoned colonisation and pleaded for the lives of the peoples who resisted oppression.[48] In one instance his opposition to slavery and capital punishment coalesced into what became his most publicly known drawing during his own lifetime. Following the failure of his appeal to the USA for the abolitionist John Brown to be spared the death penalty, Hugo agreed that one of the drawings he had made in 1854 against the condemnation of John Tapner (see Rose Thompson, p. 104) could be reproduced bearing Brown's name. Brown's fellow abolitionist Frederick Douglass (who had tried to dissuade Brown from the disastrous Harpers Ferry Raid in 1859) valued Hugo's literature and came to hold *Les Misérables* in high esteem. Hugo went on to make further images of hangings as a mechanism to look horror in the eye (fig. 13): 'I saw it in the Pyrenees when I was a child. [...] The smugglers used it as a bridge and the authorities as a scaffold. [...] It was also called: "They walk above / And dance below".'[49]

Drawing

From 1861 Hugo resumed his summer travels in Europe and his mode of sketching on the spot to engage anew with familiar places, for instance revisiting the Devil's Table at Kaltenbach in the Rhineland Palatinate (fig. 14), a geological phenomenon camouflaged as fantastical architecture amid his other drawings. The rock's height is greatly exaggerated, apparently sprouting from the trees below in an expression of hybridity. Vernacular architecture continued

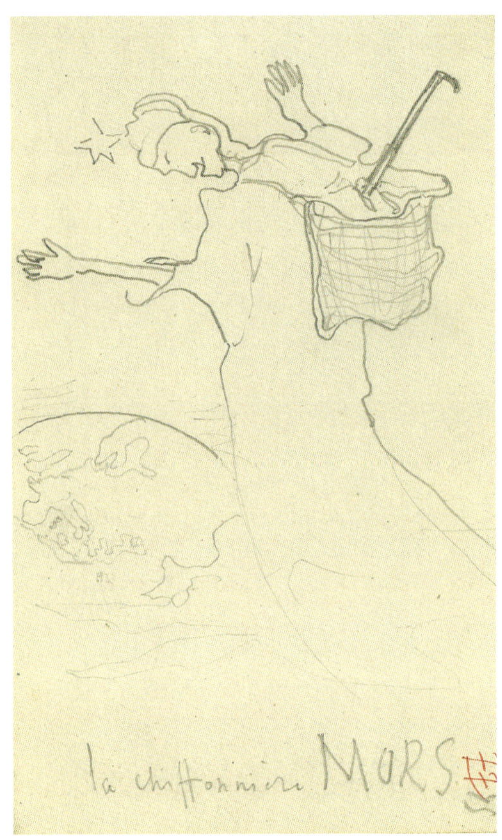
la chiffonnière MORS

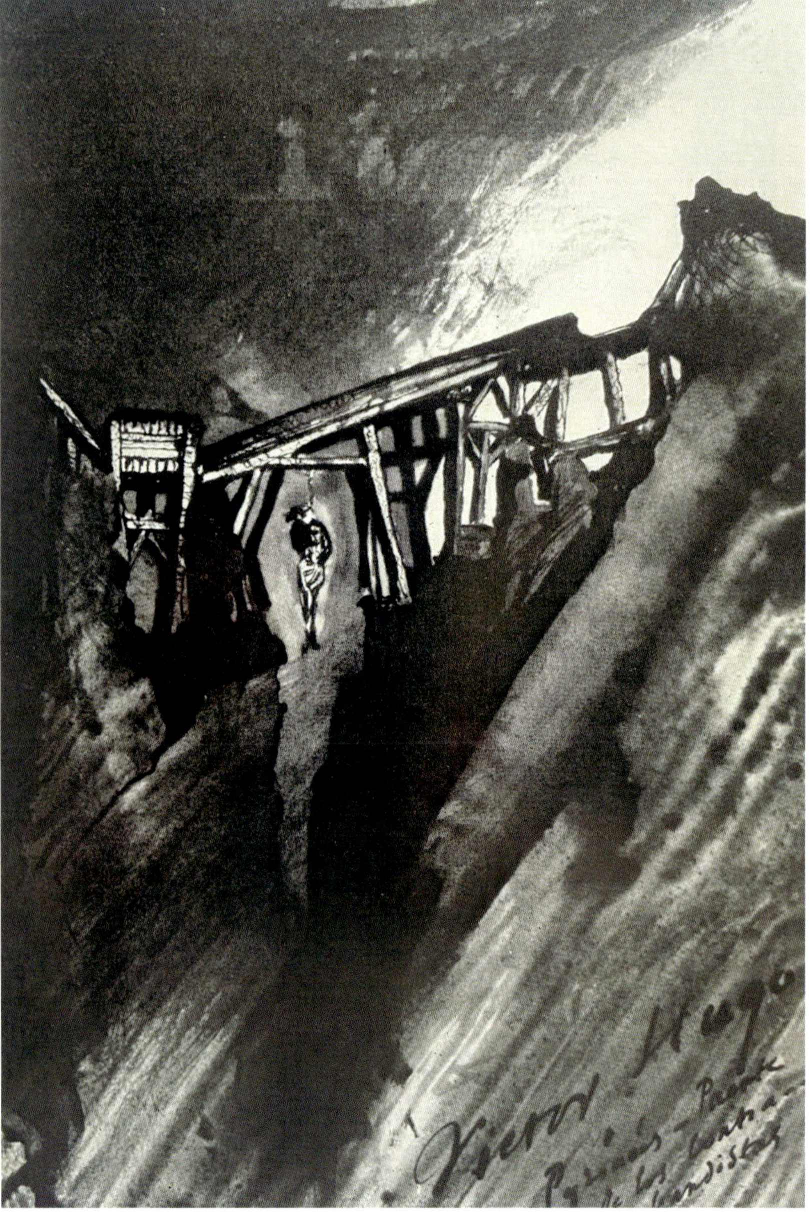

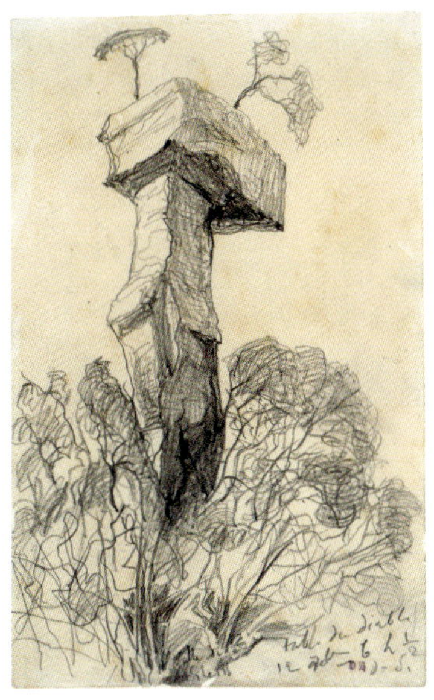

Fig. 14

Devil's Table, 12 September 1865. Graphite pencil on wove paper, 27.1 x 17.2 cm. Maisons de Victor Hugo, Paris / Guernsey, inv. no. 20

Fig. 12

La chiffonnière MORS, folio 77r of cat. 33, *Sketchbook Depicting Imaginary Creatures (Human, Animal, Plant) and Musicians*, 15 March – 18 April 1856. Sketchbook, 10 x 16 x 1.5 cm (closed). Bibliothèque nationale de France, Paris, Département des Manuscrits, inv. no. NAF 13447

Fig. 13

Smugglers Bridge, 30–31 December 1868. Pen, brown ink and Indian ink wash on white paper, dimensions unknown. Private collection

to catch Hugo's observational eye, both the improbable (cat. 18) and the ordinary. In *Walcourt* (cat. 19) an energetic line connects all parts of the composition, integrating shading with a fluid confidence born of decades of drawing, internalising the staircase motif that reappears in epic form in *The Lighthouse at Casquets, Guernsey* (cat. 75). Hugo could turn his hand easily to mixing memory, observation and invention in whichever stylistic approach he selected, often governed by the materials that he had to hand.

The output of his Guernsey years (1855–70) is marked by a closer association between the imagistic writing of his novels and the subjects of his drawings, notably in those associated with *The Toilers of the Sea* (*Les Travailleurs de la mer*) (1866). His works from this period, made in the 'Lookout' at Hauteville, were informed by his constant companion, the ocean, which was also the model that Hugo used to frame his literary work and continues to offer a paradigm to understand it;[50] indeed, some of his last drawings are evocative seascapes (cat. 77). Yet one of the materials that most inspired him was wood, its bark, knots and grain offering up images like ink *taches*. The heavy solidity of Hauteville's interior is the antithesis to the open view; to experience the house from the ground upwards is a passage from darkness into light. Hugo decorated wooden frames for his drawings, sometimes in the act of dedicating or presenting work, often as a means to integrate them into interior schemes and occasionally as the focus of the artwork itself. *Mirror with Birds* (cat. 58), a gift for Juliette Drouet's birthday made shortly before Hugo's initially triumphant return to Paris, represents the fence surrounding the base of a fountain he created in the garden at Hauteville, to protect his grandchildren from the open water. The square reflective surface imitates the basin, and the ivy and swallows are seen as if from a bird's-eye view; an invitation to avian visitors is inscribed on a *trompe-l'oeil* sign, echoing one on the fence surrounding the real pool.[51] Hugo's earlier poem 'La Nature' had staged a dialogue with a tree, which agrees to be a log for the hearth, a tiller for the plough, the pillar of a house, the mast of a ship, but refuses, outraged, to be a set of gallows.[52] Some of Hugo's most enigmatic drawings lend this shape-shifting quality to a single entity: can we say with any certainty, despite the numerous suggestions it offers, what on earth the object depicted in the ink drawing known as *Boat without Sails* (cat. 73) really is?

Hugo also used drawings as presents or to make dedications. He embellished Paul Meurice's copy of *Songs of the Streets and Woods* (1865) with *The Nest* (cat. 5). He inscribed Charles Baudelaire's copy of the same work: 'jungamus dextras' (Let's join hands). In 1859, having seen *The Castle with the Cross* (1850; Maisons de Victor Hugo, Paris / Guernsey, inv. no. 40) and other drawings at Meurice's home, Baudelaire had praised 'the magnificent imagination which flows through the drawings of Hugo as mystery flows through the sky'.[53] Later, embittered by Hugo's cultural 'dictatorship', he remarked 'the ocean itself got bored with him'.[54] The strained relationship between these two ideologically opposed poets was noted, from an early twentieth-century perspective, by Walter Benjamin, who digressed from his subject ('The Paris of the Second Empire in Baudelaire', part of his *Arcades Project*) to devote several pages to Hugo. He compared the two poets' attitudes to the crowd, noting Hugo's tendency towards collective titles for his literary works. Benjamin interpreted Hugo's contact with the spirit world as 'a contact with the masses which the poet necessarily missed in exile'; it was 'primarily a public' that gave him 'a foretaste of the immeasurable acclaim which was to await him at home in his old age' (after the death of his sons, Hugo and his grandchildren became the Third Republic's adored equivalent of a royal family). Benjamin also identified the crowd as the model for Hugo's engagement with what Benjamin called the 'natural-supernatural'; he aligned Hugo's willingness to lose himself in 'the promiscuity at work among the multitude of living things' with contemplation of 'the impenetrable obscurity of mass existence'.[55] More recently, building upon Robb's attention to the impact of this 'self-hypnosis' on Hugo's language and form in which 'things and even concepts become sentient creatures', Karen Quandt has noted the influence of Hugo's 'symbiotic dialogue with his surroundings' on *Les Contemplations* and *Les Misérables*, finding in Hugo's poetry and prose a proto-environmentalist awareness of nature as an ecosystem and a recognition that 'humans are just an intermediary in the entangled web that exists between nature and a divine force.'[56]

For Hugo, the act of drawing was bound up with his relationships to people and to the natural world, a meditative activity that allowed a free play between the self and the cosmos. The image of the ragpicker evoked in immense, cosmic terms by Hugo's terrifying idle sketches (fig. 12) is an apt one in the concrete sense that Hugo cherished the slightest scraps of everything he wrote or drew: the sheets of notes he dubbed *copeaux* (wood shavings) for example (fig. 15), each one a crowd of thoughts ensuring that no observation or idea was wasted. The figure of the ragpicker is also resonant with an understanding of history put forward by Benjamin in the *Arcades Project*: that leftovers, accidents and fragments hold the potential for memory, meaning and renewal, a model very different to the linear progress Hugo exalted in his public speeches, but one which resounds in the temporal complexities of the subjects and methods of Hugo's drawings.

Hugo's gently dismissive description in 1863 of 'these things people insist on calling my drawings', 'made in the margins or on the covers of manuscripts during hours of almost unconscious reverie with what remained of the ink in my pen', belies the effort he had made to train his eye and hand, and the sophistication of the multiple modes of drawing he developed, honed and returned to.[57] Yet his description of his drawings as 'things' rings true; he was a bricoleur of objects, images and words, and the haptic process of making drawings offered unique modes of cognition to his creativity, not only as an artist but also as a writer. Combining contemplation, observation, fantasy, memory and meditation in new ways, the metaphysical space of the blank page could cohere transforming scales and the ebb and flow between fiction, personal experience and historical events, while the physicality of the practice of drawing helped to ensure that 'one toe always remains in contact with reality'.[58] Drawing offered Hugo a temporary refuge – a mental garden – in which he could exercise or rest his ceaselessly searching mind's eye.

Fig. 15

Copeau (wood shaving) for *The Toilers of the Sea*, c.1864–65. Ink on wove paper, 34.3 x 28.2 cm. Maisons de Victor Hugo, Paris / Guernsey, inv. no. ah929

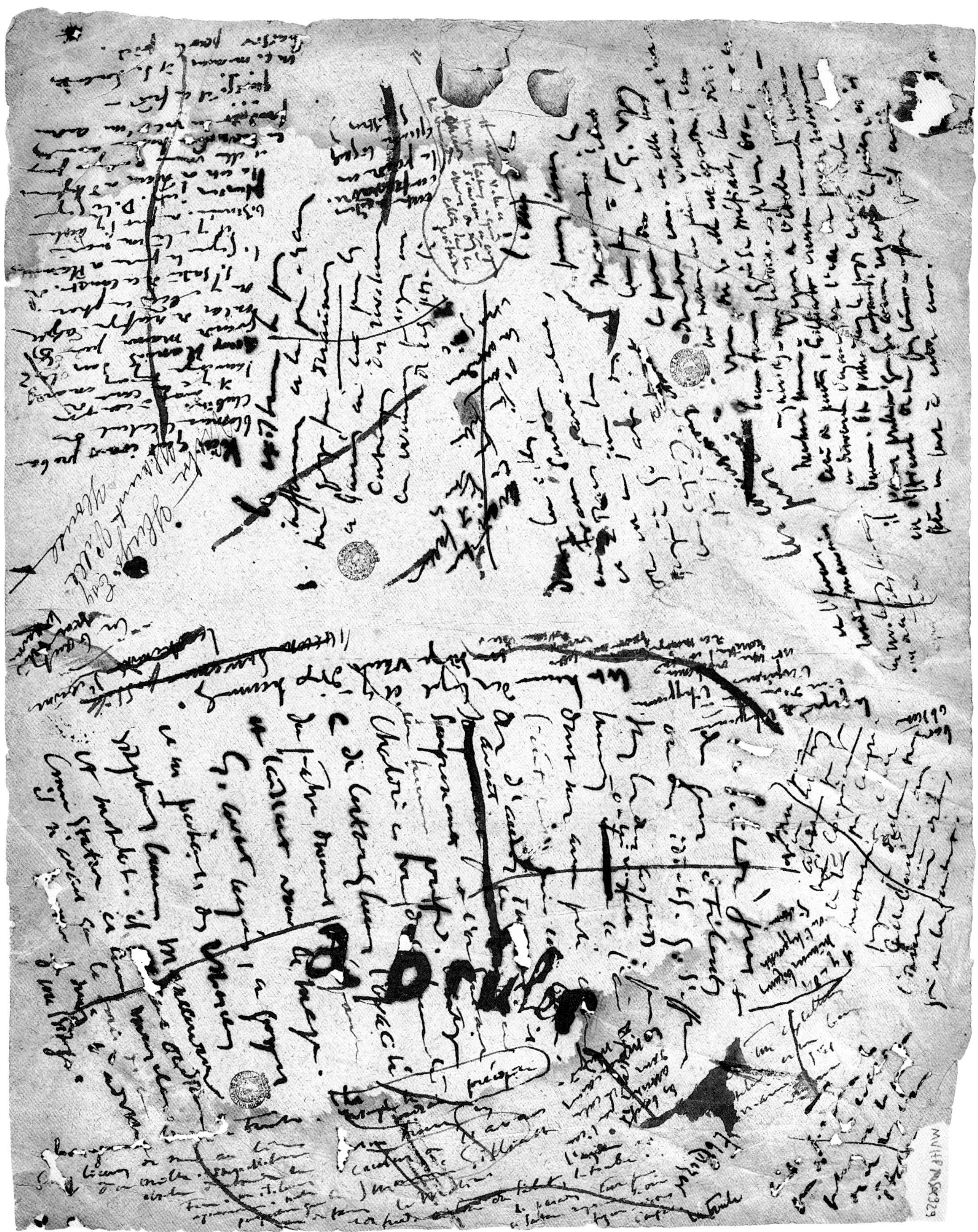

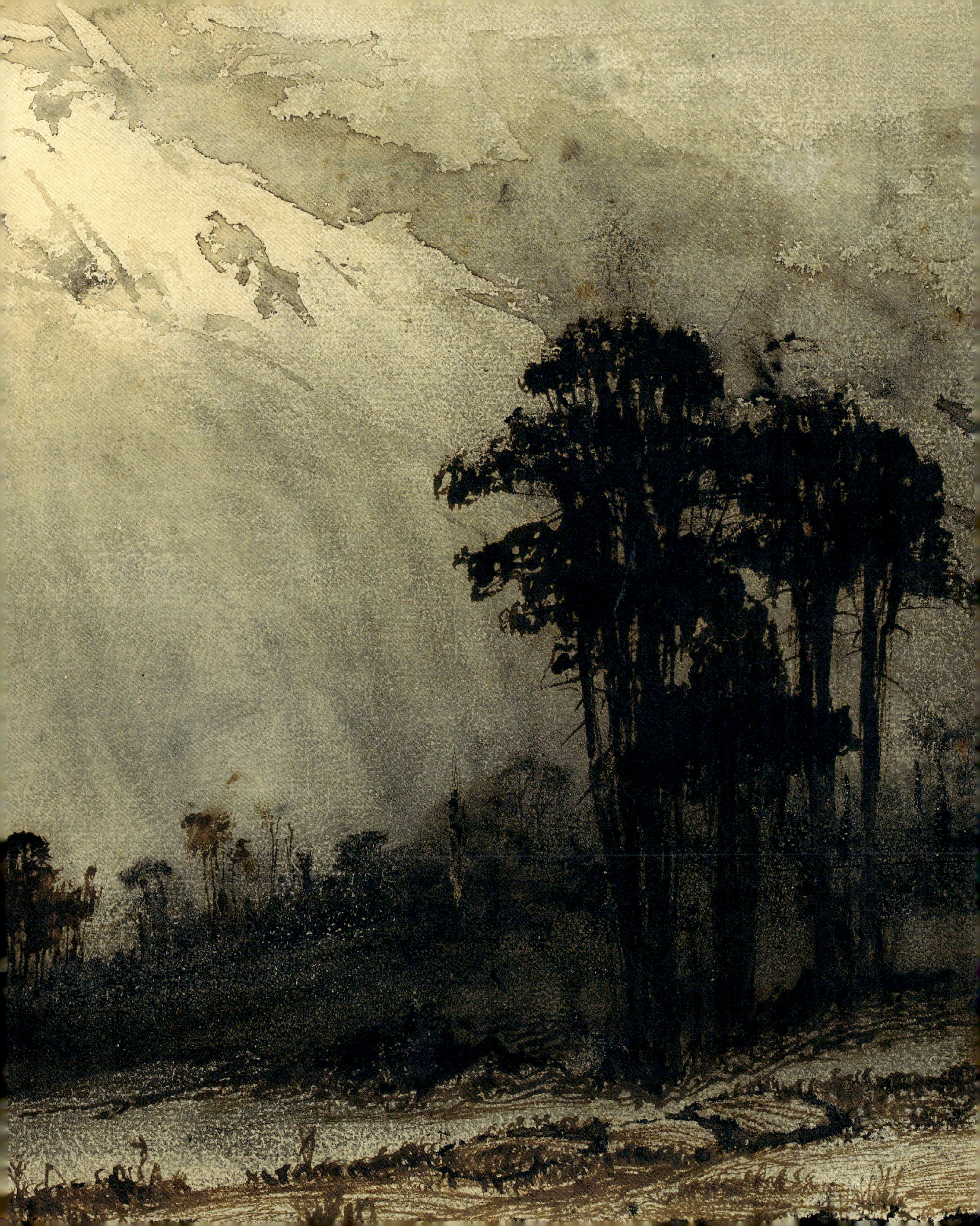

How a Poet Becomes a Painter

GÉRARD AUDINET

How does one become a draughtsman? Or rather, how, from being a writer who draws, like many other writers, does one become a fully fledged draughtsman, whose work is worthy of being written into the history of art?

Victor Hugo was one of these exceptional people: his work as a draughtsman has won him a reputation almost equal to that of his renown as a writer, although this recognition developed late, over the course of the twentieth century. Hugo himself enjoyed an ambiguous relationship with his graphic work, presenting it as simply a form of relaxation, keeping it relatively close and yet authorising its reproduction.

Hugo took up the fashionable art of caricature (cat. 3) during the 1830s, in defence of Romanticism against Classicism. After 1834, during summer holidays with his mistress Juliette Drouet, he made pencil sketches of monuments and sites under the pretext of documentation. As the years went by, his drawings became more and more elaborate, although they remained the work of a gifted amateur (see, for example, *Furteneck in Mist*, cat. 20). The death of his daughter Léopoldine in 1843 put an end to his summer trips as he entered a period of mourning.

After this, Hugo did not plan to publish any more books. In 1845 he was appointed Pair de France (Peer of the Realm). In his journal he recorded long conversations with King Louis Philippe, which seem to have constituted his political education. Was Hugo dreaming of becoming a statesman like Chateaubriand? But in early July 1845 he was surprised in the act of adultery with Léonie Biard (née d'Aunet), the wife of a painter who was also close to Louis Philippe. Although the scandal was more or less successfully hushed up, Hugo was advised to make himself scarce for a few months. He shut himself away in his apartment and began writing what was later to become *Les Misérables* (1862). He worked on it until the Revolution of February 1848.

In September 1845 he made a trip to Chelles and Montfermeil, east of Paris, to see the places where he had described Cosette living as a child with the Thénardier family, and the woods dotted with ponds through which Jean Valjean was to lead her. In September 1846 he finally found the courage to visit Léopoldine's grave at Villequier, on the banks of the Seine in Normandy (fig. 21).

A few drawings belong explicitly to this journey of 1845, others by hypothesis, and the same goes for his trip to Villequier in 1846.[1] But there is a time lag. When Juliette's letters refer to a drawing from the summer of 1846, they inform us, in colourful language, that it was above all in July 1847 that Hugo began his more intensive production: 'While I wait for the happy moment to arrive, I look at the array of beautiful drawings you have done at my house and I open my GOB really wide and my eyes as wide as the Porte Saint-Denis.'[2] From this we can surmise that it was not until the following summer that Hugo, availing himself of some free time, made drawings of what he had seen the preceding autumn. But to this time lag could be added a reinvigorated, more sophisticated technique. A double revolution had taken place.

're-done the drawing of the Rhine'

First, a Copernican revolution. By now, as mentioned above, Hugo no longer drew from life, on the spot, as he had during his earlier travels. No sketchbooks or pencil drawings survive from 1845, 1846 or 1847, and, as Drouet suggests, the drawings seem to have been executed several months later. This time lag is hinted at in the titles given to the drawings: genuine 'souvenirs' begin to appear, titled as such, for example *Souvenir of the Pond in the Woods of Bellevue. 1845* (1847) (fig. 16) or *Souvenir of Chelles. 1845* (1858).[3] The term 'souvenir' may have been borrowed from André Durand, who engraved two of Hugo's drawings and who used the word frequently in the titles he gave his own landscapes.

Simultaneously, and in another innovation, Hugo picked up some compositions dating from his travels along the Rhine in 1839 and 1840; these engendered *La Tour des Rats* (cat. 17), his major drawing of 1847, an important year. On 20 July 1847 Hugo wrote in his journal: 're-done the drawing of the Rhine'. Not a very explicit message, perhaps, but the extreme rarity of such a piece of information suggests that it refers to a drawing of great importance to him, even if only by virtue of its format: *La Tour des Rats* was the largest drawing Hugo had made up until this date.

His new technique is perfectly realised here: the charcoal, the various inks, the rubbed areas of wax crayon, the ink pulled with a cloth to represent teeming rain. If we compare this with the original drawing (fig. 17), which seems to depict the same picturesque view as in his engravings, this new version presents us with a true dramatisation of the landscape; this is neither an illustration nor even a literary equivalent of the letter XX from *The Rhine* (1842), describing the Mäuseturm,[4] but a transcription of the strangeness and poetic colour of that text.

From now on, for Hugo, drawing became essentially an act of memory, distanced from the object as seen in favour of the object as remembered, in other words a paraphrase of memory – and moving ever closer to an invented or imagined object, thus undergoing a kind of mental filtration. The true origin of the drawing was transfigured. It was Hugo's new technique that made this possible.

Fig. 16

Souvenir of the Pond in the Woods of Bellevue. 1845, c. 1847. Pen and brown ink wash on laid paper, 7.5 x 12 cm. Maisons de Victor Hugo, Paris / Guernsey, inv. no. 895

Fig. 17

La Tour des Rats, 27 September 1840. Pen and brown ink wash on paper, 16 x 30 cm. Collection Louis-Antoine Prat, Paris

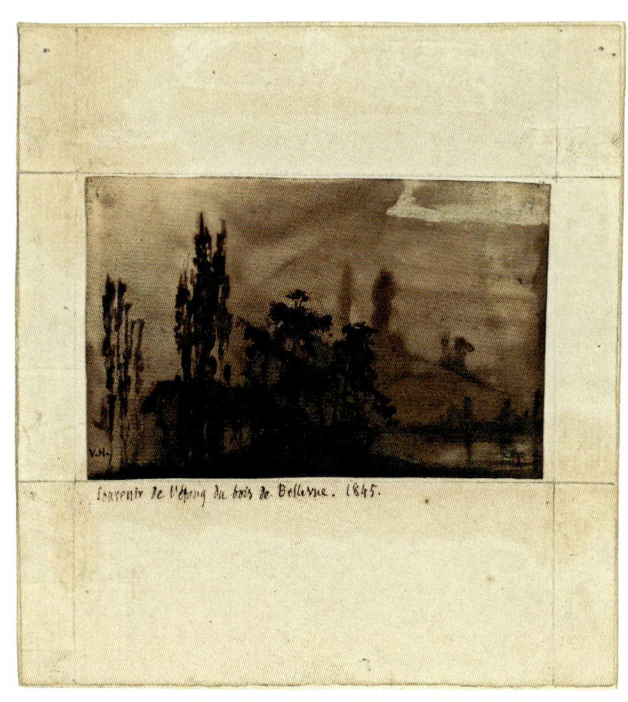
Souvenir de l'étang du bois de Bellevue. 1845.

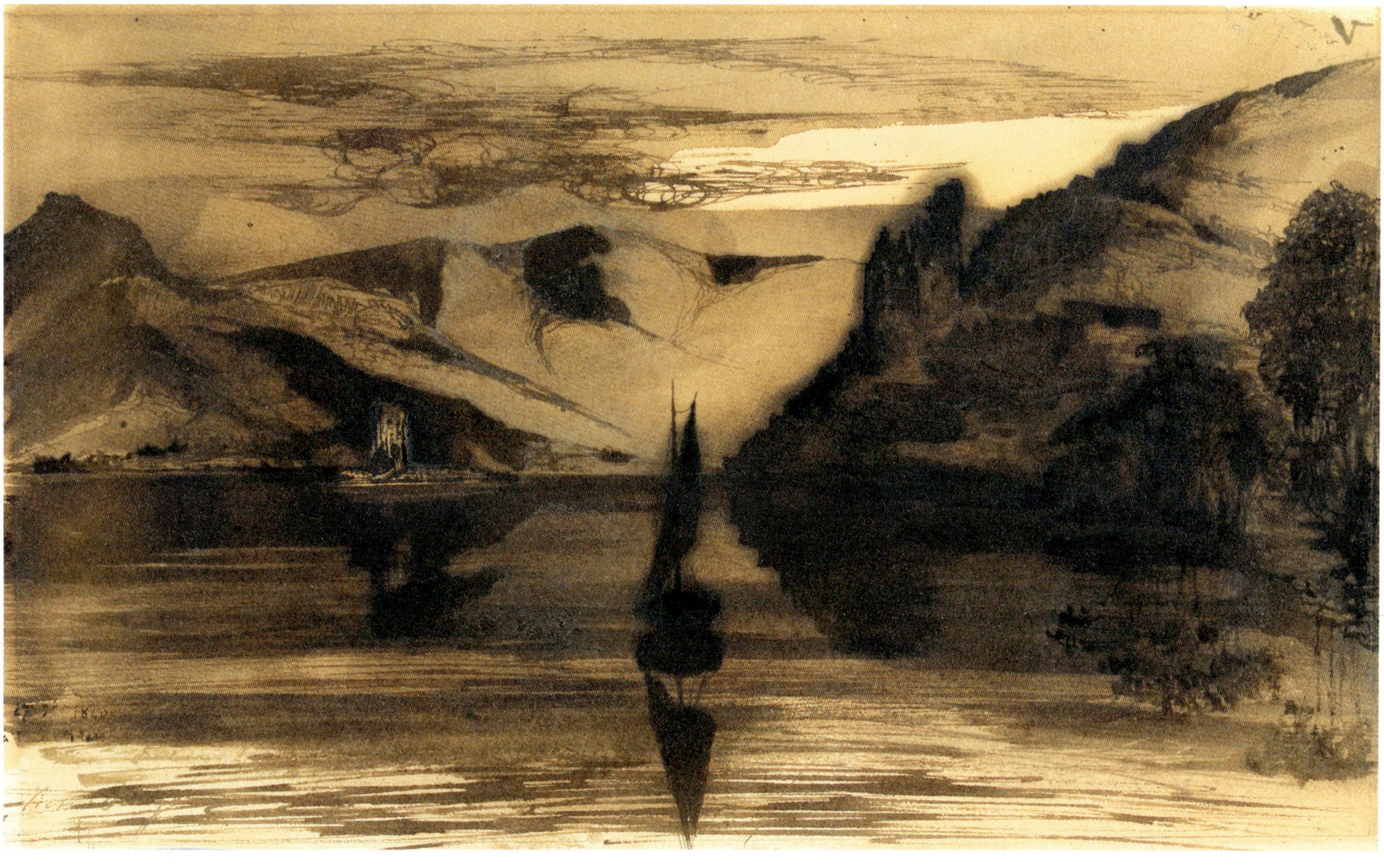

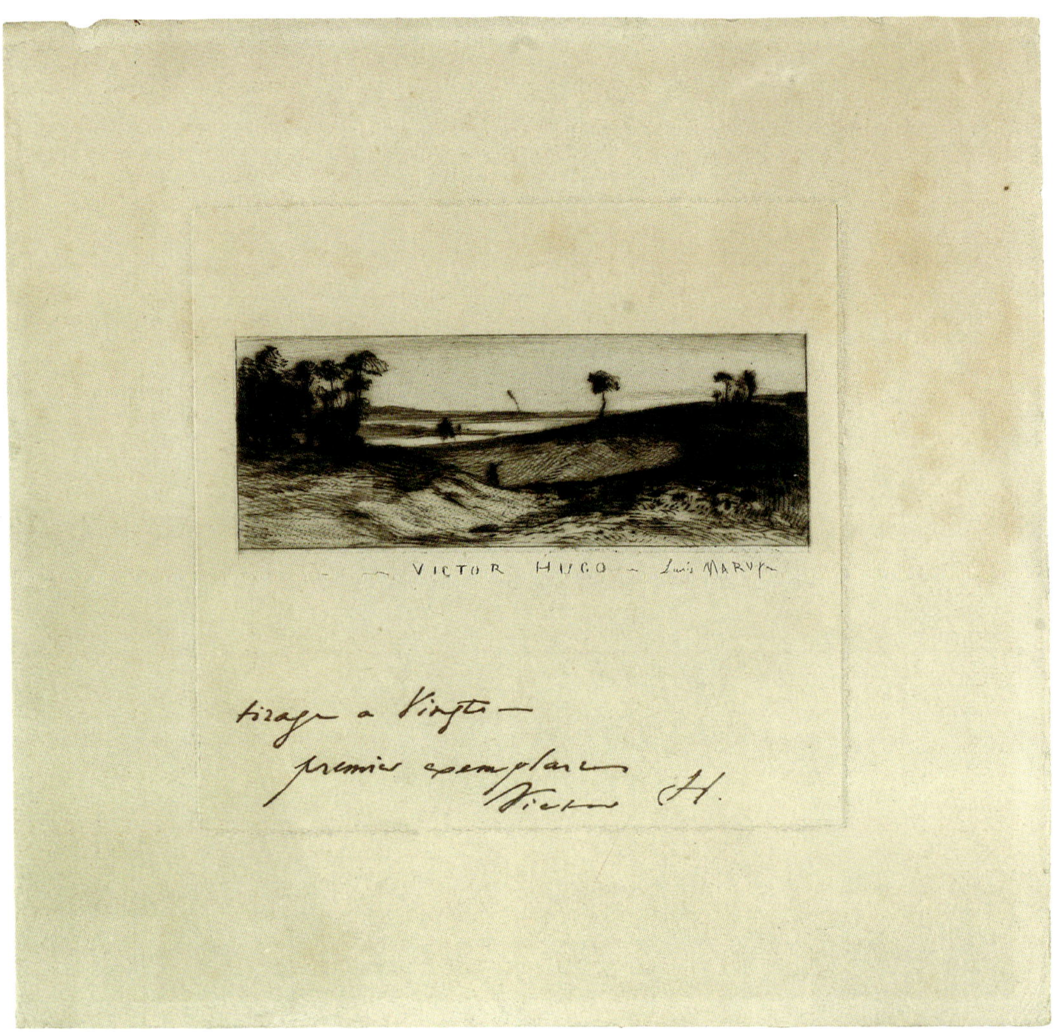
VICTOR HUGO — Luis MARVY
tirage à Vingt —
premier exemplaire
Victor H.

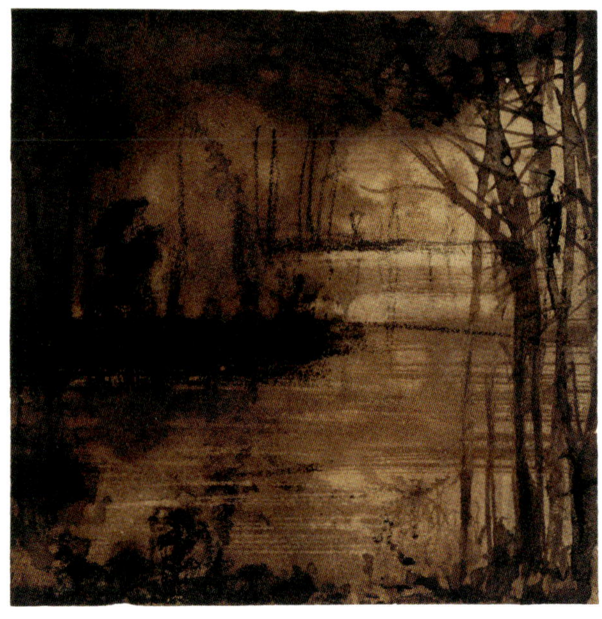

'I rely on your generosity to give it to me once the engraver has copied it'

The second revolution was technical in nature. Hugo was no longer satisfied with his writer's ink or with the stroke of the pen and the colour wash. He resorted to wetting his drawings, bathing them in water in order to obtain blended, vaporous effects. Above all, he now turned to other materials: he rubbed some areas with charcoal or soft black crayon, and filled other areas with drawing in wax crayon or lithographic pencils. These dark highlights were probably suggested to him by Célestin Nanteuil (1813–1873); they had produced their first travel album together in 1836, *Travel Sketchbook: Cliff at Bois-Rosé, Fécamp* (cat. 15).

Between these two 'layers', Hugo varied his inking, using sometimes quite dense contrasting expanses of brown and black ink. Whereas ink wash traditionally exploits the transparent lightness of the ink and the luminous areas where the paper is left blank, Hugo instead used a veritable lamination of materials, superimposing charcoal, ink and wax crayon, leaving very little or nothing blank. Worth noting also is that charcoal and pencil, coupled with the blending effect of wetting, contribute to the more graphic appearance of the pencil drawing, a long way now from the fluidity of the pure ink wash.

On 21 July 1846 Drouet wrote twice to Hugo. When she got out of bed: 'This morning when I awoke my first concern was to look at your ravishing drawing. I regret not being rich enough to buy it. I rely on your generosity to give it to me once the engraver has copied it'.[5] Then, in the afternoon: 'Anyway, all this is nothing but a dodge to sneak my drawing to the engraver in your name, in place of your drawing.'[6] At this date the engraver in question was in all probability Louis Marvy (1815–1850); we know of four prints by him dated 1847 (fig. 18) that appeared as lots in an auction in aid of the charitable works of the Duchesse d'Orléans, organised at Hugo's house.[7] Drouet's letter suggests that we should date these to July 1846. Only one of these engraved drawings has been identified: this is a castle on the Rhine, *The Cat*[8] (a pendant to *The Mouse* (*Velmich*), cat. 2), but the others also seem to be close to the drawings executed during Hugo's Rhineland trips, and more particularly in Belgium.

Marvy practised acid etching but is mainly famous for soft varnish, a technique by which a sheet of paper is stuck onto the varnish that covers the copper plate; a drawing is made on the paper and acid used to bite into the plate. When printed, the impression resembles a pencil drawing.

We might ask ourselves whether this technique, which Hugo must have observed, with its superimpositions (copper, varnish, paper, pencil) and its result – the crayoning of the artist's proof – could have perhaps been not so far from the crayoned look that Hugo gave his ink washes with charcoal, wax crayons and the wetting technique described above.

In addition, Marvy was willing to work on small plates. And in Hugo's undated output attributable to the years 1846–47, we notice a number of tiny drawings, for example *Undergrowth* (cat. 24), which seem to constitute a laboratory for the poet-draughtsman, as much for their technique as for their poetic effect (fig. 19).

Alas, no documentary evidence survives of the exchanges between Hugo and Marvy at that time, but years later, in 1863, in a letter to Philippe Burty, Hugo remembered the engraver with great appreciation: 'You are right to value Marvy so highly; he was for me in particular an admirable translator'.[9] Was he really no more than a translator?

Fig. 18

Louis Marvy (1815–1850), after Victor Hugo, *Plain with Clump of Trees*, 1846. Etching, 18.8 x 20.1 cm. Maisons de Victor Hugo, Paris / Guernsey, inv. no. 621.1

Fig. 19

The Pond, c. 1847. Pen and brown ink wash, black pencil and scratching on wove paper, 11.5 x 11.5 cm. Maisons de Victor Hugo, Paris / Guernsey, inv. no. 912

'All the vague phantoms, smiling or solemn'

Hugo adapted techniques borrowed from others to his own needs and use. One drawing, *The Cheerful Castle* (cat. 38), datable to *c.* 1847 by comparing it with another, *The City with the Broken Bridge*,[10] reveals his extraordinary inventiveness and freedom, both technical and aesthetic. This sheet also belongs to his revival of Rhineland castles and landscapes, but the tonalities are very different; indeed, they are almost the opposite of those in *La Tour des Rats*. The 'burg' here is bathed in light. Where areas are worked over with wax crayon, the brown ink is lightly applied. Blank areas play a major role, complementing the areas of grey charcoal. Most importantly, Hugo had the idea of lifting off layers of the paper, which, thus removed, produced fluffy, luminous clouds. The very fine, precise details of the towers suggest that the draughtsman was absorbed in his dream. The castles on the Rhine were to become Hugo's favourite subject. Drawn over and over again, they translate all the nuances, all the variations of reverie and remembrance. Sunlit though it is, and the total reverse of the gloomy drawings of 1847, *The Cheerful Castle* remains emblematic of Hugo's new language, so well suited to the expression of all the emotions.

The genuine skill that he now made his own opened the door to the fertile fields of his imagination and his visions. A double revolution had taken place and everything was set for Hugo's graphic work to show to the fullest extent what he was capable of achieving. His progress was to be slowed, however, by another revolution, that of 1848, which involved him – newly Republican and newly representative of the people – in political activity. At the end of the summer of 1850, it was to bear fruit. This was a difficult year for the politician – at odds with his party, heckled in the National Assembly, unwell – but he was to find an outlet in his drawing. He installed his studio in Drouet's dining room, in Rue Rodier, and there he found his fullest graphic expression, producing his most ambitious drawings and greatest masterpieces, among them *The Castle with the Cross* (*Le Burg à la Croix*),[11] *Mushroom* (cat. 8), *Hic clavis, alias porta* (*Here the key, elsewhere the door*) (cat. 22), *The Two Castles* (cat. 44), *The Dead City* (cat. 23), *Causeway* (cat. 65) and *Architecture Renaissance* (cat. 21). All expand on the technique he had adopted in 1847 and impress with the strength of their dramatic intensity. All are bathed in an atmosphere of twilight.

'The dusk rendered pallid his handsome brow and covered his eyes with shadows'[12]

This technical revolution, however, occurred in response to an aesthetic need. Hugo was aiming to transpose subjects that were not in themselves picturesque and to achieve a poetic version of drawing. A drawing should say more than it shows. This translates as a new repertoire, or at least an enriched repertoire – lakes, rivers, riverbanks and the edges of woodland (for example, *Undergrowth*, cat. 24) – and a new light: twilight. Indeed, Hugo was fascinated by this moment when light still remains but the light source is hidden beneath the horizon. Dusk in the evening, dawn in the morning; this can be identified from at least the summer of 1837.[13] Hugo wrote in a letter: 'I've always loved these journeys at dusk. This is the moment when nature takes on strange shapes and becomes fantastic.'[14]

This is the moment when imagined forms can take over nature. This theme was to return regularly to Hugo's pen and brush over subsequent decades. But from 1845 onwards, dusk took on a special importance during the writing of *Les Misérables*, particularly the second draft in 1847. This rewrite brought to the novel its poetic and psychological weight. All the decisive moments in the destiny of Jean Valjean – then still 'Jean Tréjean' – take place at dusk. Dusk is the hour of destiny.

By remarkable coincidence, 1847 – such a key year in the writing of *Les Misérables* – was also to be a decisive year in Hugo's drawing career. As he worked on the style of *Les Misères*, he worked on the style of his drawings too.

'My soul was in mourning; it was the hour of the shadows'[15]

The connection between the twilight in *Les Misérables*, the repetition of the Rhine drawings, the lakes and ponds of Montfermeil and the riverbanks might seem quite loose, but Hugo's imagination and invention never functioned in a strictly logical, discursive fashion, rather according to a desultory dreamlike discourse, or the leaps and bounds of sudden grief.

Like death, dusk means the passing from light to dark. To the father whose favourite daughter had plunged to her death in the Seine, all such expanses of water, lakes or rivers, became the image of death (fig. 20).

Mourning for Léopoldine certainly forged the links between these disparate elements. Mourning returned on 21 June 1846 with the death of Claire Pradier, Juliette Drouet's daughter; then from 25 to 28 September, when Hugo found the courage to visit for the first time his own daughter's grave at Villequier (fig. 21) as well as the place where she had drowned. In the same year, 1846, Hugo composed at least four poems on the subject of night and sunset;[16] in October and November, after his trip to Villequier, he began writing poems for the second part of *Les Contemplations*, and these he dedicated to Léopoldine, followed by four more in 1847. This marked his poetic confrontation with mourning.

Possibly Hugo's most important collection of poems, *Les Contemplations* is a kind of autobiography articulated around the date of Léopoldine's death in 1843, marking a 'before' and an 'after'.[17] The poet described his project thus: 'What are *Les Contemplations*? They are what one might call, if the work had no pretention, "The Memoirs of a Soul"', a lapidary heading that he followed with an explanatory list: 'They are, in fact, all the impressions, all the memories, all the realities, all the vague phantoms, smiling or solemn, that the conscience can retain – returned and remembered, gleam by gleam, sigh by sigh, mixed together in the same dark cloud.'[18]

The title of the collection, *Les Contemplations*, encourages us to pursue the parallel development observed in 1846 and 1847 between the writing of *Les Misérables*, the poems and the drawings with their new technique, between written and drawn twilights, and to witness the emergence not only of Hugo's mature graphic work but also an unrecognised relationship between his writing and his drawing. Having acquired his means of poetic expression through technique, drawing could for Hugo also be the 'memoirs of a soul'. The 'impressions', 'memories', 'realities' and 'phantoms' banking up within his soul could be drawn

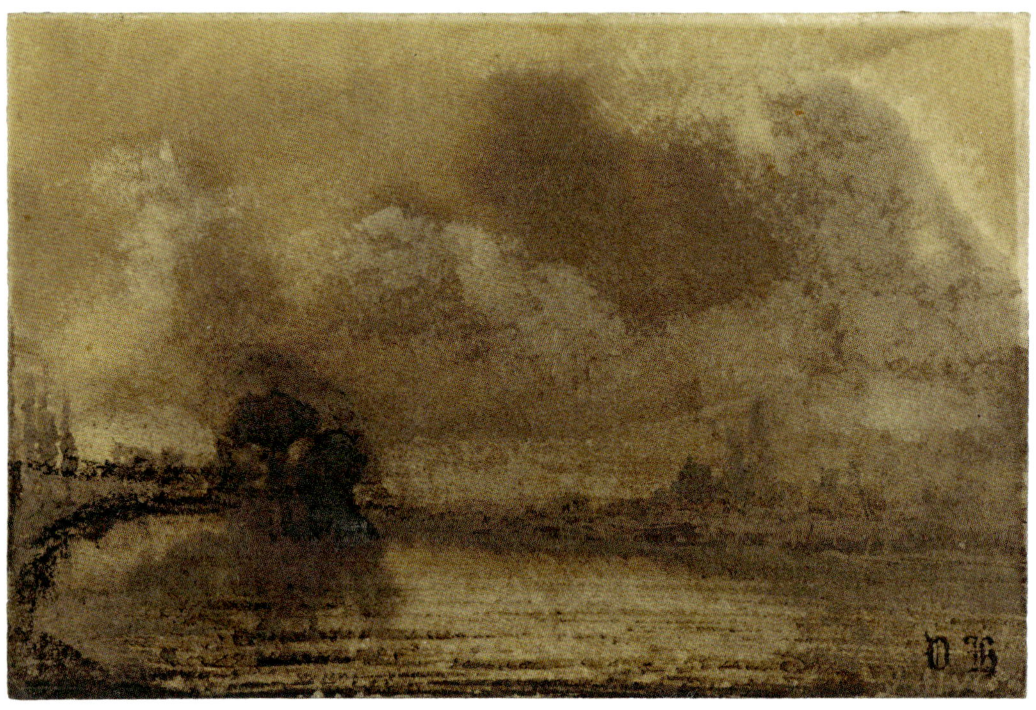

Fig. 20

At the Edge of a Lake or River, c. 1847. Ink, scratching and black pencil on paper, 6.2 x 9.5 cm. Maisons de Victor Hugo, Paris / Guernsey, inv. no. 910

Fig. 21

Landscape (Villequier), 1847. Pen, brush, brown ink and wash, black ink wash, graphite pencil and wax crayon on beige paper, 28.9 x 48.9 cm. Maisons de Victor Hugo, Paris / Guernsey, inv. no. 919

upon either for his writing or for his drawing, or indeed for both at once. Filtered by their distance in the memory or their passage through his soul, torn between 'yesterday' and 'today', Hugo's drawings henceforward are on an equal footing with the poems in *Les Contemplations*.

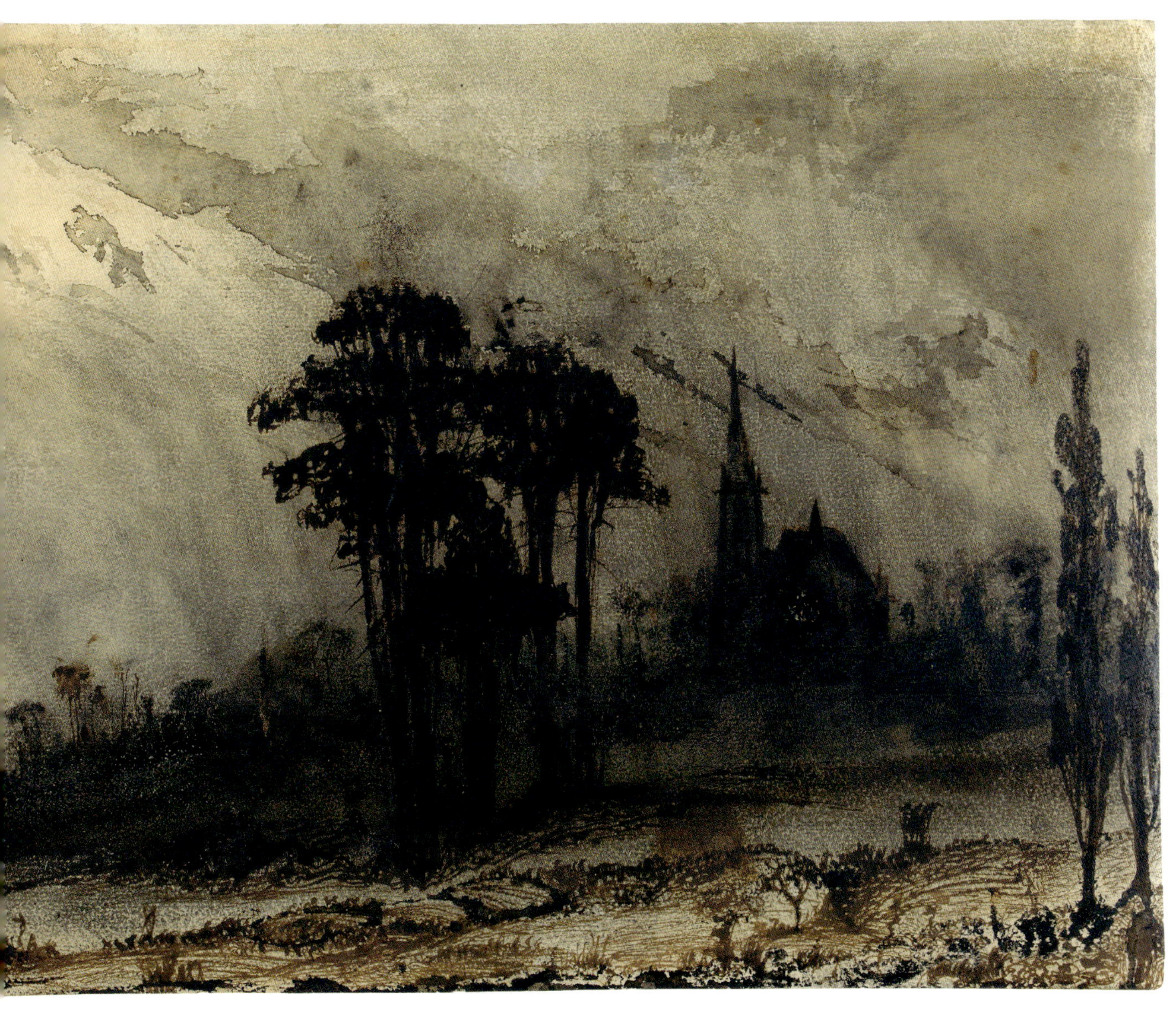

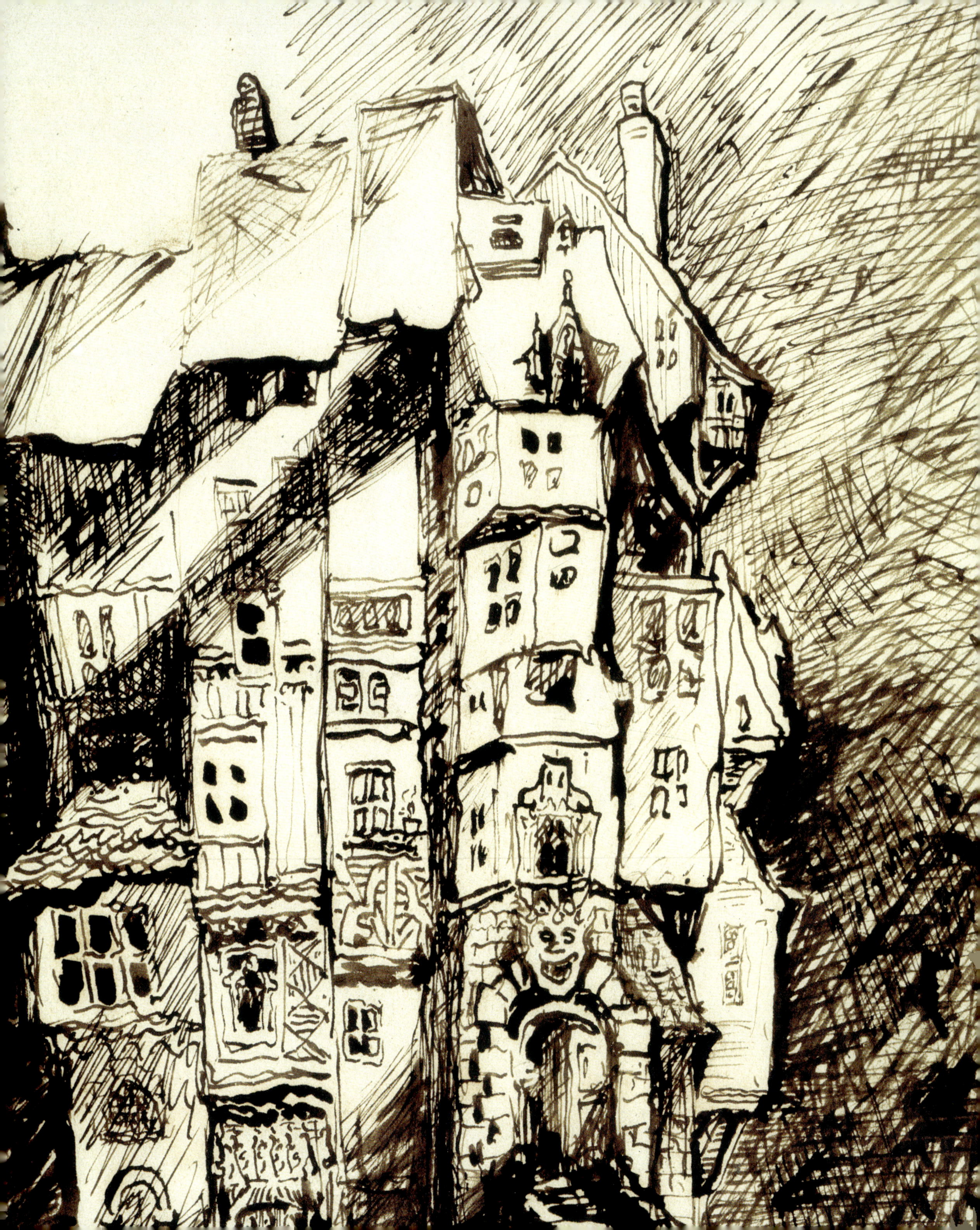

Architecture in the Drawings of Victor Hugo

THOMAS CAZENTRE

Architecture and the human figure: these are the most oft-repeated subjects in the graphic works of Victor Hugo. His curiosity was constantly aroused by man-made constructions: they fed his imagination, inspired his pencil or pen, and stimulated his experiments with graphic art. From his earliest travel diaries of the 1830s to his last stay in Luxembourg in 1871, Hugo never ceased to represent buildings, whether real, reinvented or entirely fanciful.

The frequent presence of imaginary architecture in Hugo's work is both fascinating and enigmatic. As a writer and a public figure, he was certainly very interested in buildings. He devoted some remarkable texts to the subject and played his part in the recognition and conservation of the architectural heritage of France; his literary work abounds in references to real or fictional buildings. But, with the obvious exception of *The Hunchback of Notre-Dame* (1831), these never constitute a central or structural element in his books. However powerfully described and rich in symbolism they may be, they remain essentially the backdrop to dramas centred around humanity, nature, the cosmos or history. There is a specificity in Hugo's graphic works that cannot be defined by literature: his images possess their own symbolic economy, their own system of signification, beyond or beside words.

From observation to fantasy

What did Hugo really know about architecture? By modern standards, not a great deal, at any rate from direct experience. During his adult life he travelled very little, even in his own country. For Hugo there was to be no voyage to the Orient, which had become a rite of passage, following Byron's example, for a number of his contemporaries (Chateaubriand, Lamartine, Nerval, Flaubert), although Hugo had occasionally expressed a vague longing

Detail of fig. 24

to follow in their footsteps. He saw the Mediterranean only once, and did not even extend his journey as far as Italy. His single trip to Spain took him no farther than the Basque Country and Navarre (cat. 14). During his eighteen-year exile in the Channel Islands, he made only the briefest excursions to England, ignoring the splendid cathedrals at Canterbury, Winchester or Salisbury that might have attracted and dazzled the author of *The Hunchback of Notre-Dame*.[1] His life as a tourist was confined to north-western France, Belgium and the Rhine Valley.

Hugo's lack of curiosity about the appearance of the real world – or, more precisely, his genuine but selective curiosity, which expected nothing to be revealed by experience – is acknowledged and justified in his 1830 poem 'To my friends L.B. and S.-B.'; these were the painter Louis Boulanger and the writer Charles-Augustin Sainte-Beuve, then on a trip to Rouen.[2] He evokes the 'town with its hundred spires', which he longs to discover yet apparently does not mind never actually seeing. He continues to evoke such places, the 'Romes', the 'Cordobas' and the 'Alhambras', that fill his mind: 'And I dream! Never will imperial cities / eclipse this dream with its idealised splendour. / Let us hang on to the illusion: it vanishes so soon', as if to admit that these architectural visions owe little to visual memory. His mental gallery was not the main source of his writing: at best, it was material that his imagination and graphic handiwork would reduce and transform, a promontory from which his dream world could set sail, as he describes it in one of his greatest poems, 'La Pente de la rêverie' (1830). The poem could stand as a visionary introduction to his entire graphic output.[3]

His scant regard for direct observation should not be mistaken for indifference, however. Hugo's eye for architecture was accurate, precise and well informed. He had read and assimilated the main scholarly works on the history of architecture available in French at the time.[4] When a building attracted his gaze, he was able to characterise it and represent it accurately, and to extol its monumentality. His travel journals are full of drawings of architecture done on the spot, in pencil, and unquestionably beautiful in their classicism (cat. 12).

Some of these drawings are enhanced with ink, which produces an immediate reinvention of the subject observed: the pen accentuates the lines, obliterating certain details while emphasising others, producing shadows and contrasts, adding vegetation and sketchy outlines of figures. A drawing of 1864 depicting Eltz Castle in Germany (fig. 22) shows this touching-up process in an unfinished state. We see the brooding vision of the foreground rising up as if to assault the architectural outline sketched in pencil.

The Rhine drawings of 1839–40 (for example *Furteneck in Mist*, cat. 20) bear layer upon layer of wash, intended to produce an effect of shadow or mist, but here manifestly more graphic than naturalistic; the wash is used to cover the building, to separate it from its surroundings and to transport it into a secondary reality. In drawings made between 1850 and 1860, such as *City on the Rhine* (cat. 16), this process becomes systematic, drowning the outlines under layers of brown wash, until the wash is almost opaque.

Other drawings bear witness to a further distancing from observation. Thus, the Gothic façade with asymmetrical towers of *Towers and Spires of a Gothic Cathedral* (cat. 13) seems at first glance to represent Chartres Cathedral, and the building was certainly Hugo's starting point: he visited it with Célestin Nanteuil in 1836, who made a drawing of it. But by subtly modifying style, composition and environment, Hugo lent the image an 'undeniably bizarre accent', as Gérard Audinet puts it, 'a completely dreamlike character'.[5]

Eltz Castle, September 1864. Pencil, pen, ink and wash on paper, 25.8 x 19.2 cm. Bibliothèque nationale de France, Paris, Département des Manuscrits, inv. no. NAF 13345, f. 2

Oriental Landscape, 1837. Pen, ink and wash on wove paper, 20.5 x 20.8 cm. Maisons de Victor Hugo, Paris / Guernsey, inv. no. 135

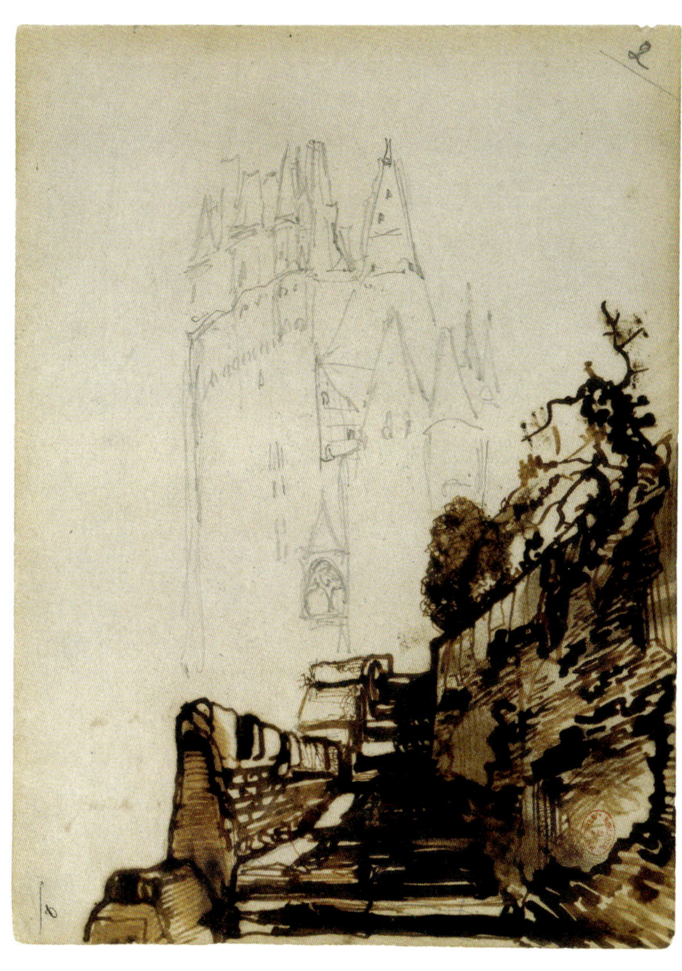

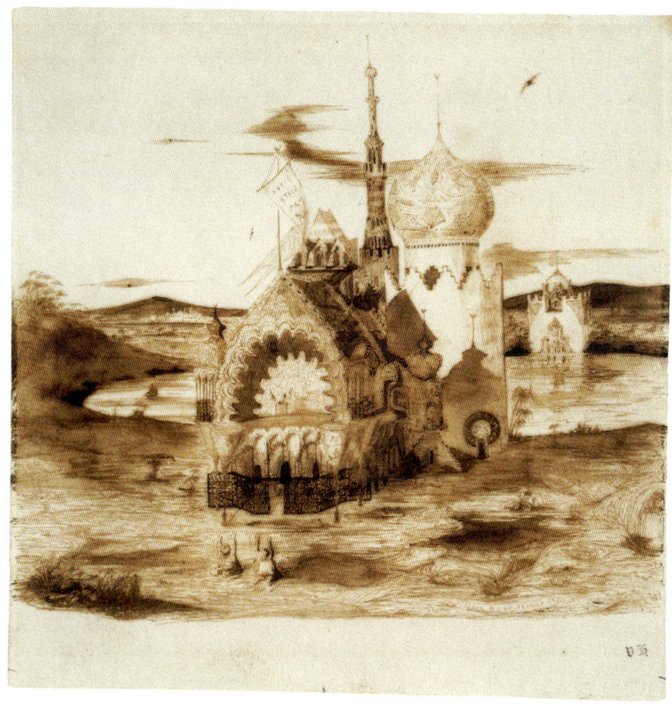

Architecture observed, reinterpreted, reinvented … the next phase was pure fantasy, consisting of fanciful buildings rendered with great precision but with no reference to any existing structure nor to any identifiable style. Hugo accomplished this decisive leap forward by the production of a brief series of 'pagodas' and 'oriental' landscapes in 1836–37. In these compositions, documentary sources can be readily identified: references to Islamic and Chinese architectural models such as Hugo may have encountered in the academic literature of the day. Yet their playful collage of elements taken from radically different civilisations and periods in history (as at the Royal Pavilion in Brighton), their tricks with proportion and their isolation in imprecise landscapes all reject any notion of genuine reference in favour of dreamlike fantasy (fig. 23).

This 'Orient', like the Orient in the collection of poems produced by Hugo in 1829, for which he devised a coloured frontispiece in about 1855 (cat. 9), makes no claim to any cultural, historical or geographical veracity. It simply depicts a province of Hugo's imagination, so infinite, so far beyond reality that the drawing can discard any mimetic intention: it is a purely created location. Drawings inspired in similar fashion, but more allusive and more painterly, can occasionally be found over the succeeding years. During the 1840s Hugo's fantasies took their inspiration from the vocabulary of European architecture, such as fantastic castles or ancient cities bristling with spires; these are executed using a more descriptive, more varied technique and were to culminate in Hugo's most powerfully evocative drawings, for example *The Cheerful Castle* (cat. 38) or *The City with the Broken Bridge*.[6]

From fantasy to form

Although these 'oriental fantasies'[7] were nothing more than a digression in his output, Hugo's extreme taste for the bizarre recurs in his architectural drawings. He was interpreting an aesthetic principle whose literary model he had found in Shakespeare and which he adopted from the preface to his 1827 play *Cromwell* onwards: a mixture of registers with unexpected, sometimes clashing associations and a fascination with composite things and beings. In the literary world, the search for the heterogeneous may claim close fidelity to real life. In architecture, it is the other way round: the heterogeneous takes on an added appearance of strangeness or marginality. Hugo enjoyed noticing the incongruous, for example a cottage surmounted by a windmill (cat. 18). It also amused him to present architectural fantasies with the pretence of literal representation: imaginary constructions that are technically impossible, defying not only aesthetic laws but also the laws of gravity. He piled things up, grafted one thing onto another, juxtaposed elements like an antiquary making fantasy creations from disparate objects or a child playing with wooden blocks, for example *The Home of 'Hugo-Tête-d'Aigle'* (cat. 56), the Eddystone Light – even though its inspiration was a realistic engraving by James Beeverell[8] – or the house at Saint-Malo populated by gangsters, beggars, prostitutes and smugglers in his novel *The Toilers of the Sea* (1866) (fig. 24).

Hugo's games with decomposition and recomposition characterise a large part of his architectural output. In his travel notebooks he frequently sketched details: a door, a watchtower, the top of a building. From 1850 he began to use these architectural fragments

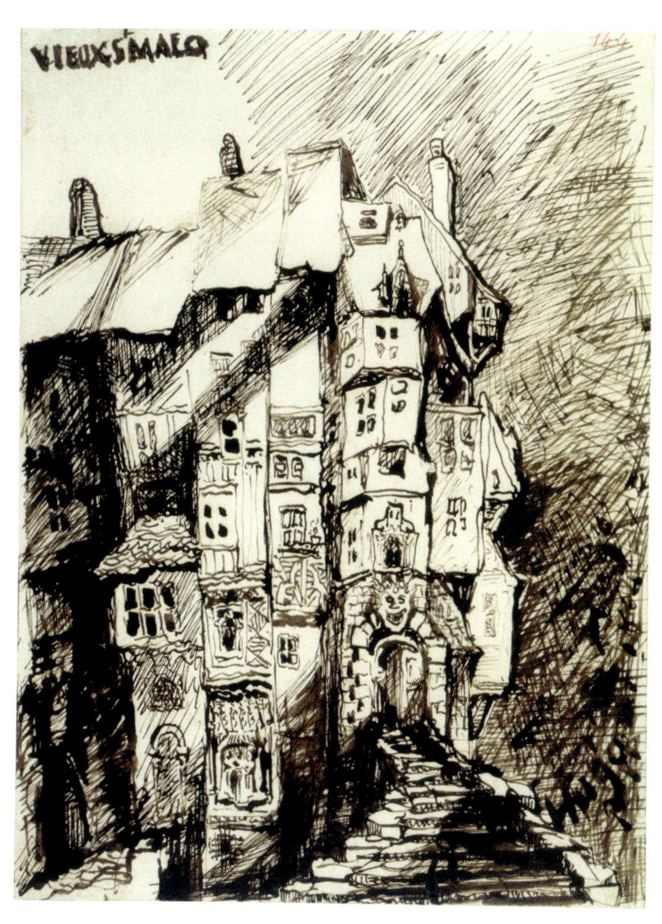
VIEUX ST MALO

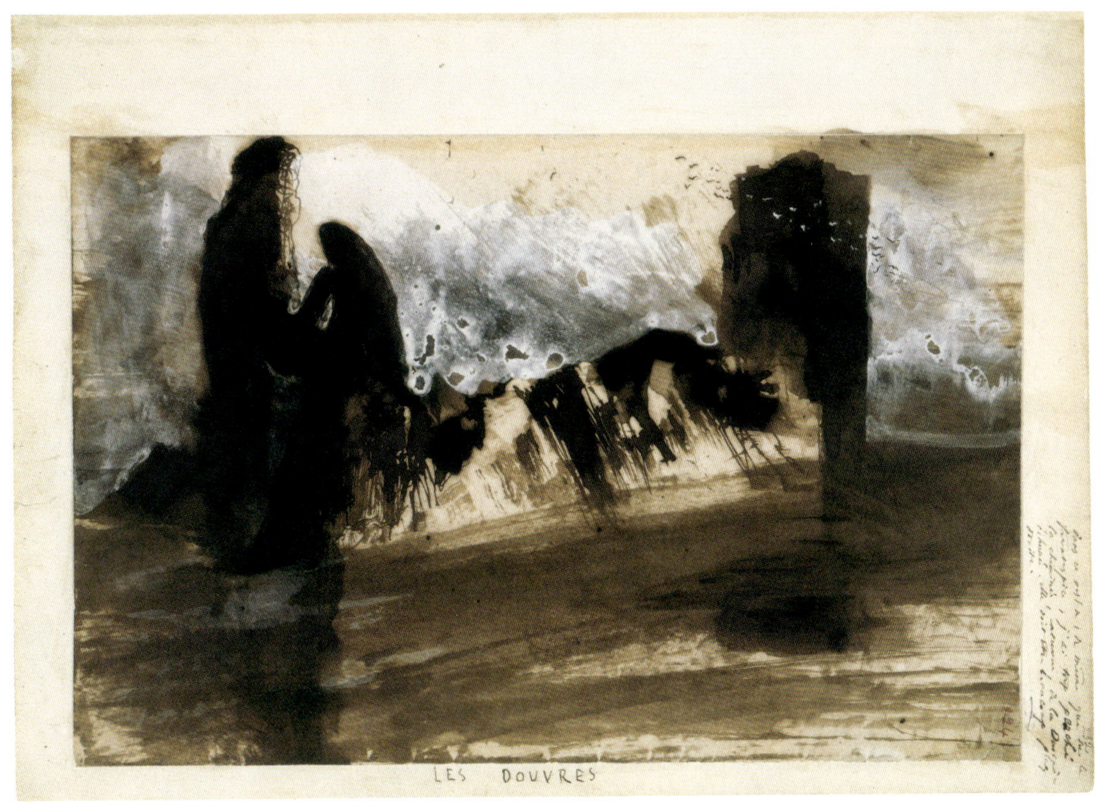
LES DOUVRES

as an inventory of forms upon which he drew in his compositions in apparently random fashion, with symbolism that is unclear. His works were by now closer to the cerebral landscapes of Giorgio de Chirico than to the classical ruins of Hubert Robert (cats 21, 22). Some of Hugo's most striking drawings show buildings apparently floating in an ill-defined space, by day or by night, in the air, on the sea or on land, as if they have been wrenched from their original environment and transported into an insubstantial space with no discernible boundaries.

The ultimate phase of this process was the reduction of architecture to its simplest forms, silhouettes that can be placed freely on the page, positive or negative, and around which the imagination, or the simple random play of the visual material, can have free rein. The use of cut paper, either to print with or as a stencil, appears in dozens of drawings and about twenty of these cut-outs survive. For the most part, they represent architectural forms: the Tower of Babel, steeples, a rock on Jersey surmounted by a chapel, but above all fortified castles, some of them identifiable (Vianden Castle, cat. 43), others purely generic (cat. 40).

At a certain point in their graphic transformation – darkening, stumping, immersion in colour wash – these forms begin to lose their architectural character. They rejoin the fluid world of universal analogy, of metamorphosis, of the non-specific that is so characteristic of Hugo's aesthetic, an aesthetic that found its most radical achievement in compositions consisting entirely of blots. We know how Hugo enjoyed spotting a forest in a cathedral, a monstrous beast in a building, a face in a tree trunk, a human or an animal profile in a mountain or a cliff face (see cat. 15); in the same fashion, in some of the drawings, the works of man and nature mingle and hybridise. Rocks, ruins and atmospheric phenomena merge into indistinct hallucinations: the silhouette of a fortress suddenly precipitated from the shadows by a flash of lightning (fig. 26); the 'Dicq' in Jersey, a man-made construction that could just as well be a forest of dead trees or an ossuary of titanic creatures (cat. 66); or the imaginary rocks near Guernsey known as the Douvres (fig. 25) in *The Toilers of the Sea*, 'these two natural towers guarding the dark city of monsters'.[9]

From form to symbol

The architectural forms in Hugo's world are weighted with significance because of their malleability and their analogical virtuality. Whether depicted in minute detail or verging on abstraction, his forms are part of a visual language that stirs up visions and brings news of another world, or other worlds; indeed, they are the richest, most identifiable register of this language. Some of the constructions, by their very nature, bear multiple symbolic meanings that are not exclusive to Hugo, even when he appropriated them and integrated them into his own universe: bridges, broken causeways (cat. 65), beacons (cat. 75). But these are far fewer in number than the edifices drawn or fashioned from Hugo's imaginary medieval worlds, the famous 'burgs'[10] (strongholds) that are the subject of his most ambitious drawings.

In an effort to approach the symbolic message of Hugo's monuments we need to read his most striking, most comprehensive piece of writing on architecture, the chapter 'Ceci tuera cela' ('This will kill that') in *The Hunchback of Notre-Dame*. Without examining all the implications of this text – which cannot in any case be attached to Hugo's graphic work as it was written at least two decades earlier and deals mainly with religious architecture, which seldom appears in the drawings – we need to bear in mind its central tenet: 'from the origin of things up to and including the fifteenth century of the Christian era, architecture was the great book of mankind, man's chief form of expression in the various stages of his development'.[11] To Hugo, architecture in its most significant manifestations goes beyond the alliance of form and function: it is a total language, the bearer of a world view that is at once political, philosophical, spiritual and mythological. Architecture began when the first stones were piled one on top of the other and, in Europe, culminated in the Gothic period. The invention of printing, enabling the wholesale diffusion of the written word, deprived architecture of its *raison d'être*, drawing it inexorably towards fatal decline into hollow formalism and pastiche. Since the Renaissance, architecture had become, for Hugo, a dead art form whose sole value was to bear archaeological witness.

Ancient monuments are the scattered remains of a vast book written before the invention of the book: to anyone who knows how to see them, to *read* them, they speak of an immemorial vanished world, more mythological than historical. It would be absurd to attempt to retrieve a coherent and unequivocal account from this long-dispersed book, many of whose pages are missing and whose language is no longer familiar to us. Like those ancient texts whose fragmentary survival increases their polysemy and prophetic power, Hugo's spectral buildings are open to endless interpretations, none of them random.

As Pierre Georgel points out when discussing *The Castle with the Cross* (*Le Burg à la Croix*) (1850; Maisons de Victor Hugo, Paris / Guernsey, inv. no. 40), in these lugubrious fortresses, in these sombre cities enclosed by their ramparts, it is possible to read '[the] dark hub of the poet's "philosophy", the tragic awareness of human disaster, the terror when faced with the inexorable pitiless closure of *ananké*'.[12] This architectural metaphor for human damnation – Hugo was undoubtedly inspired by Piranesi's prisons or John Martin's apocalyptic scenes – is evident in some of the drawings and is based on very explicit literary references.

Yet, other architectural visions tell other stories in other drawings: thus, in Hugo's 'fantastical' work described above, the airy, exuberant architecture seems to connect us with the fabled cities of fairy tales or the *Thousand and One Nights*; or with the bird's-eye view of Paris relived by the narrator from atop the towers of Notre-Dame;[13] or with those 'beautiful old cities of Spain' depicted from imagination in the preface to *Les Orientales* (1829). Nostalgia mingles with utopia: Hugo's world predates the emergence of political and economic modernity and their translation into aesthetics. Reverie, fantasy and adventure have a free hand.

Finally, we should return to the genesis of the 'burg' as a subject in the preface to *Les Burgraves* (1843), in which Hugo describes his travels in the Rhine Valley a few years earlier. He compares the landscape to Thessaly, where the Greek poets saw all the vestiges of the Titans' struggles against the gods. The Rhineland castles bear a similar message: solitary and proud, they bear witness to the struggles of heroic human beings before the advent of empires, whose literary incarnations are the 'wandering knights' of *La Légende des siècles* (1859). Conscious of their own inevitable defeat, of the death sentence threatened by the march of history, they defend their savage liberty and the pursuit of their ideals: a mythological aristocracy with whom the poet-painter clearly strongly identified.

It is revealing that Hugo should have devoted his last series of large drawings to Vianden Castle in Luxembourg in the summer of 1871. He represented it close up, from below, in all its power, or projected against the sky as the backdrop to a monumental

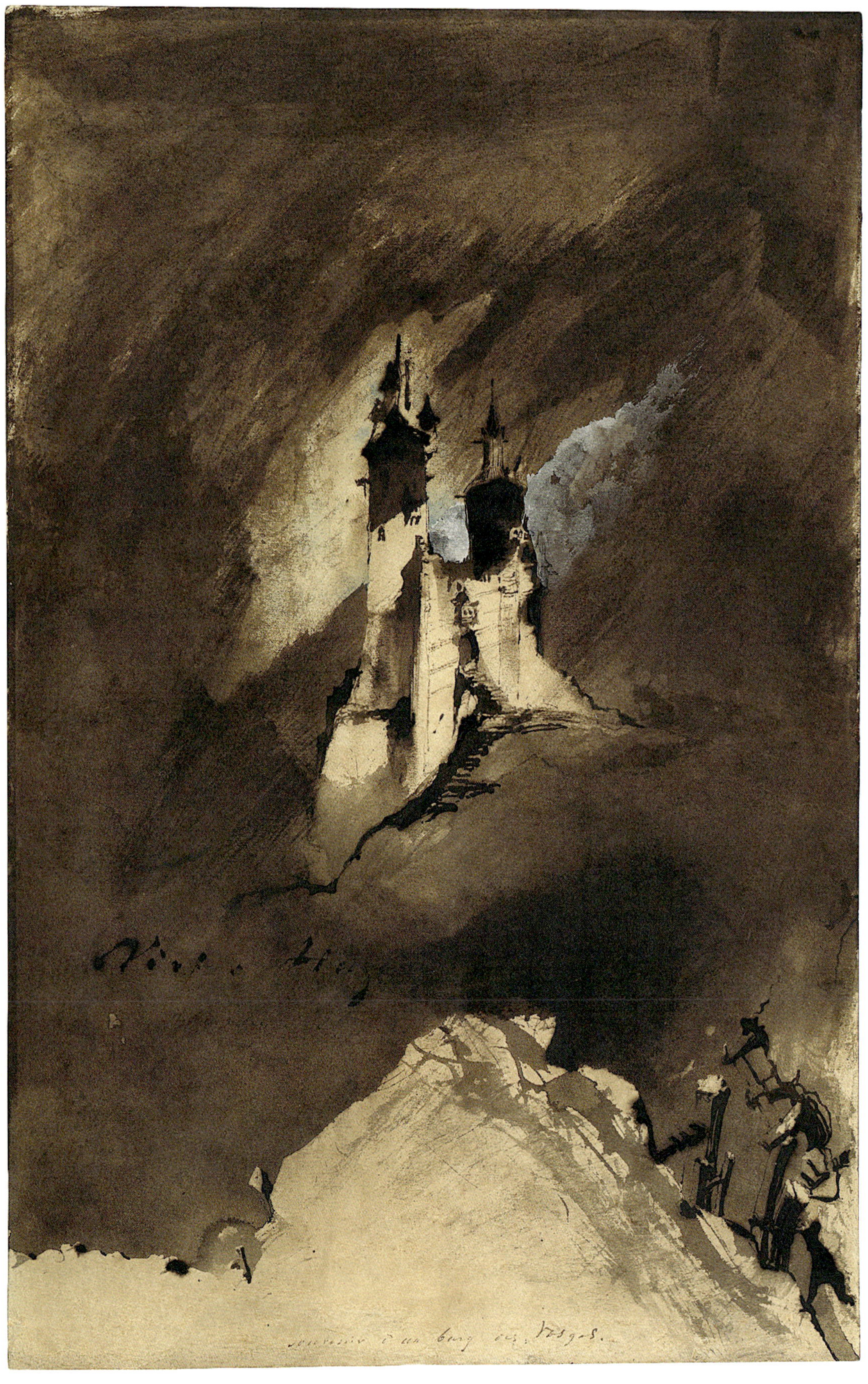
Victor Hugo
souvenir d'un burg des Vosges.

stone cross (cat. 45). Or, by contrast, reduced by mist and moonlight to a ghostly silhouette (cat. 43); or even obscured by an immense spider's web to which any number of interpretations might be pinned (cat. 10). Having returned from twenty years of exile, unvanquished and bathed in glory, Hugo was overwhelmed by the loss of loved ones, by being excluded from France and Belgium by war and political rivalries; he was also conscious of approaching the last stage of his journey and his final meeting with the unknown. Hugo came to find a kind of consolation in his solitary confrontation with this formidable fortress. In his search for peace, he sketched on the fragile paper support, for the last time, the visions that had haunted him since his early drawings: an act of faith in human accomplishment, faith in that part of eternity to which we may all aspire.

Fig. 26

Souvenir of a Castle in Vosges, 1857. Brush and iron gall washes, pen and iron gall ink, and white gouache on paper, 47 x 31 cm. The Metropolitan Museum of Art, New York, Purchase, Harris Brisbane Dick Fund, Donald Young Foundation Gift, Harry G. Sperling Fund, and Mr. and Mrs. David M. Tobey Gift, 2012, inv. no. 2012.17

Writing and Drawing

Victor Hugo is thought to have produced more than 4,000 drawings during his lifetime, of which approximately 3,000 survive today. Although Hugo gave many to family and friends, the majority are now in the collection of the Maisons de Victor Hugo, Paris / Guernsey, with additional works held as part of the legacy of Hugo's manuscripts at the Bibliothèque nationale de France in Paris. Drawing was a largely private activity for Hugo, but it remained a significant aspect of his creative practice throughout his life and informed the writing he presented to a public audience.

Hugo enjoyed creating caricatures and continued to draw them among friends even when he had become a household name, thanks to his career as a writer and as a politician. He participated privately in a wider public vogue for caricatures in Paris, which manifested itself in satirical publications such as *Le Charivari*. The writer and poet Antoine Fontaney wrote in 1832 of an evening spent with Hugo: 'we stay until midnight in Victor's office chatting and debating; … Victor also drawing, making little caricatures … which he places every evening on his children's bed and which they find when they wake up in the morning, to their great joy.'[1] Although Hugo's own caricatures, for example *The Art Lover* (cat. 3), recount the struggles between classicists and Romantics that are the focus of his early poems and plays, such as *Les Orientales* (1829) and *Hernani* (1830), his own fame and political standing made him a favourite subject for other caricaturists; indeed, he was one of the most frequently depicted figures in nineteenth-century France, often appearing in newspapers and magazines.

Writing and drawing went hand in hand for Hugo. In *A Visiting Card for the New Year, Guernsey* (cat. 4), which was possibly sent as a greeting card, he depicted the ruins of a church, or a castle encircled in foreboding darkness. He made this drawing while on Guernsey, in exile from France due to his outspoken attacks against Napoléon III, who had seized power by force. As became his habit, Hugo added his surname in the foreground of the composition, overshadowing the large building in the background.

An example of the convergence and interrelationship of Hugo's literary and artistic practices can be seen in *The Nest* (cat. 5). Opposite the title page of a copy of his volume of poetry *Songs of the Streets and Woods* (1865) given to his friend the novelist and playwright Paul Meurice,[2] and as a sort of unofficial frontispiece, there is a drawing of a nesting bird, possibly a swift, signed 'VH' and with a dedication in brown ink reading 'To Paul Meurice / Victor Hugo / Hauteville House / January 1, 1868'. The drawing was later engraved and reproduced in the 1886 edition of the book.

Hugo often used the theme of nature as a metaphorical structure in which to work through and present ideas on history, culture, humanity and the passing of time. His interest in drawing subjects of great scale, both natural and man-made, a characteristic that emerges in his drawings of such motifs as ruins, castles and mountains, may relate to the self-mythology of his own towering persona. In *Le Mythen* (cat. 7) his inscription states, 'Drawn at / the Summit / of Rigi / On 11 July 1839 / at sunset / 5,676 feet above sea level'.[3] Although it is unclear which mountain Hugo was referring to,[4] an earlier sketch for this drawing is inscribed to a trip to Mount Rigi in Switzerland in 1839. However, the present composition is thought to have been completed much later in his career, during his period of exile in Jersey (1852–55). The layering of places and times is characteristic of Hugo's work. *Le Mythen* has been linked to many moments in his life. It is thought it might reflect a story told by his father that he was conceived 'almost in mid-air', on 'one of the highest peaks of the Vosges mountains',[5] but has also been linked to a poem, 'Les Montagnes (Désintéressement)', from a collection of poems entitled *La Légende des siècles* (written intermittently between 1855 and 1876), which perhaps suggests that he may have revisited this drawing as inspiration for his written work.[6]

Moving from the sublime monumentality of mountains to a much smaller scale, *Mushroom* (cat. 8) is perhaps one of Hugo's most enigmatic drawings. Very little is known about his depiction of a poisonous mushroom. In a seemingly post-apocalyptic landscape, the drawing reveals a hidden secret: a ghostly human face trapped within the mushroom's stem. Despite the diminutive nature of its subject this is one of Hugo's largest drawings, made in a year when he started to draw complex and surprising compositions at a bigger scale.

Likewise, in *The Town of Vianden Seen through a Spider's Web* (cat. 10), Hugo plays with the idea of scale and turbulence. He wrote of the drawing, made while he was staying in Luxembourg for a few months after being forced out of Belgium, and after his decision not to return to France following the suppression of the Paris Commune by the French army: 'August 13, 1871. I drew in my travel book the large spider's web through which we see the ruin of Vianden like a spectre.'[7] *Rose Thompson*

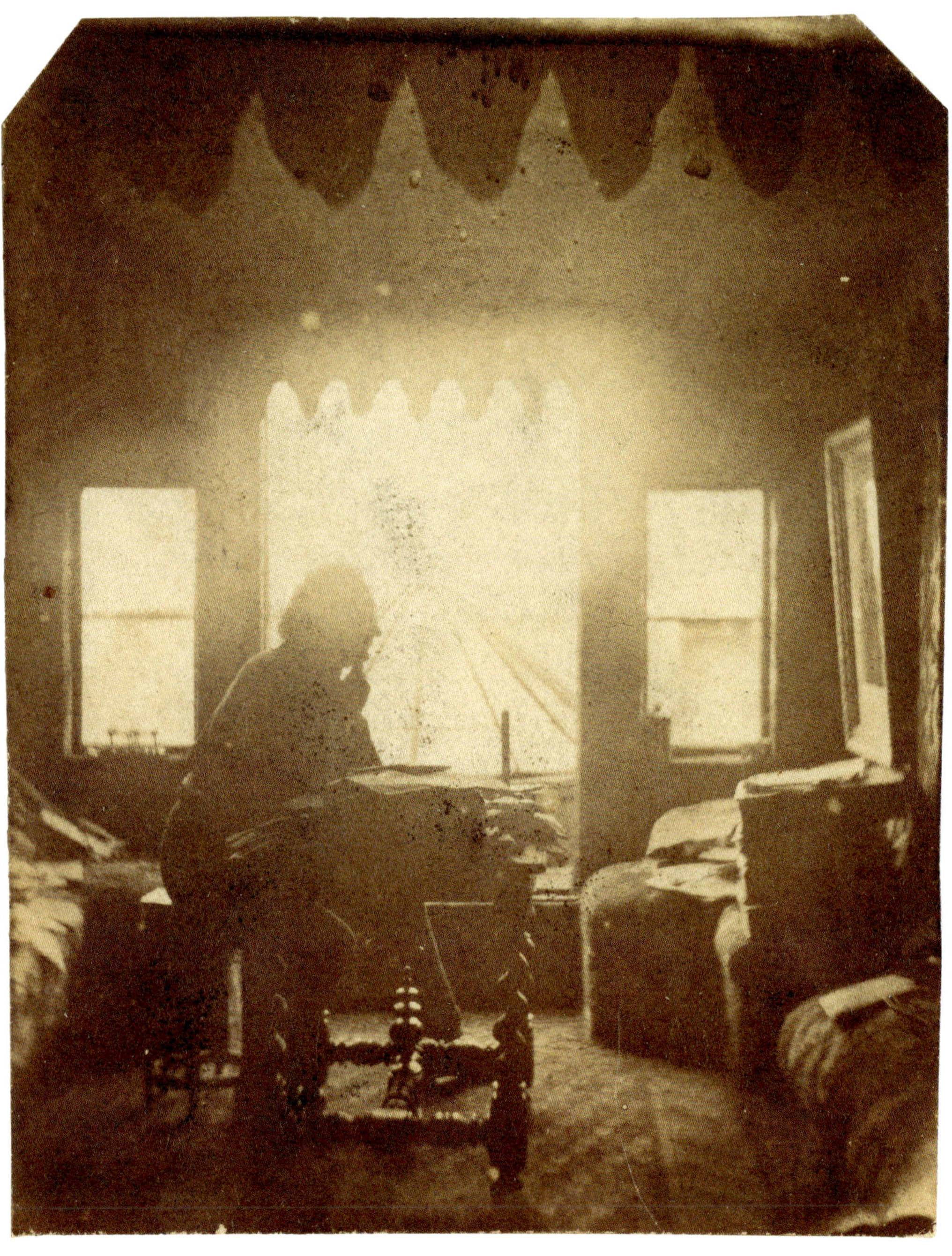

1

Charles Alexandre Leballeur-Villiers
(1815–1870)
*Victor Hugo in His Study at Hauteville
House, Guernsey, before the Construction
of the 'Lookout'*, 1860–61
Print on albumen paper, 8.7 x 6.8 cm
Maisons de Victor Hugo, Paris / Guernsey,
inv. no. 1322.2b

2

The Mouse (*Velmich*), 1840
Pen and brown ink wash, pencil
and graphite on paper, 27.5 x 22 cm
Maisons de Victor Hugo, Paris / Guernsey,
inv. no. ah433

tiens-toi, ne te [...] ne [...] pourvoir. Maintenant voilà les
vacances presque finies, nous n'avons plus que quelques jours et
peu, je vous fais [...] de ma décision.

Si tu as lu ma lettre, mon Charles, tu sais que je [...]
que le chat et la souris, je donne le chat à Toto, je
t'envoie la souris. Ici, [...] le courage de la [...]
la souris en beaucoup [...] grosse en beaucoup plus,
[...] que le chat [...] où je l'ai dessiné, le lit
où elle se perdait avec [...] quelque chose de violent et
de tumultueux.

Tu remarqueras au bas de la [...] violer le masque
de géant avec sa bouche [...] je l'ai dessiné très [...]
tu as vu géant fort [...].

J'ai fait [...] cela avec [...] mes enfants, en pensant
à vous, afin de vous amuser [...] rendre heureux. Mes
[...] d'un [...] comme mes [...] de [...] la nuit,
c'est pour vous.

Je ne sais pas trop dans quel état arriveront tous les dessins que
je vous envoie. Les encres d'auberge changent de couleur du jour
au lendemain avec une fâcheuse facilité.

J'ai beaucoup travaillé pendant les vacances, mon Charles, j'espère
que tu en as fait un peu autant de ton côté. J'ai sans cesse
pensé à toi, mon fils bien-aimé; j'espère que de ton côté tu as
songé à ton petit papa qui t'aime du fond de l'âme
comme je vous [...] que je vous et que j'embrasse sur vos
deux bonnes joues.

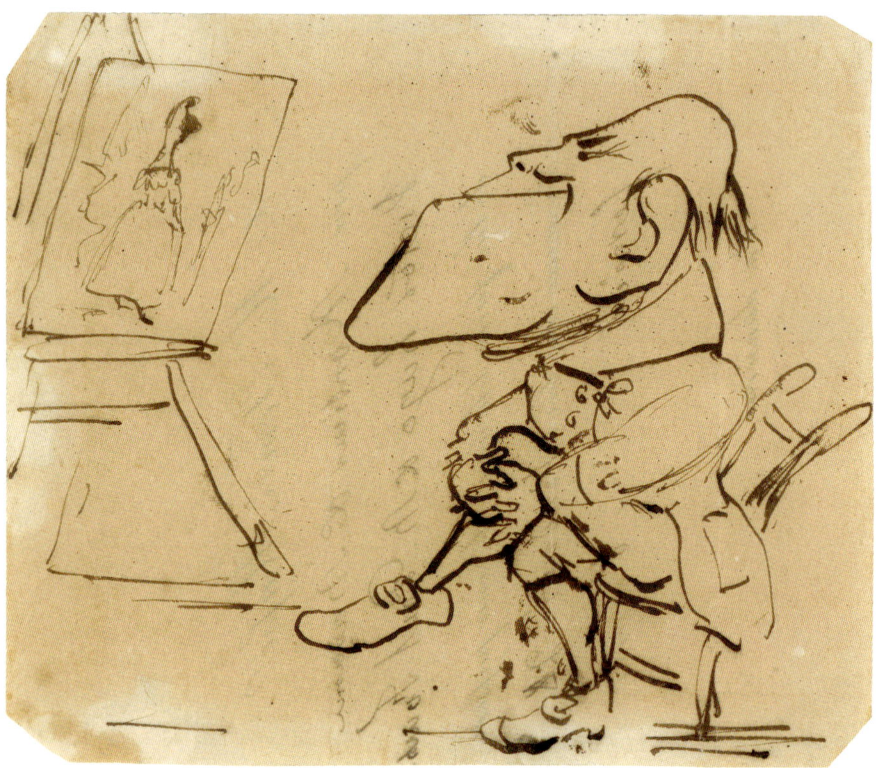

3

The Art Lover, 1834
Ink and pen on paper, 11.5 x 14 cm
Maisons de Victor Hugo, Paris / Guernsey,
inv. no. 3227

4

*A Visiting Card for the New Year,
Guernsey*, 1 January 1856
Pen and brown wash, watercolour,
gouache, charcoal and lace imprint
on paper, 13.1 x 9.9 cm
Courtesy of The University of Manchester,
inv. no. MH/7/10

Drawn by

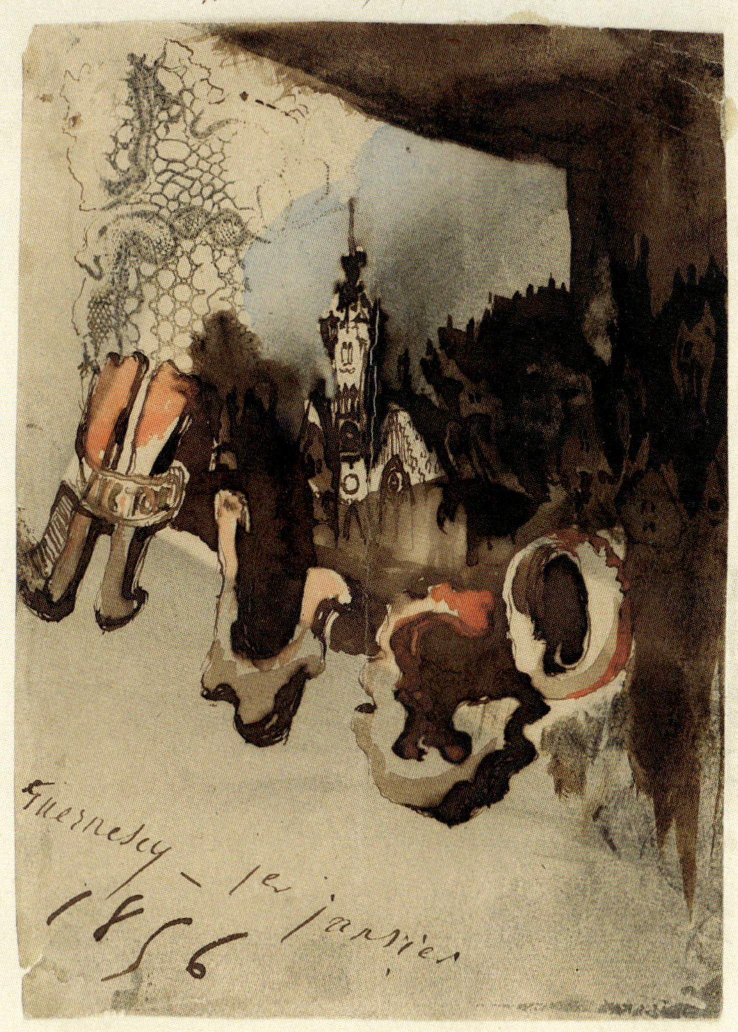

Victor Hugo
Born Feb: 26th 1802. Died May 22nd 1885

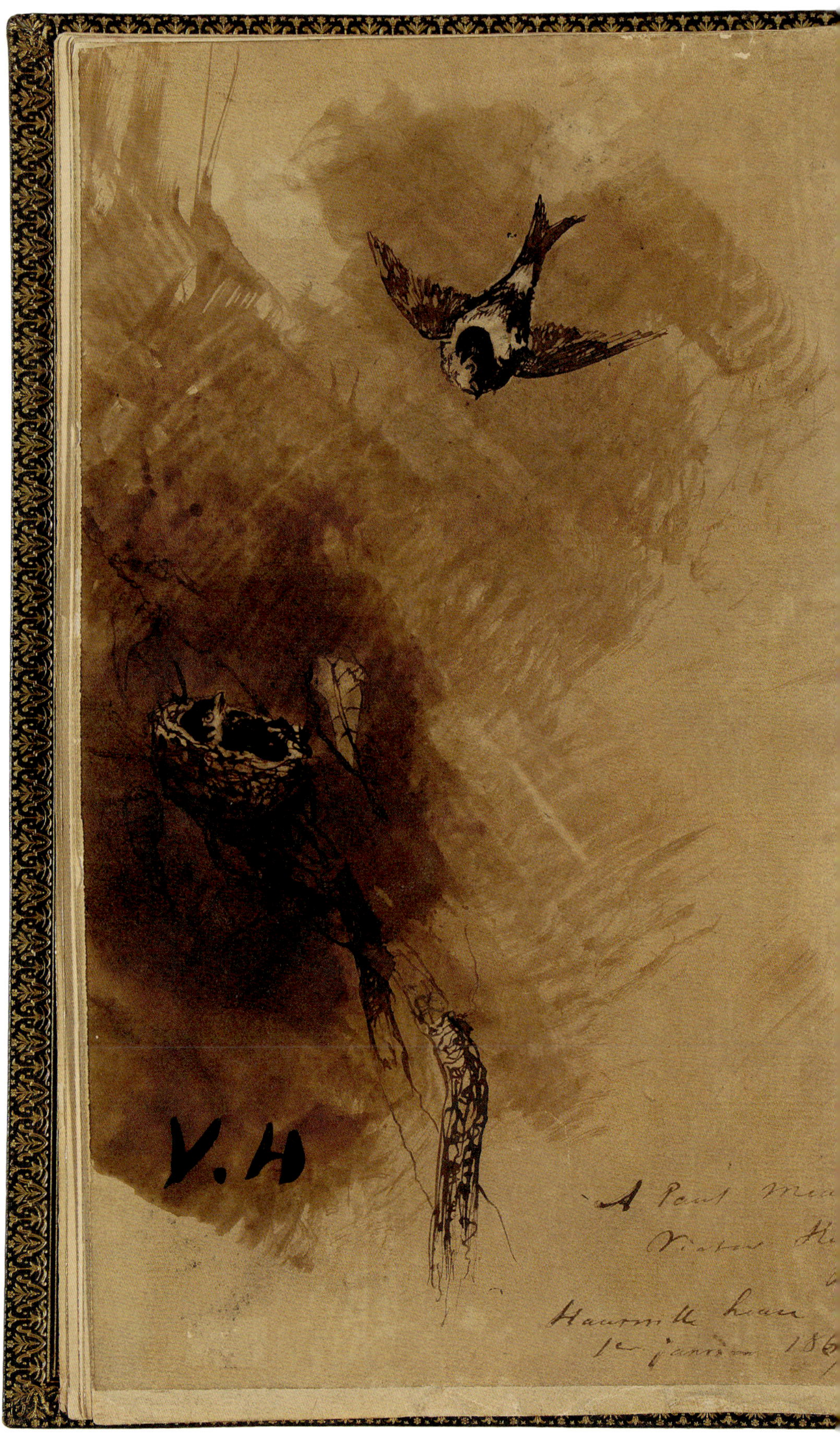

5

The Nest, 1867, the frontispiece of
Paul Meurice's copy of *Chansons des rues
et des bois* (*Songs of the Streets and Woods*)
Pen and brown ink wash and graphite
pencil on paper, 22.5 x 14.5 cm
Maisons de Victor Hugo, Paris / Guernsey,
inv. no. 186

VICTOR HUGO

LES CHANSONS

DES RUES ET DES BOIS

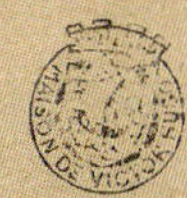

PARIS

LIBRAIRIE INTERNATIONALE

15, BOULEVARD MONTMARTRE

A. LACROIX, VERBOECKHOVEN ET Cⁱᵉ, ÉDITEURS

A BRUXELLES, A LEIPZIG ET A LIVOURNE

—

1866

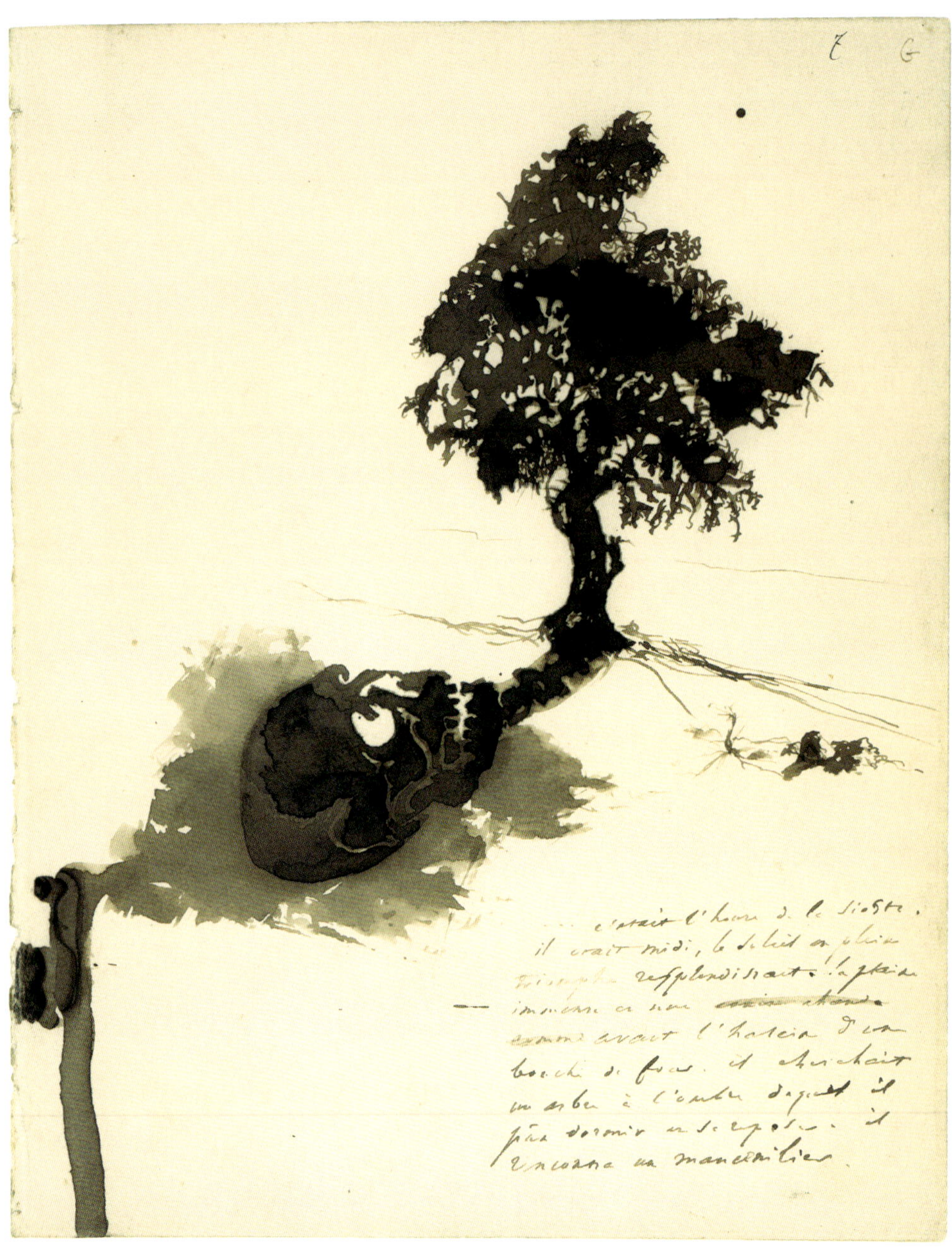

6

The Shade of the Manchineel Tree
(*Notes from a Trip to the Pyrenees
and Spain*), 1856
Pen, brown ink and wash on paper,
29.5 x 23.7 cm
Bibliothèque nationale de France, Paris,
Département des Manuscrits,
inv. no. NAF 13350, fol. 7

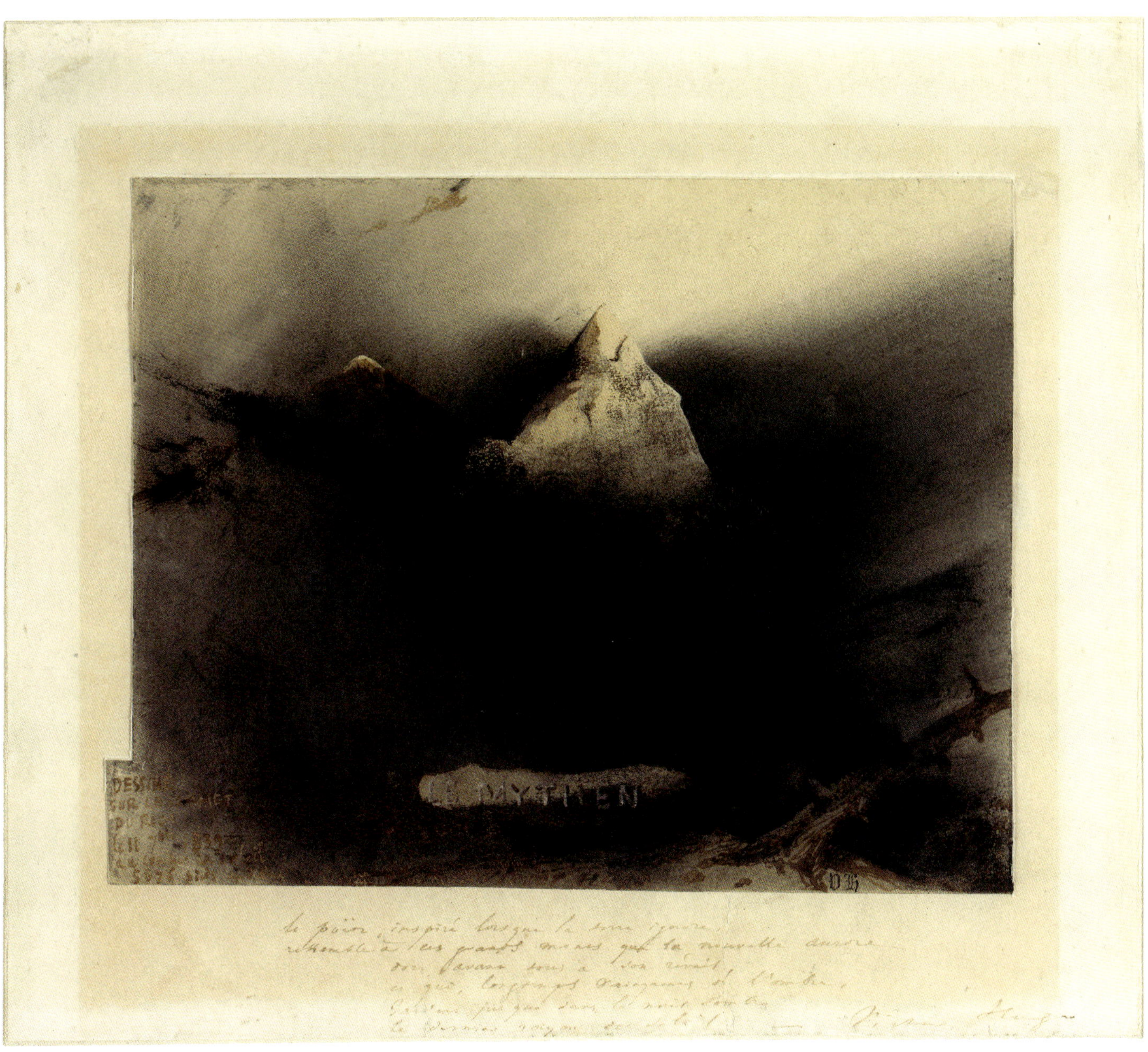

7

Le Mythen, c. 1855
Pen and brown ink wash, graphite
pencil, black ink, charcoal, black chalk
and gold on paper, 22.1 x 29.5 cm
Maisons de Victor Hugo, Paris / Guernsey,
inv. no. 921

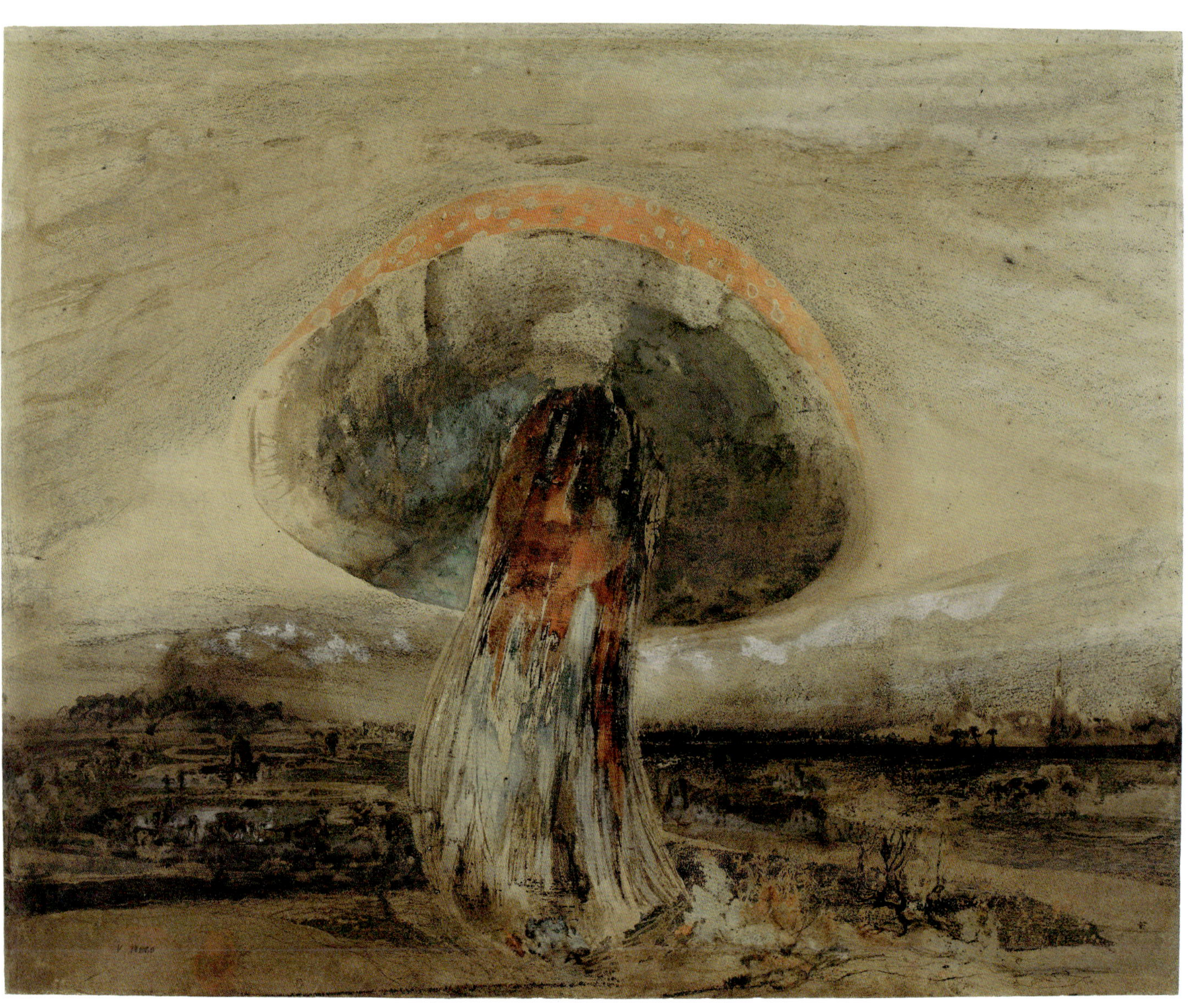

8

Mushroom, 1850
Pen, brown ink and wash, charcoal,
crayon and green, red and white gouache
on paper, 47.4 x 60.8 cm
Maisons de Victor Hugo, Paris / Guernsey,
inv. no. 812

9

Les Orientales, c. 1855–56
Charcoal, pen, brown ink and wash, white,
blue, green and red gouache and lace
imprint on paper, 17.9 x 11 cm
Bibliothèque nationale de France, Paris,
Département des Manuscrits,
inv. no. NAF 13351, fol. 8

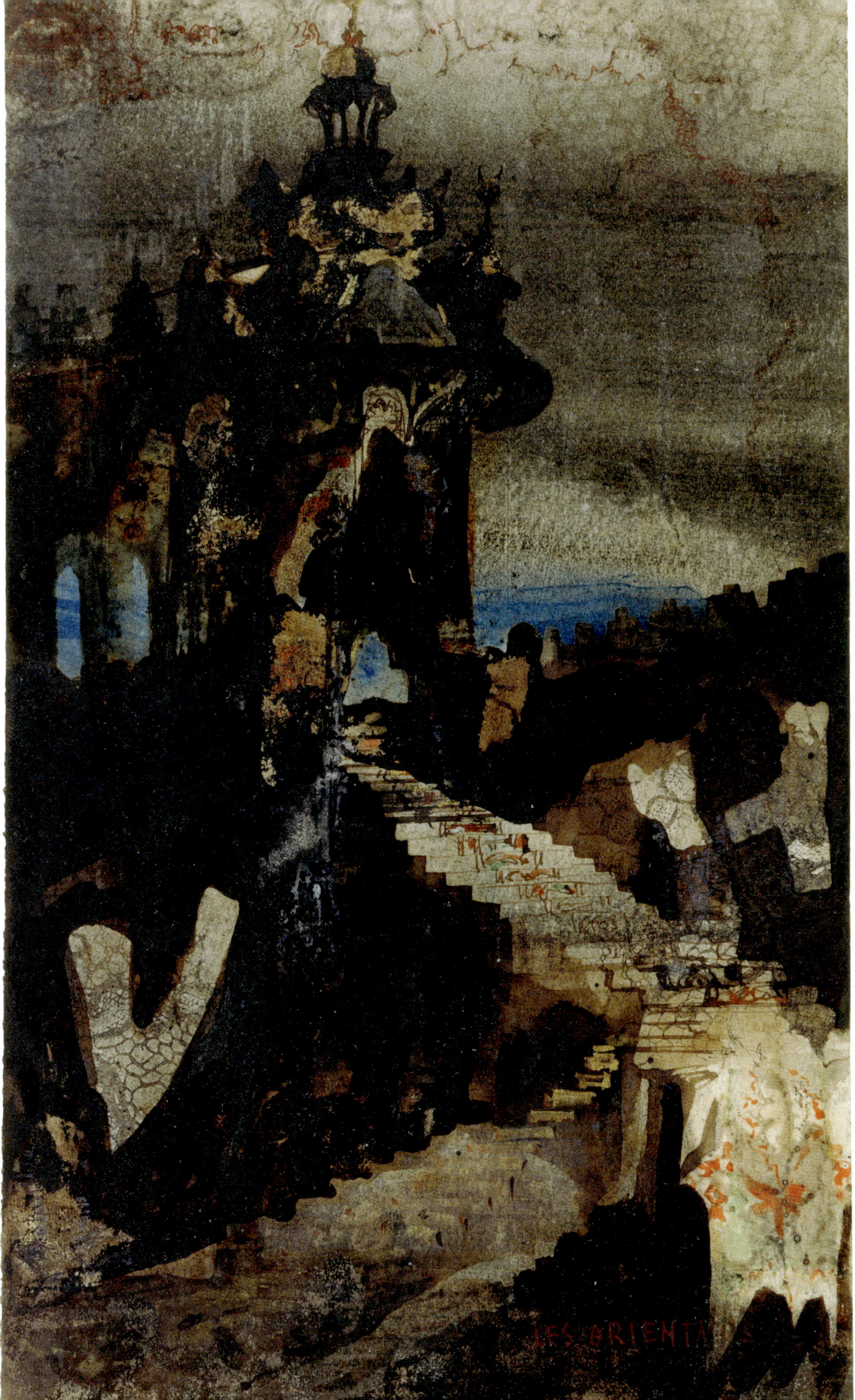

LES ORIENTALES

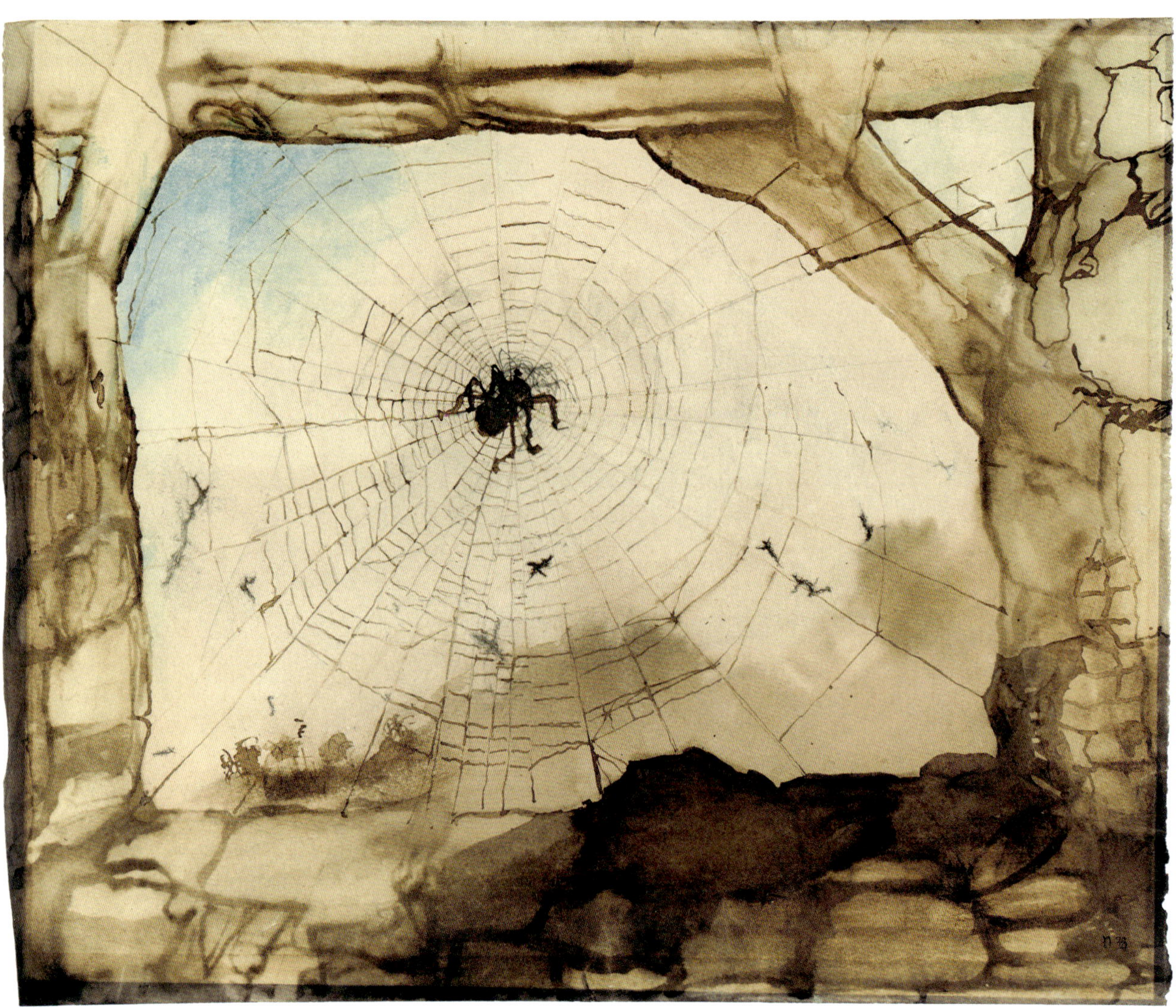

10

*The Town of Vianden Seen
through a Spider's Web*, 1871
Brown ink and wash and blue watercolour
over graphite on paper, 25.5 x 30.3 cm
Maisons de Victor Hugo, Paris / Guernsey,
inv. no. 83

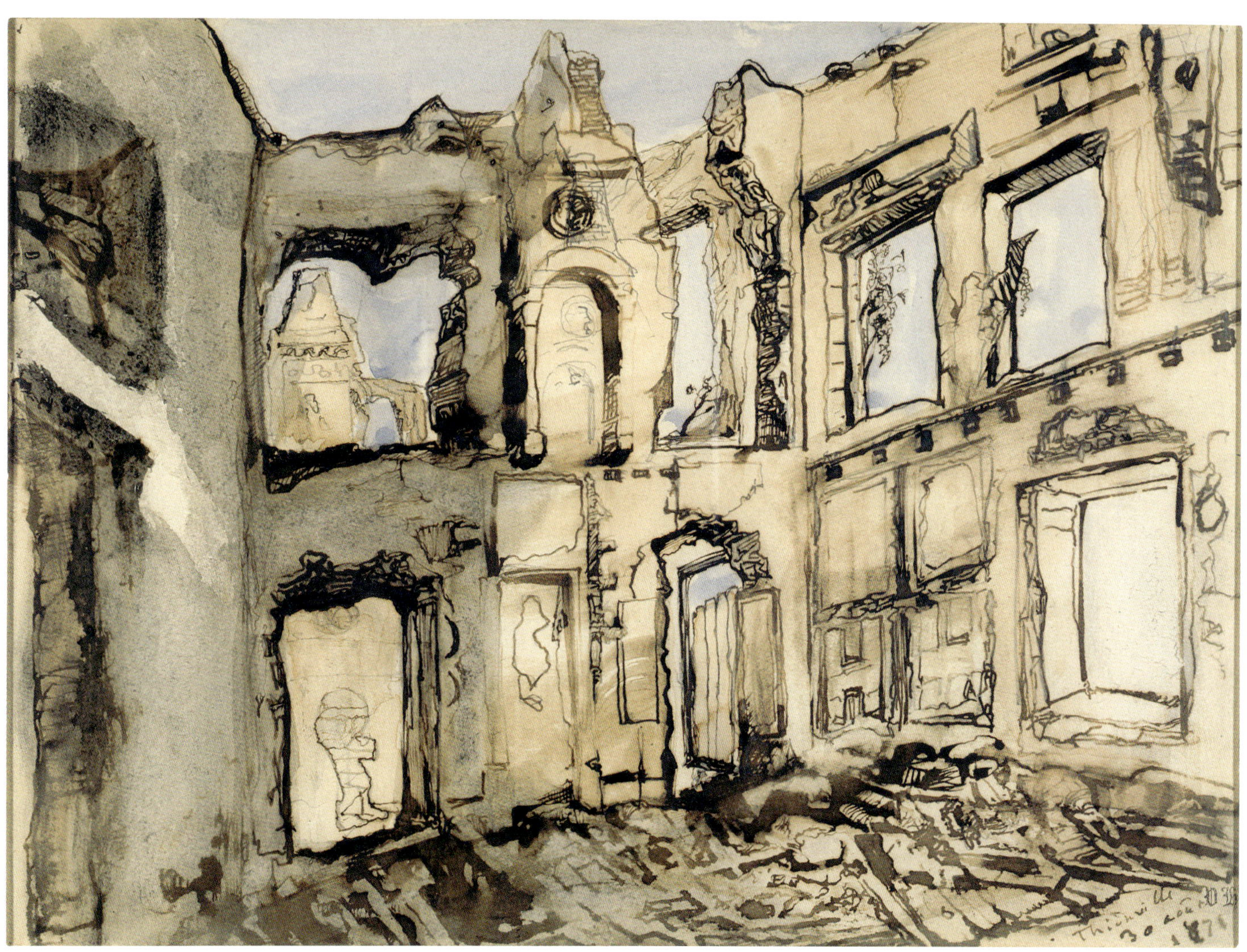

11

Meeting Room of the Municipal
Council of Thionville, after the
Entry of the Prussians, 1871
Pen, brown and purple ink wash,
graphite, black ink and watercolour
on paper, 25.6 x 35.2 cm
Maisons de Victor Hugo, Paris / Guernsey,
inv. no. 11

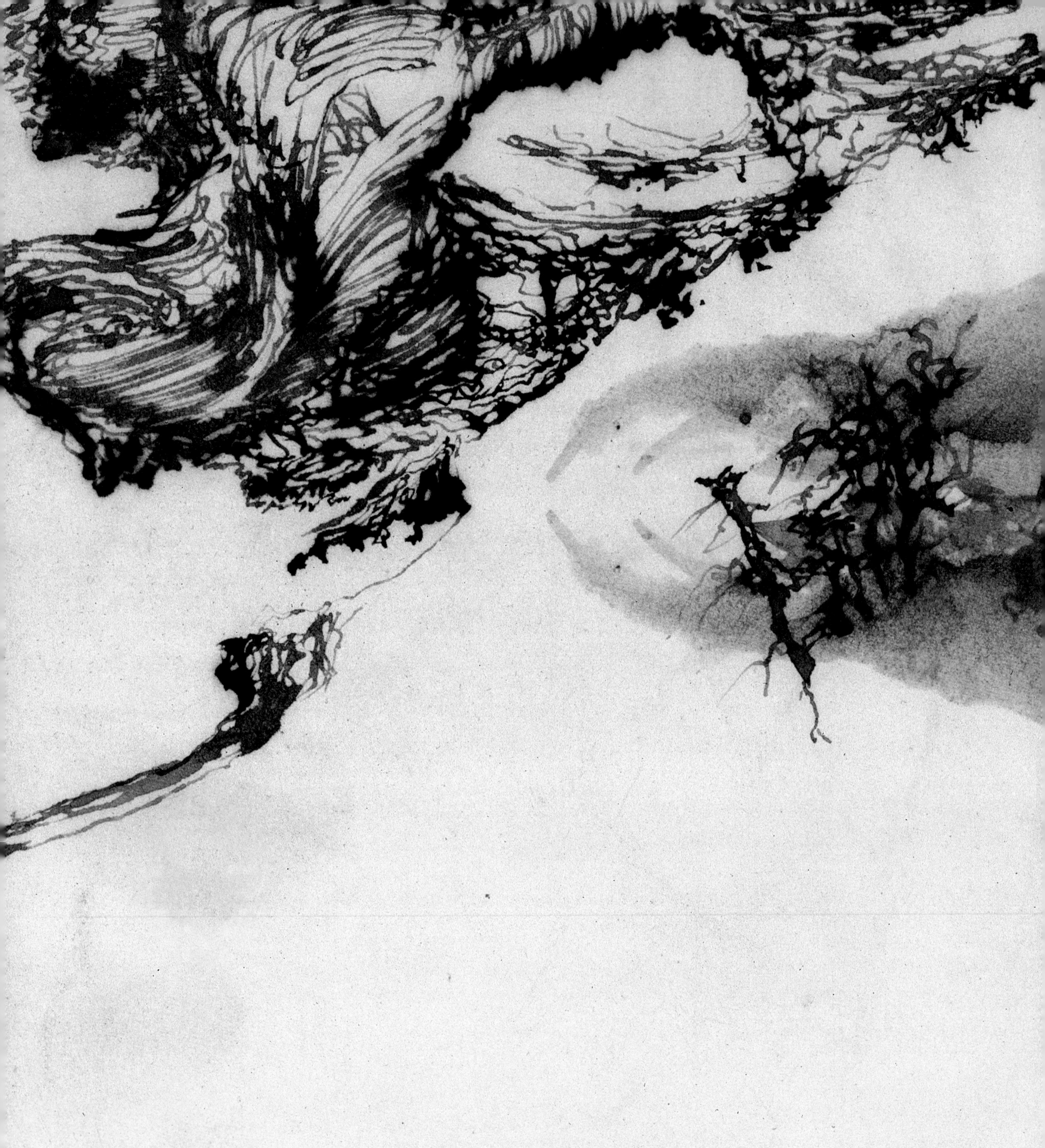

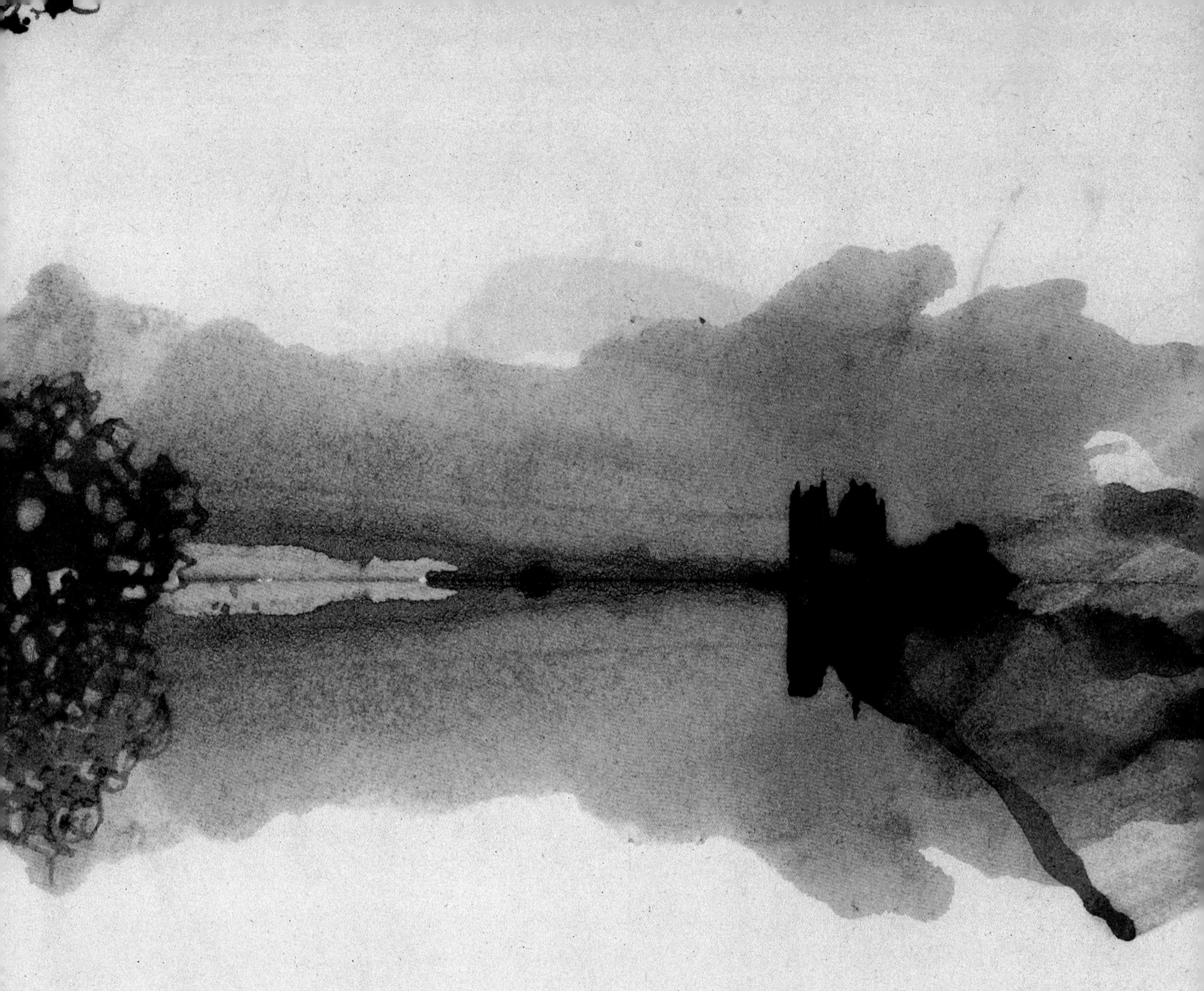

Observation and Imagination

Architecture

From 1834 Hugo began making travel journals to remind himself of places and, specifically, architectural details that had caught his eye. He would fill sketchbooks with meticulously detailed drawings, usually in pencil, and would sometimes later copy them in ink; some of these he would send to his children. The *Travel Sketchbook VII: Trip to the Pyrenees* (cat. 14) is filled with pages of handwritten text describing his travels, interspersed with miniature sketches of cobbled streets, floorplans of buildings – some stuck in like a scrapbook or photo album, others drawn directly on the page – and full-page drawings of castles; the opening shown in cat. 14 is an unfinished sketch of the buildings surrounding the port of Pasaia in northern Spain.

In some of these architectural drawings Hugo was sketching from life, inspired by real buildings that he had come across on his travels. It is believed that he spent several days drawing Chartres Cathedral, which in part inspired *Towers and Spires of a Gothic Cathedral* (cat. 13) in pen and ink, precisely documenting the details of the doorways and spires.[8] Architectural similarities may lead us to believe that he had Notre-Dame in Paris in mind, and indeed his novel of the same name, known in English as *The Hunchback of Notre-Dame*, had been published in 1831, just a few years before. In fact, this novel was to inspire the restoration of Paris's great cathedral between 1844 and 1864. Of particular interest in this drawing is the fusion of architecture and nature. Not only has Hugo meticulously imagined details of the cathedral, but alongside the building he has also drawn a small grove of trees with an interlaced network of leaves and branches.

Sometimes Hugo was inspired by real buildings because of their very ability to seem fantastical. In *Windmill on the Roof of a Farmhouse near Courtray* (cat. 18) he records a windmill atop a farmhouse near the Belgian city of Courtray. It is believed that he must have seen this extraordinary assemblage, although it does not seem to exist today.

Nature and Landscape

As well as architecture, nature and landscape were important motifs in Hugo's work. Although it was drawn at around the same time as *Towers and Spires of a Gothic Cathedral*, the style of the *Travel Sketchbook: Cliff at Bois-Rosé, Fécamp* (cat. 15) is very different. Taken from another of Hugo's many travel journals, the drawing depicts the cliffs in Normandy in a much freer composition, using charcoal or soft black crayon, and wax crayon or lithographic pencils. The progression of Hugo's drawing style was not so straightforward. This image reveals that he incorporated the darker, moodier style of drawing generally associated with his later works, such as the use of heavier lines and shading in ink and charcoal, into his practice throughout his life. *The Abandoned Park* (cat. 25) is a particularly curious composition. A tiny drawing (4.4 x 3.5 cm), it is similar in style to an earlier sketch, *Undergrowth* (cat. 24). At its centre *The Abandoned Park* appears to show a statue or a monument that has returned to nature, overgrown with shrubbery and trees. Hugo is believed to have given the drawing to the artist Jules Laurens in April 1854 when he visited him on Jersey. Laurens later engraved it and published it in the magazine *L'Artiste* in September 1855, where it was presented alongside a few verses by Auguste Vacquerie who, like Hugo, had been exiled to Jersey. The drawing shows Hugo's defiance in the face of imperial censorship and his questioning of the idea of monuments to the great and powerful.

Hugo's artistic journey took him from painstakingly observed and crafted drawings of landscapes and buildings, in which he grappled with such challenges as linear perspective, to deliberate use of methods that limited manual control, including blots, rubbings, imprints of ink-soaked lace, washes and even automatic writing, the latter reflecting his interest in the irrational, spiritualism and table-turning. In these, we can see Hugo's playfulness as he combined a variety of familiar artists' materials, among them charcoal, graphite and ink, with materials that he might have had to hand, such as coffee grounds and soot, and in some drawings made unconventional use of stencils, even his own fingerprints, to produce abstracted compositions. In *Ink-blackened Page with Half-moon and Fingerprints* (cat. 30), the title depicting his method, Hugo experiments with these techniques. The page is saturated with an ink stain but at the top there is a demi-lune opening, where perhaps 'fingerprints become heads peering down a well'.[9]

Taches

One of Hugo's larger works, possibly made as early as 1850, *Taches-Planètes* (cat. 35) is an example of his method of using *taches*, roughly translated in English as stains. In a letter about this drawing to Charles Baudelaire, Hugo wrote, 'I ended up mixing pencil, charcoal, sepia, coal, soot, all kinds of bizarre mixtures that come up to render more or less what is in my eye and especially in my mind.'[10] A number of similar scale drawings from around this date may indicate that this work predates Hugo's exile and could

have been made in a makeshift studio he shared with his mistress Juliette Drouet. He appears to have soaked the paper in water, applying pools of ink to its surface to create marbled, abstract stains interspersed with perfect circles, which indicate the application of stencils, and have been likened to planets within a solar system.

While exiled in Jersey (1852–55), Hugo and his family became interested in table-turning, the spiritualist practice of using a table to communicate with the spirit world, which had been brought to the island by the writer Delphine de Girardin. With his son Charles Hugo acting as medium, Victor Hugo, his wife Adèle and their family believed that they communicated with the spirits of Léopoldine, their daughter who had drowned a decade earlier, as well as famous historical figures including Moses, Jesus, Shakespeare, Joan of Arc and Napoléon, and such allegorical characters as Tragedy, Comedy, Death and the Ocean.[11] Hugo's relationship with the spirit world and unconscious creativity is reflected in some of the drawings he produced in Jersey and later during his exile on Guernsey (1855–70). In *Tache on Folded Paper, Retouched with a Pen* (cat. 32) comparison could be made with the game known as 'Exquisite Corpse' (*Cadavre exquis*), popularised by the Surrealists in the 1920s, in which players draw on a sheet of paper in turn, fold it to conceal their contribution, and then pass it on to the next player to add to it. And yet Hugo's work far predates the Surrealists. He folded his page in half, causing a mirror image of an ink stain to appear on the blank side. Within these stains hide mysterious characters, which Hugo teases out with a pen, manipulating the stains to reveal ghostly, spectral figures. *Rose Thompson*

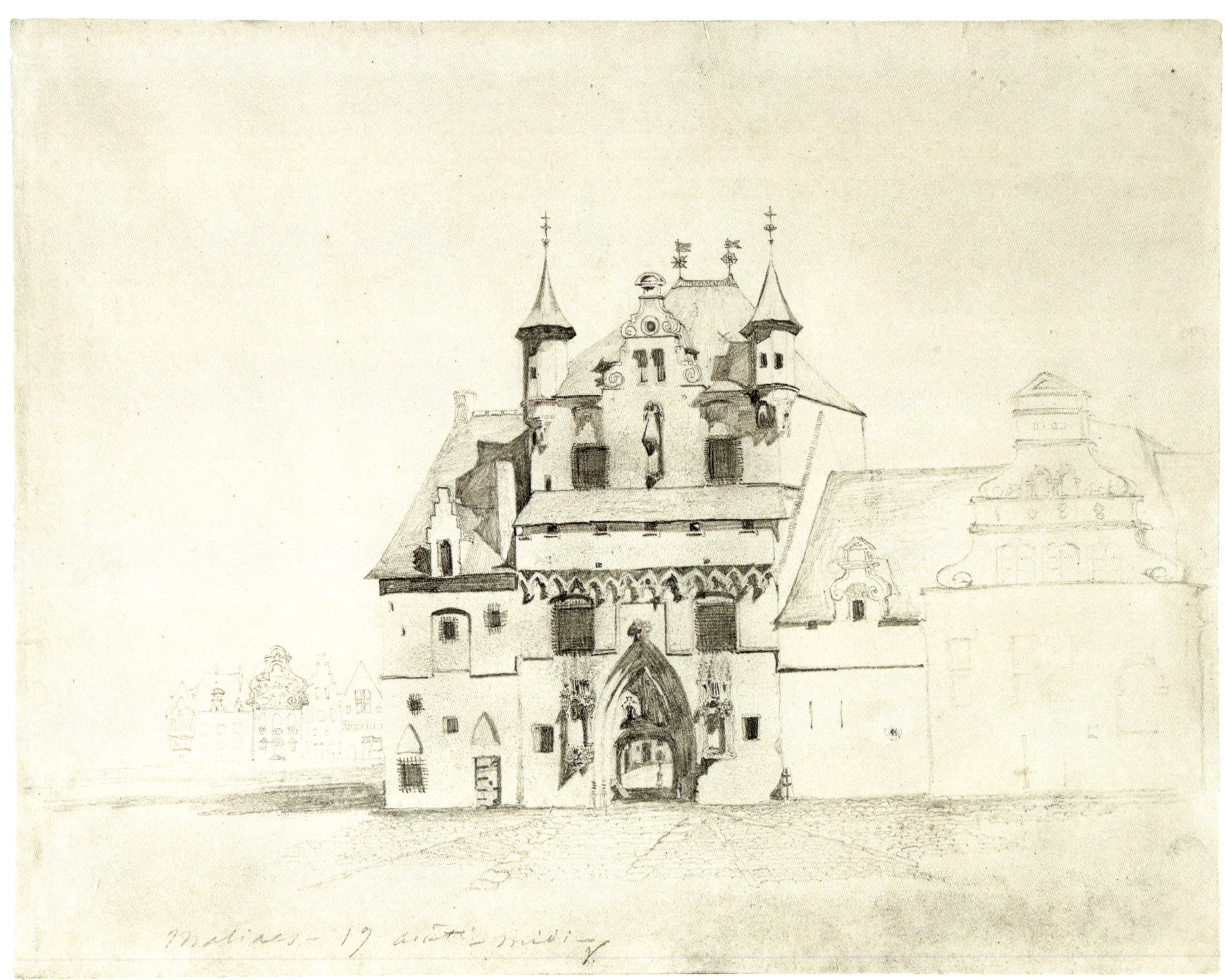

12

Malines, 19 August 1837
Graphite pencil on paper, 22.9 x 29.8 cm
Maisons de Victor Hugo, Paris / Guernsey,
inv. no. 810

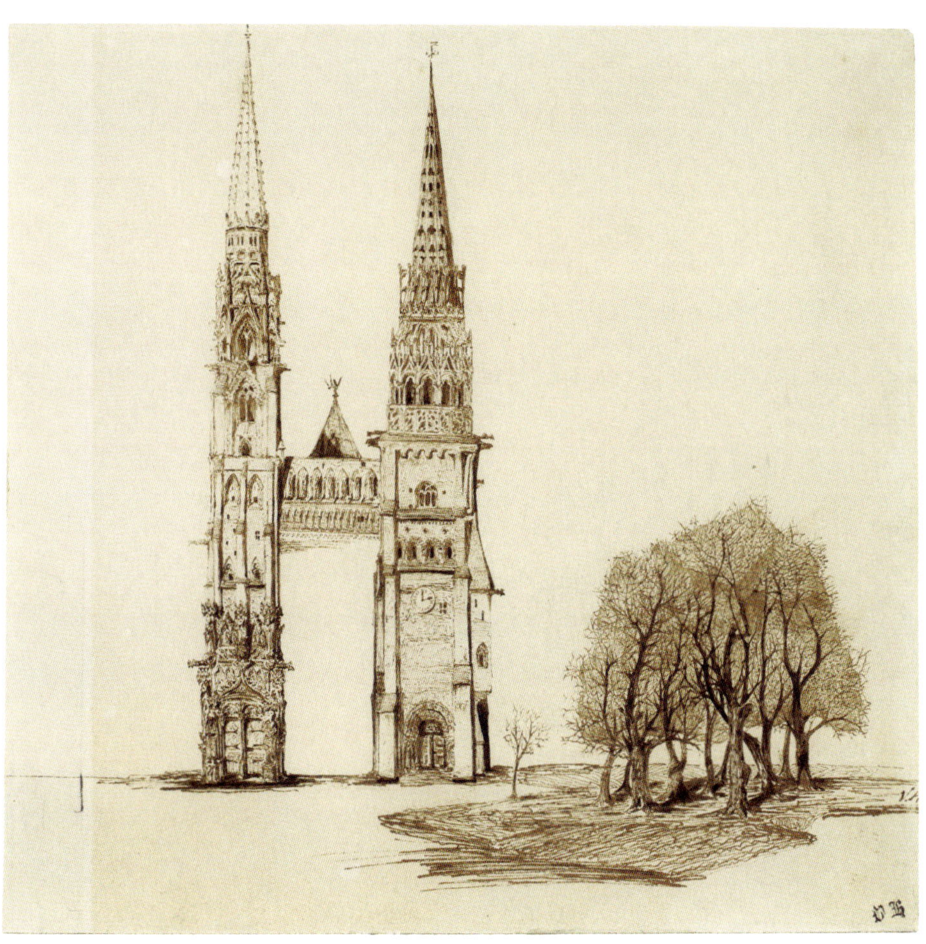

13

Towers and Spires of a Gothic Cathedral,
c. 1836–37
Pen and brown ink on paper, 19.4 x 20.2 cm
Maisons de Victor Hugo, Paris / Guernsey,
inv. no. 884

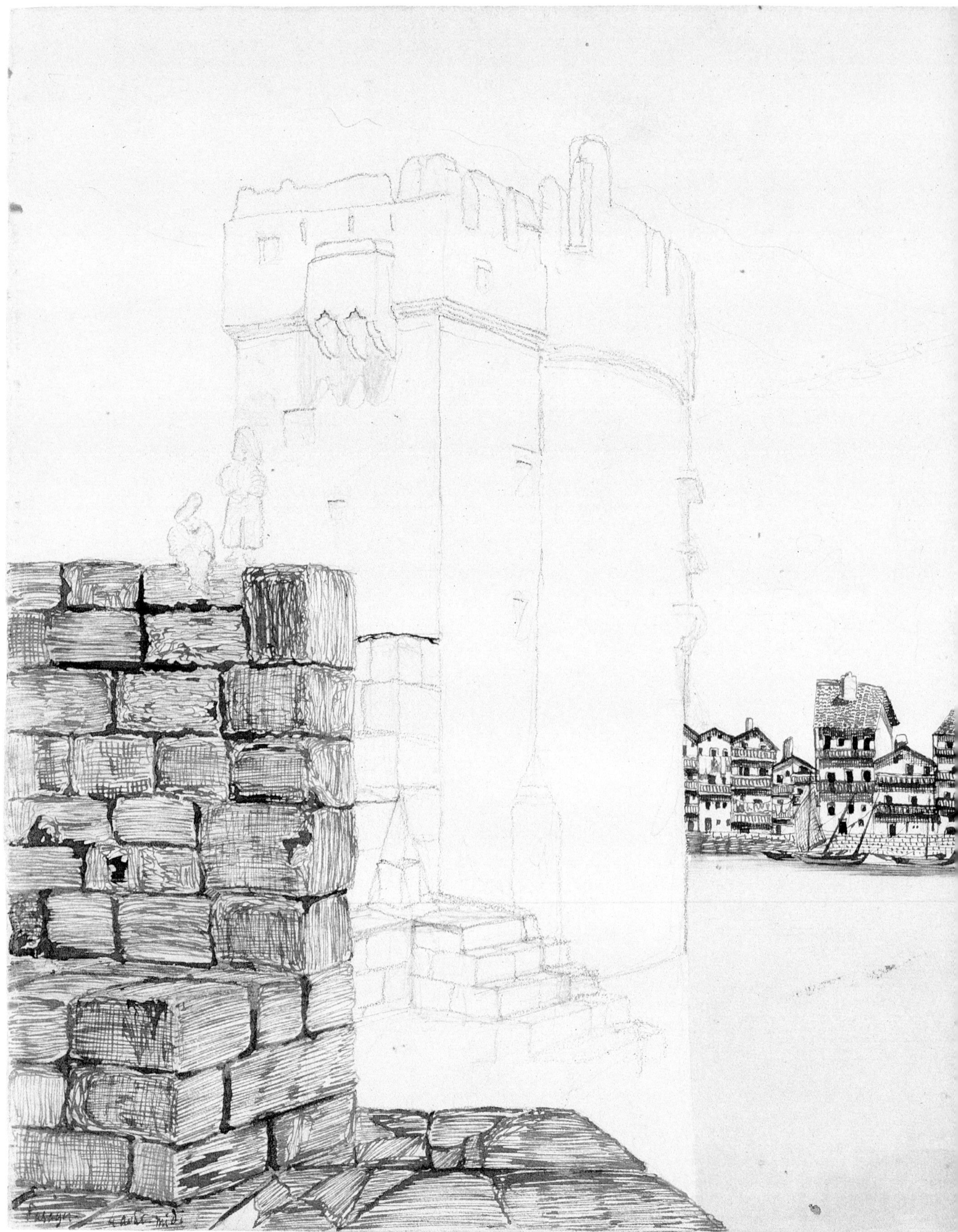

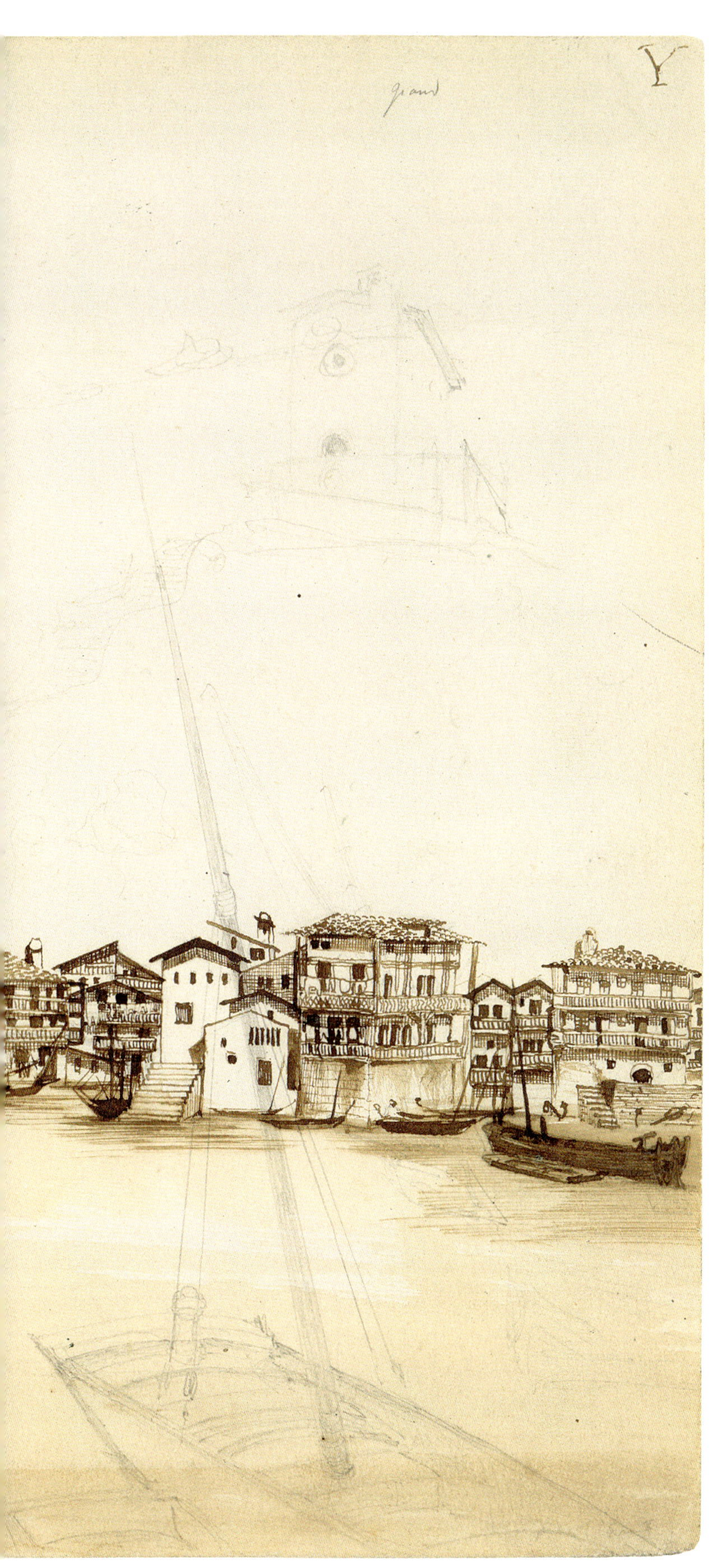

14

Travel Sketchbook VII:
Trip to the Pyrenees, 1843
Inscribed: 'Pasages, 4 août, midi' (the
Spanish town of Pasaia, 4 August, noon)
Bound sketchbook with drawings
in brown ink, wash and graphite
on paper, 24 x 65 cm (open)
Bibliothèque nationale de France, Paris,
Département des Manuscrits,
inv. no. NAF 13346, fol. 25

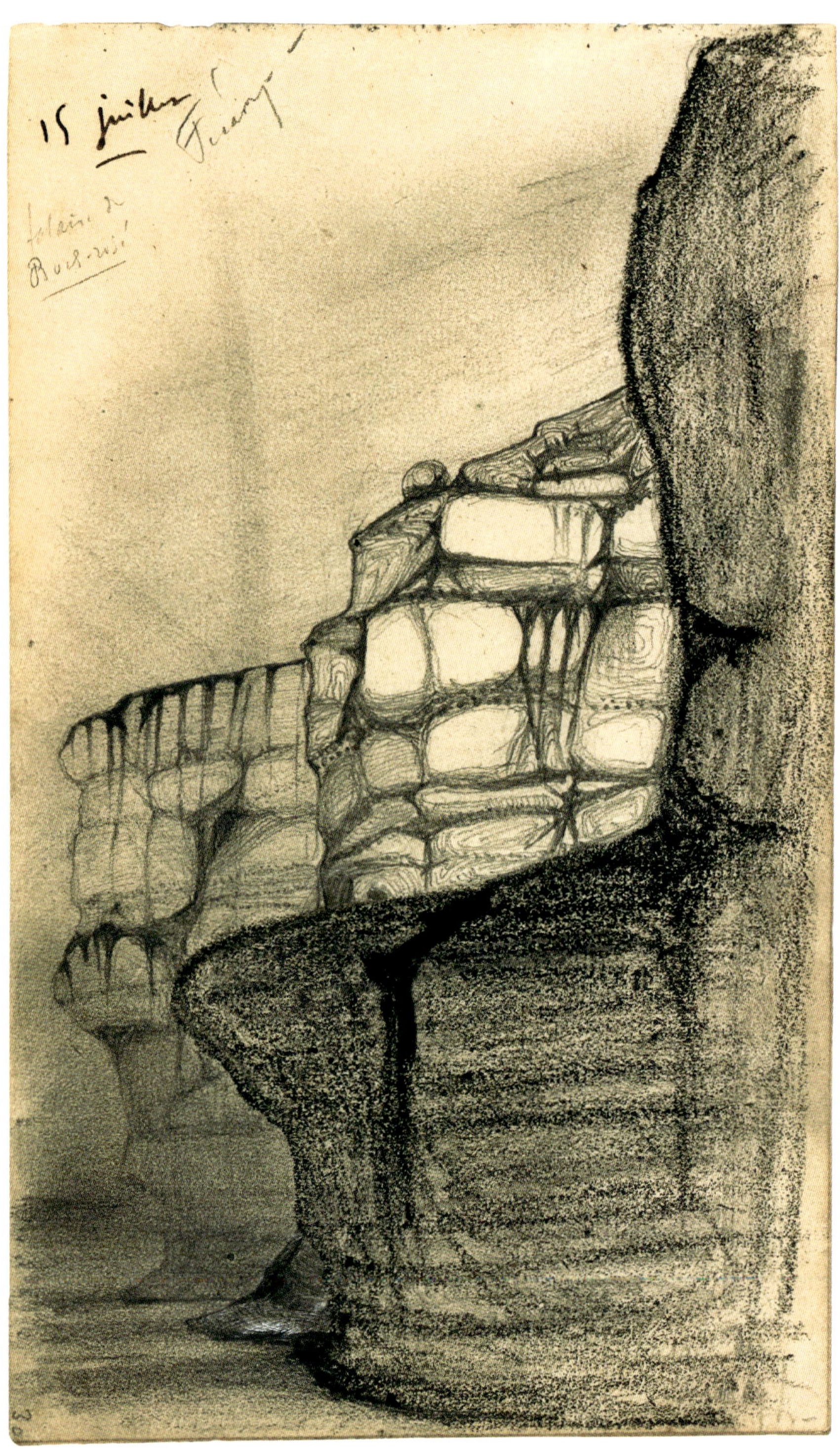

15

*Travel Sketchbook: Cliff at Bois-Rosé,
Fécamp*, 16 June – 19 July 1836
Graphite pencil, black pencil and
brown ink on paper, 38 x 11.5 cm (open)
Maisons de Victor Hugo, Paris / Guernsey,
inv. no. 970, fol. 30

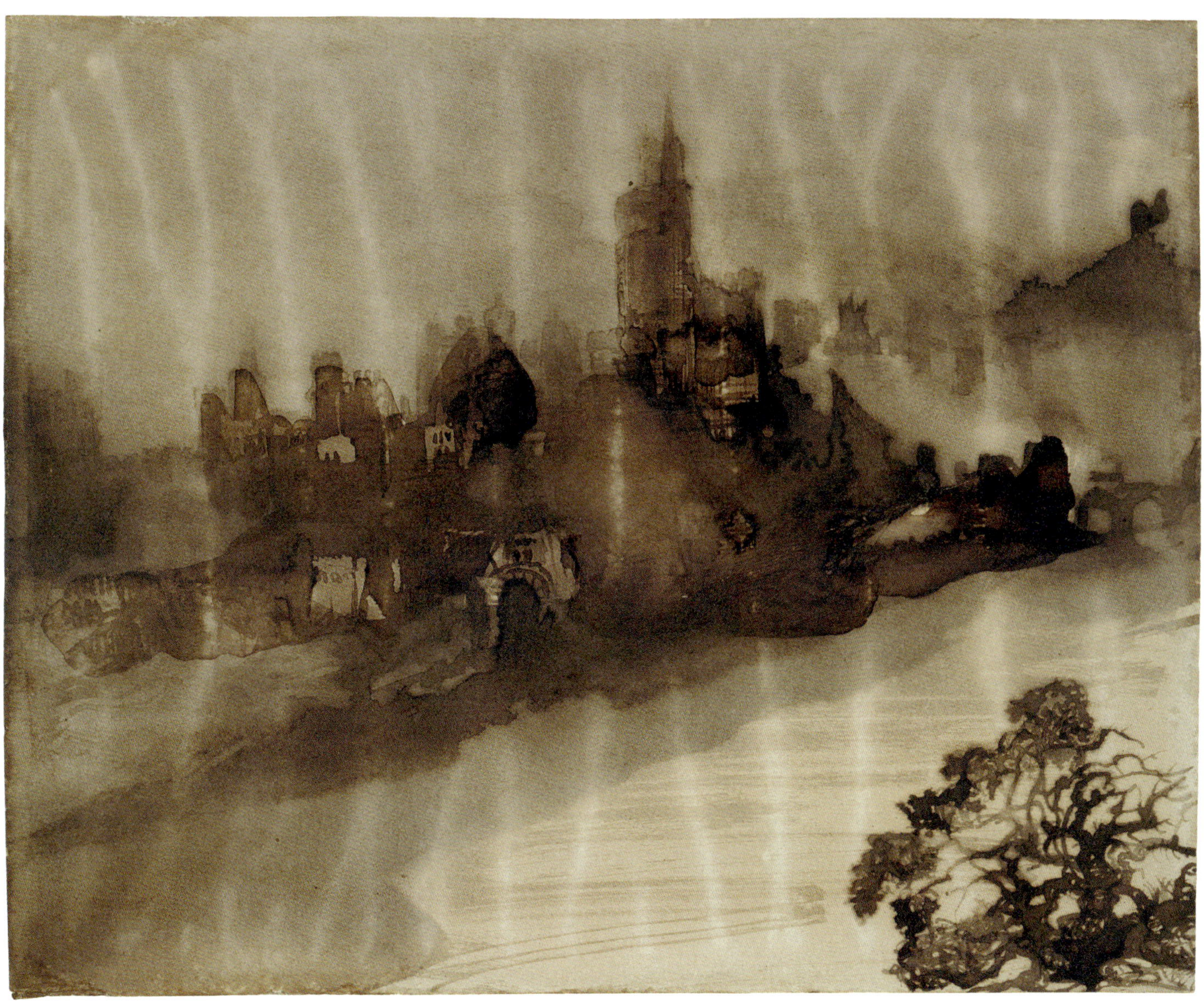

16

City on the Rhine, undated
Pen and brown ink wash
on paper, 19 x 23.9 cm
Maisons de Victor Hugo, Paris / Guernsey,
inv. no. 63

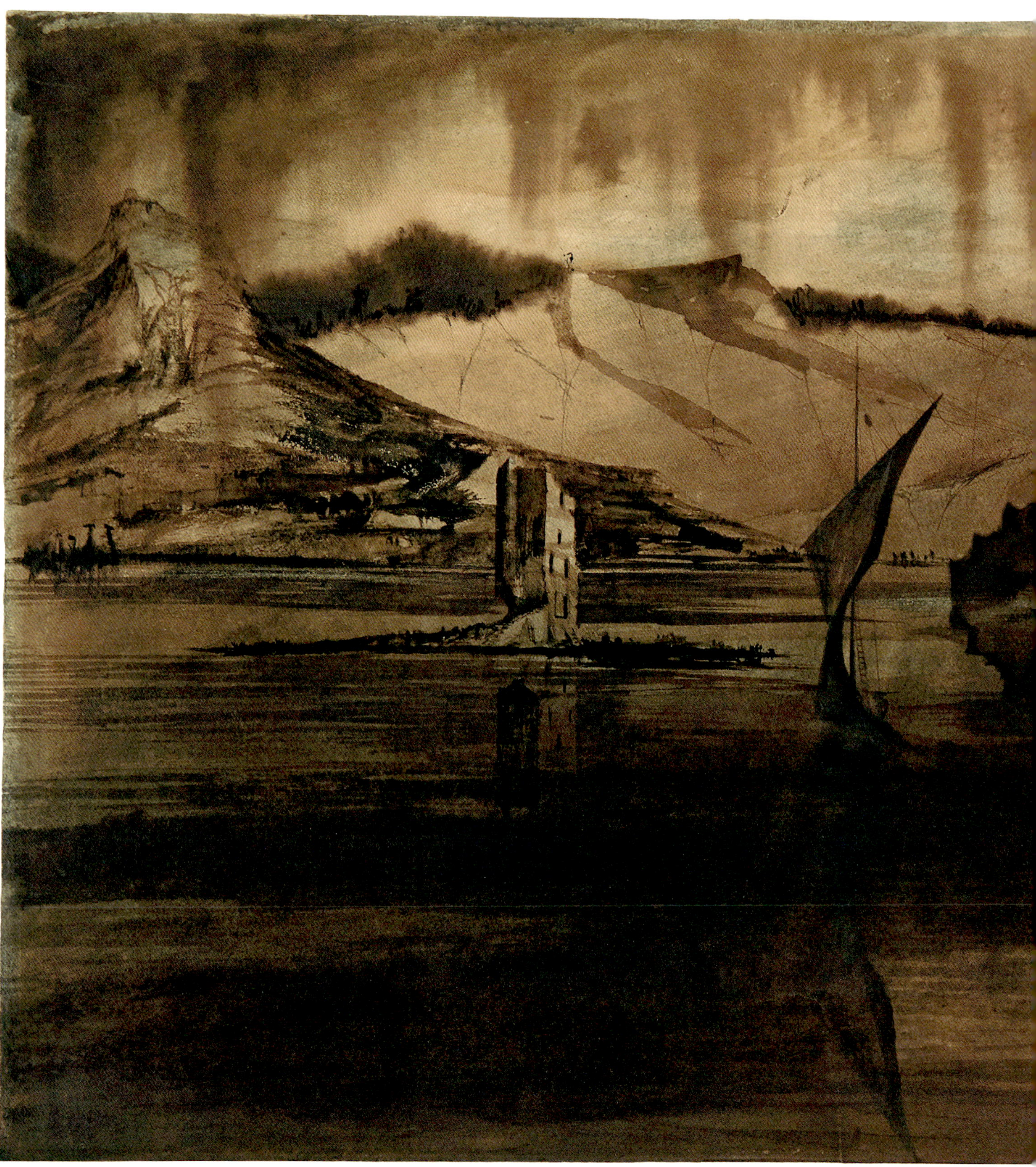

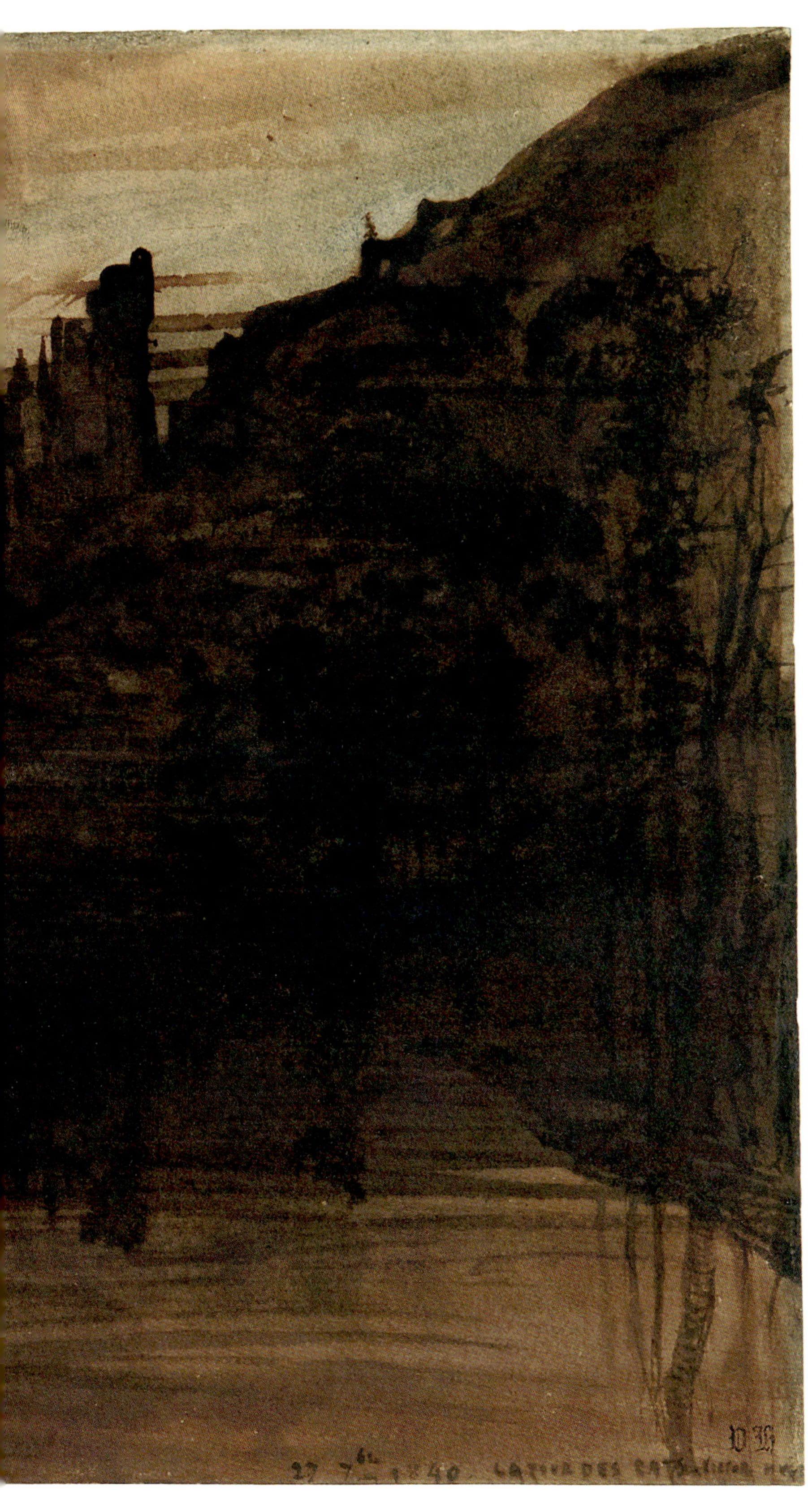

17

La Tour des Rats, 1847
Pen and brown ink wash over
graphite pencil, black ink and charcoal
on paper, 28.5 x 44.8 cm
Maisons de Victor Hugo, Paris / Guernsey,
inv. no. 12

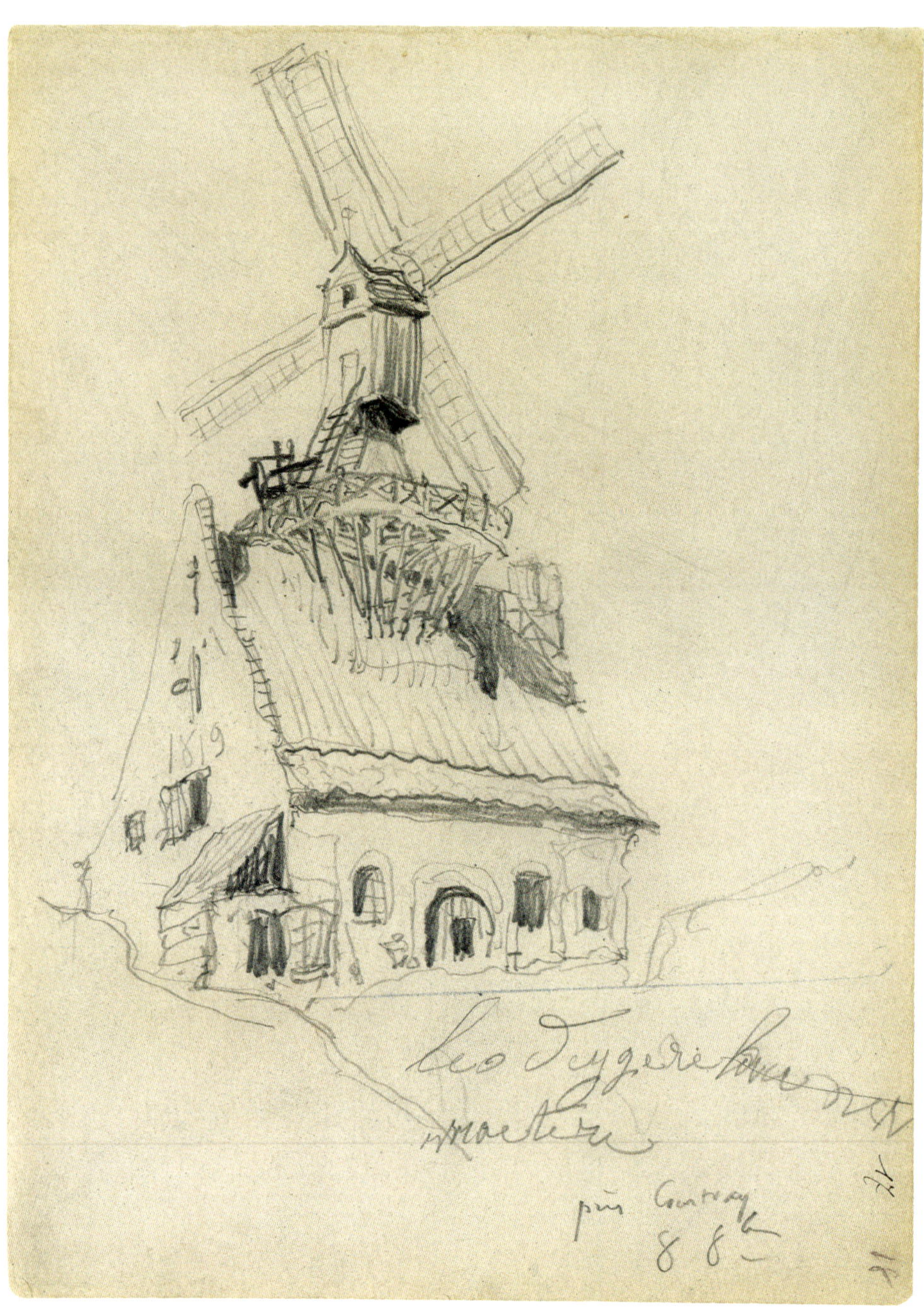

18

*Windmill on the Roof of a Farmhouse
near Courtray*, 8 October 1864
Graphite pencil on paper, 25.8 x 19.2 cm
Bibliothèque nationale de France, Paris,
Département des Manuscrits,
NAF 13345, fol. 17

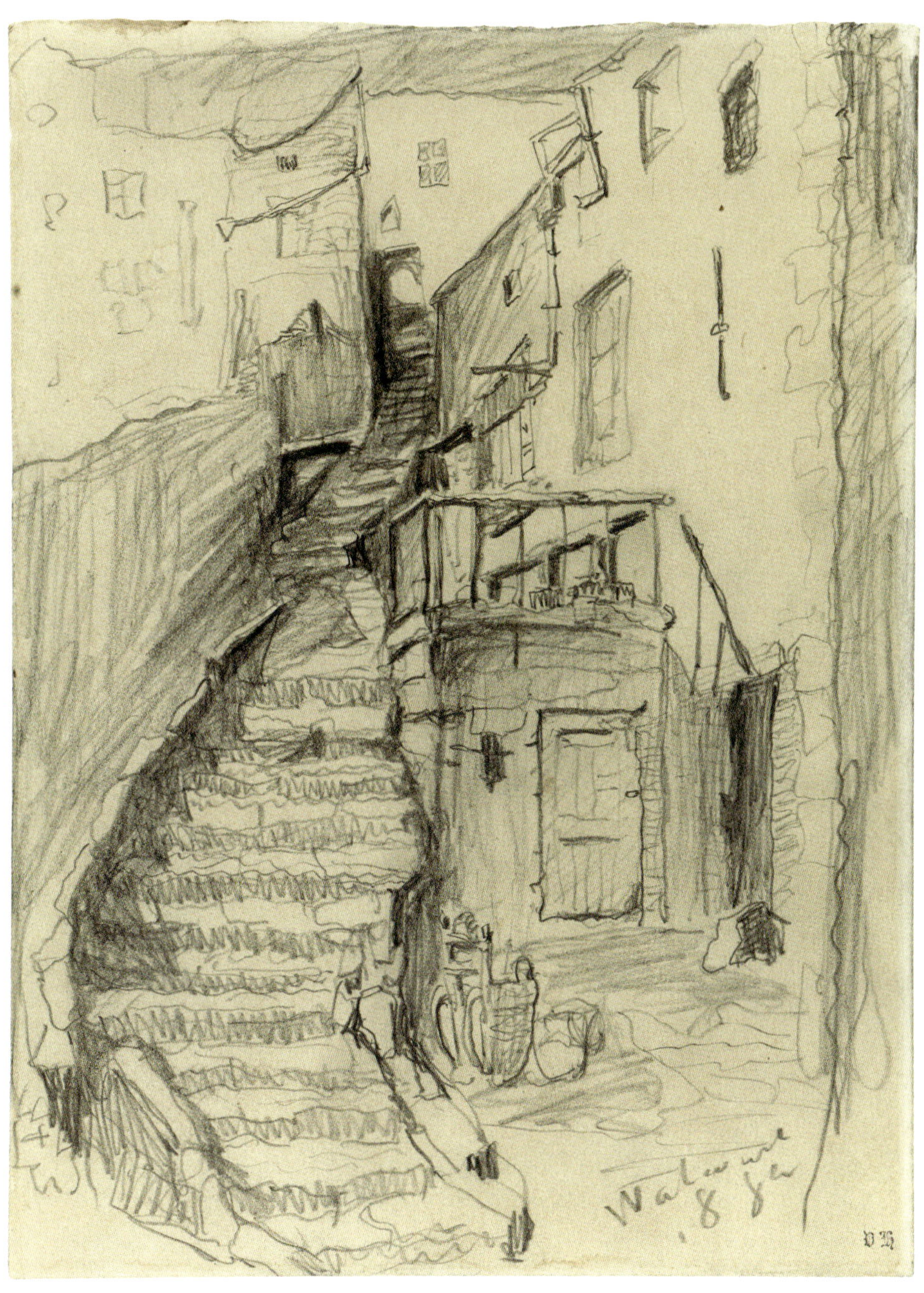

19

Walcourt, 1864
Graphite pencil on paper, 25.7 x 19.3 cm
Maisons de Victor Hugo, Paris / Guernsey,
inv. no. 19

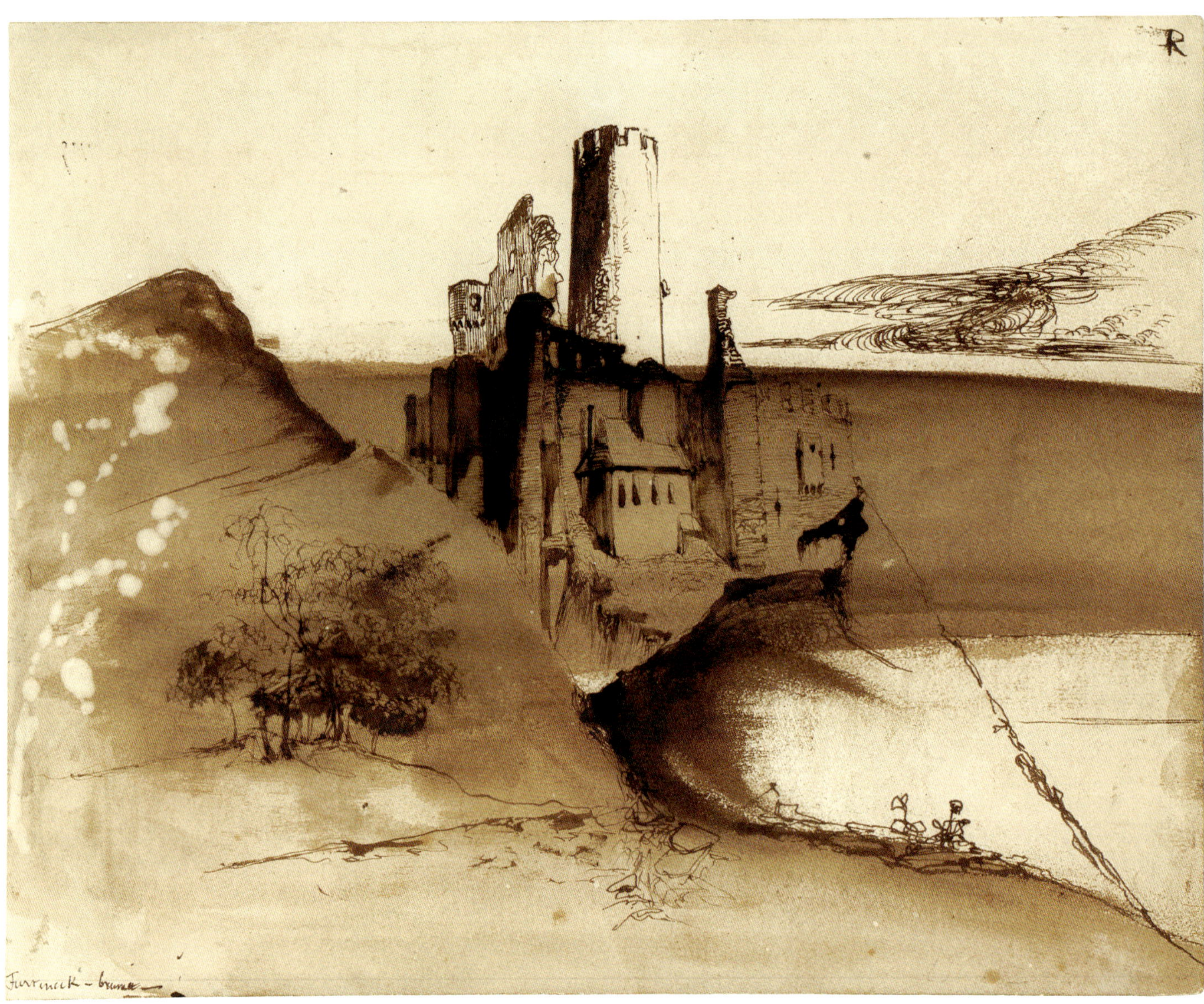

20

Furteneck in Mist, 1840
Pen and brown ink wash on paper,
29.8 x 23.6 cm
Maisons de Victor Hugo, Paris / Guernsey,
inv. no. 17

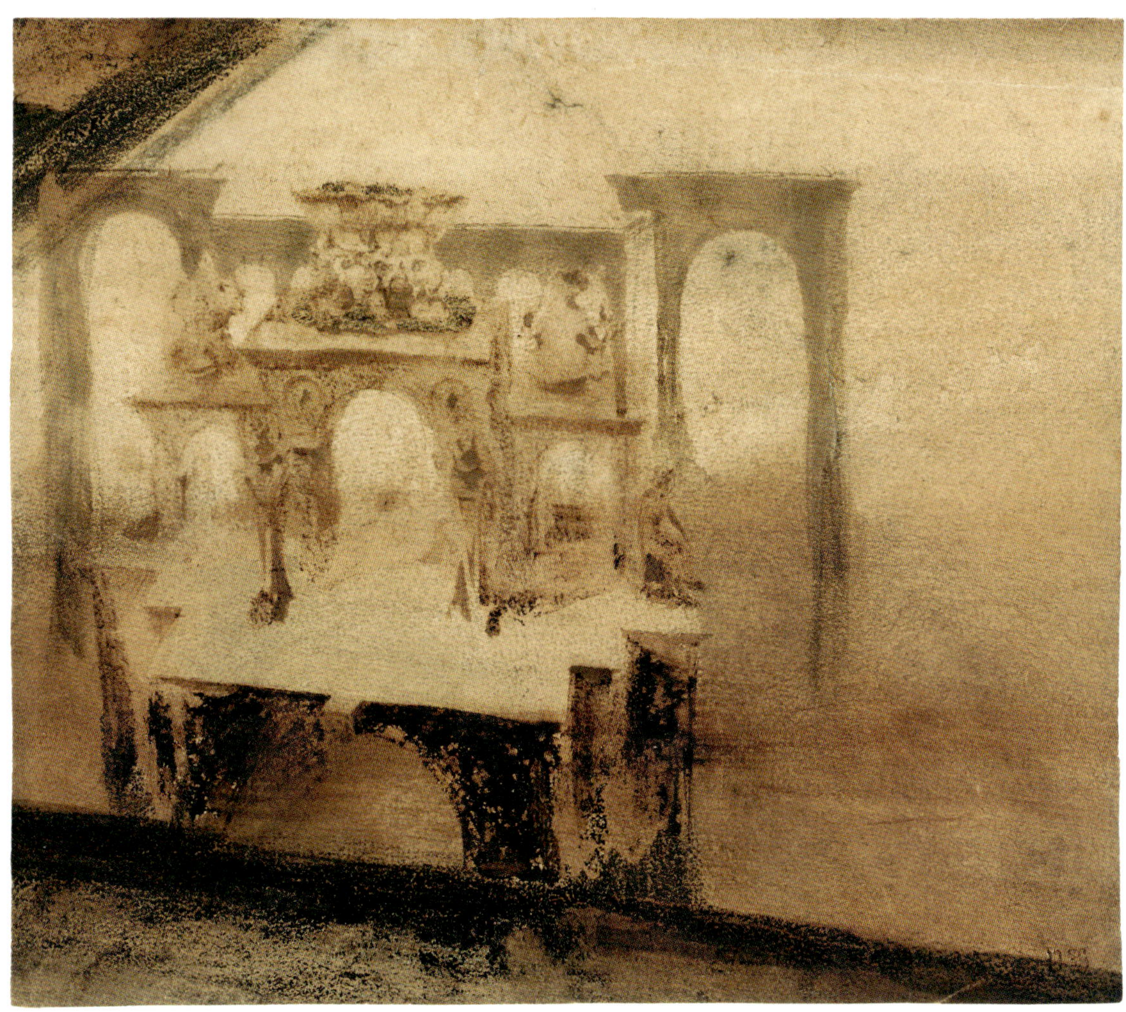

21

Architecture Renaissance, c. 1847–50
Brown ink, charcoal and black pencil
on paper, 20.7 x 24.4 cm
Maisons de Victor Hugo, Paris / Guernsey,
inv. no. 935

22

Hic clavis, alias porta (*Here the key, elsewhere the door*), 1850
Pen, brown ink and wash, black ink wash, graphite pencil, crayon, charcoal and white gouache on paper, 47 x 47.8 cm
Maisons de Victor Hugo, Paris / Guernsey, inv. no. 126

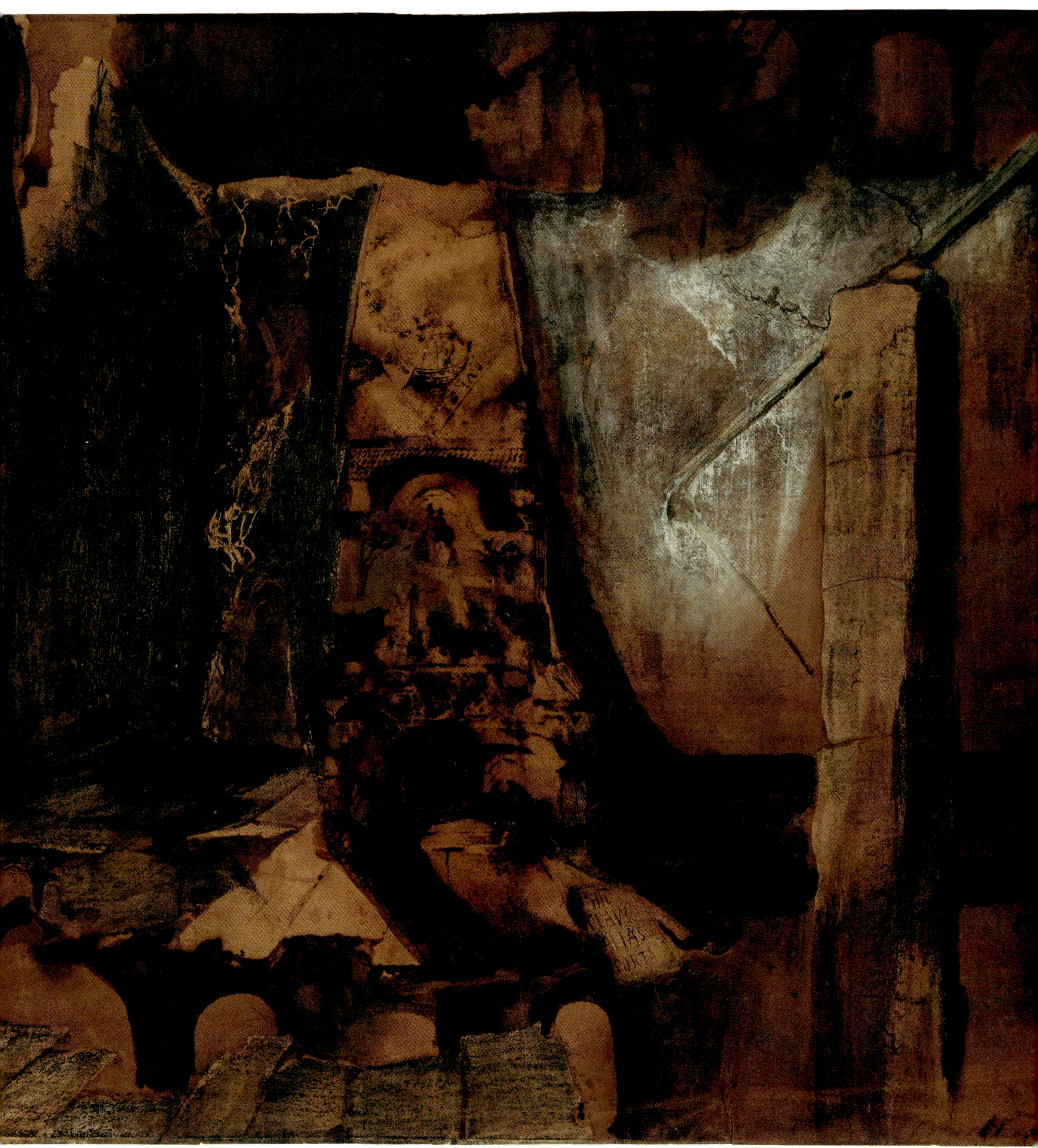

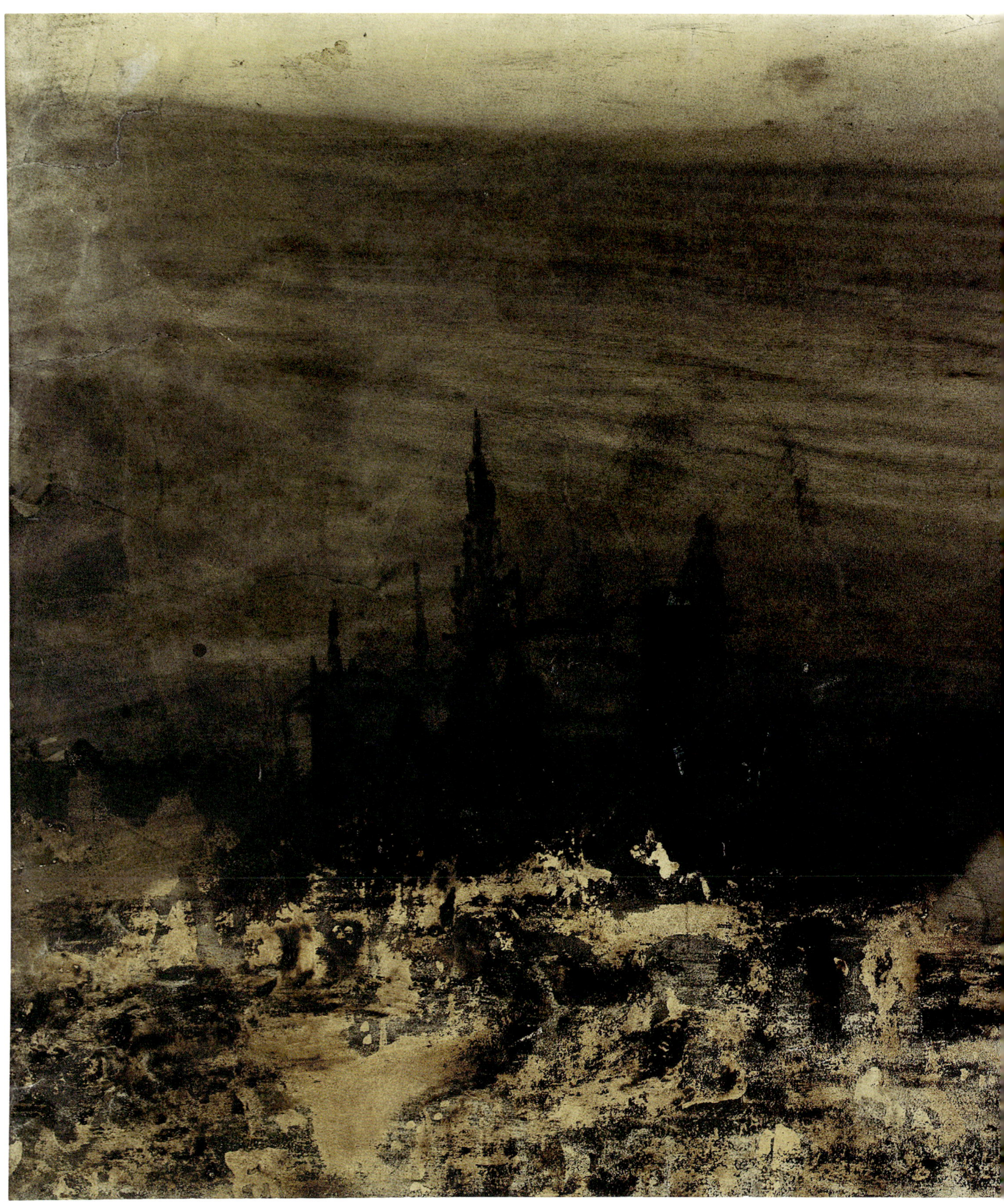

23

The Dead City, c. 1850
Black ink, graphite and Indian ink
on paper, 43.8 x 66.8 cm
Maisons de Victor Hugo, Paris / Guernsey,
inv. no. 2779

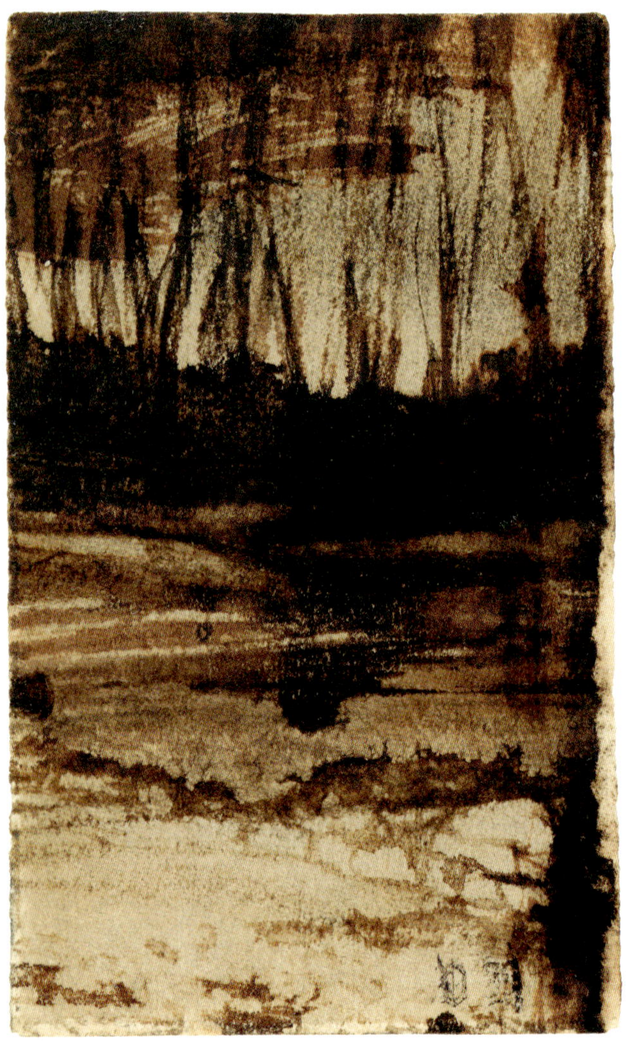

24

Undergrowth, c. 1847
Pen and brown ink wash
on paper, 7.3 x 4.5 cm
Maisons de Victor Hugo, Paris / Guernsey,
inv. no. 842

25

The Abandoned Park, before 1855
Pen and brown ink wash and black
pencil on paper, 4.4 x 3.5 cm
Maisons de Victor Hugo, Paris / Guernsey,
inv. no. 883

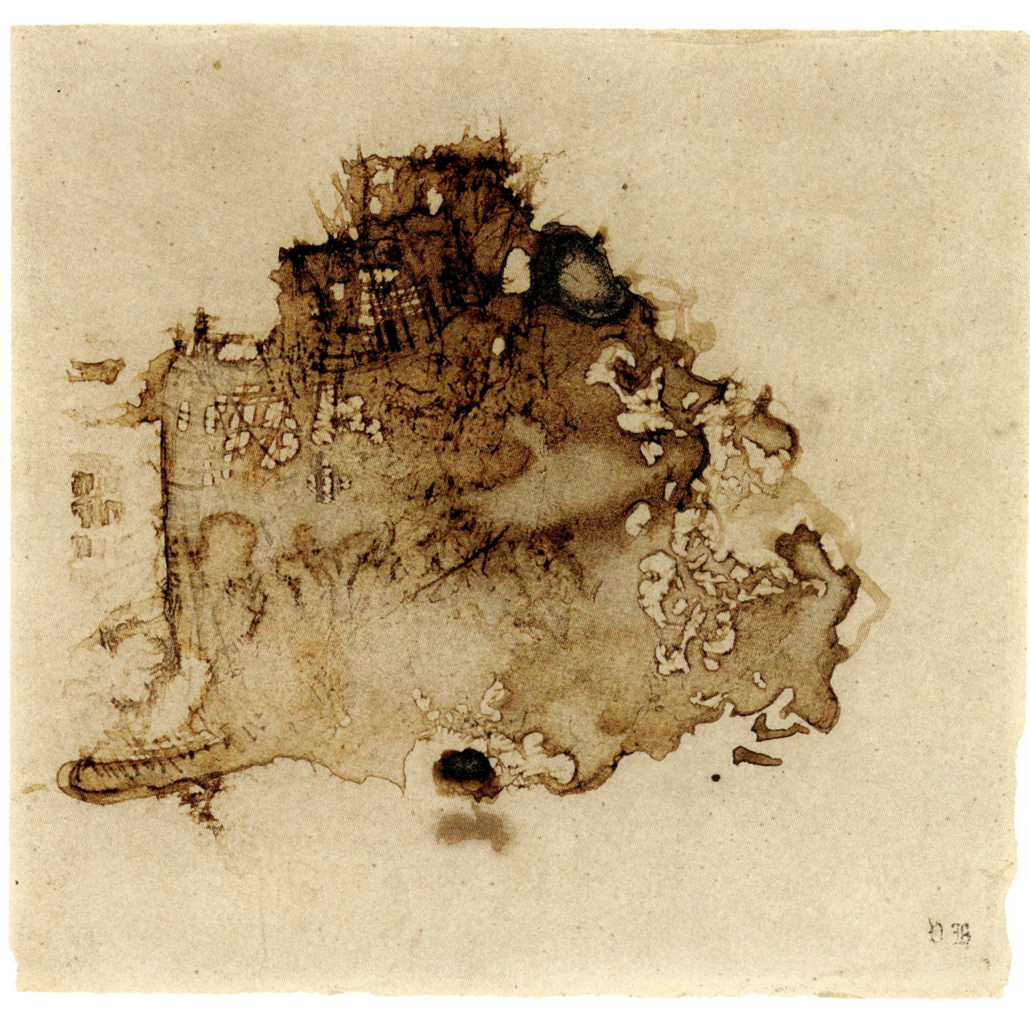

26

'twilight, stubborn, black, hideous', c. 1859
Pen and brown ink wash on paper,
14.3 x 16.5 cm
Maisons de Victor Hugo, Paris / Guernsey,
inv. no. 841

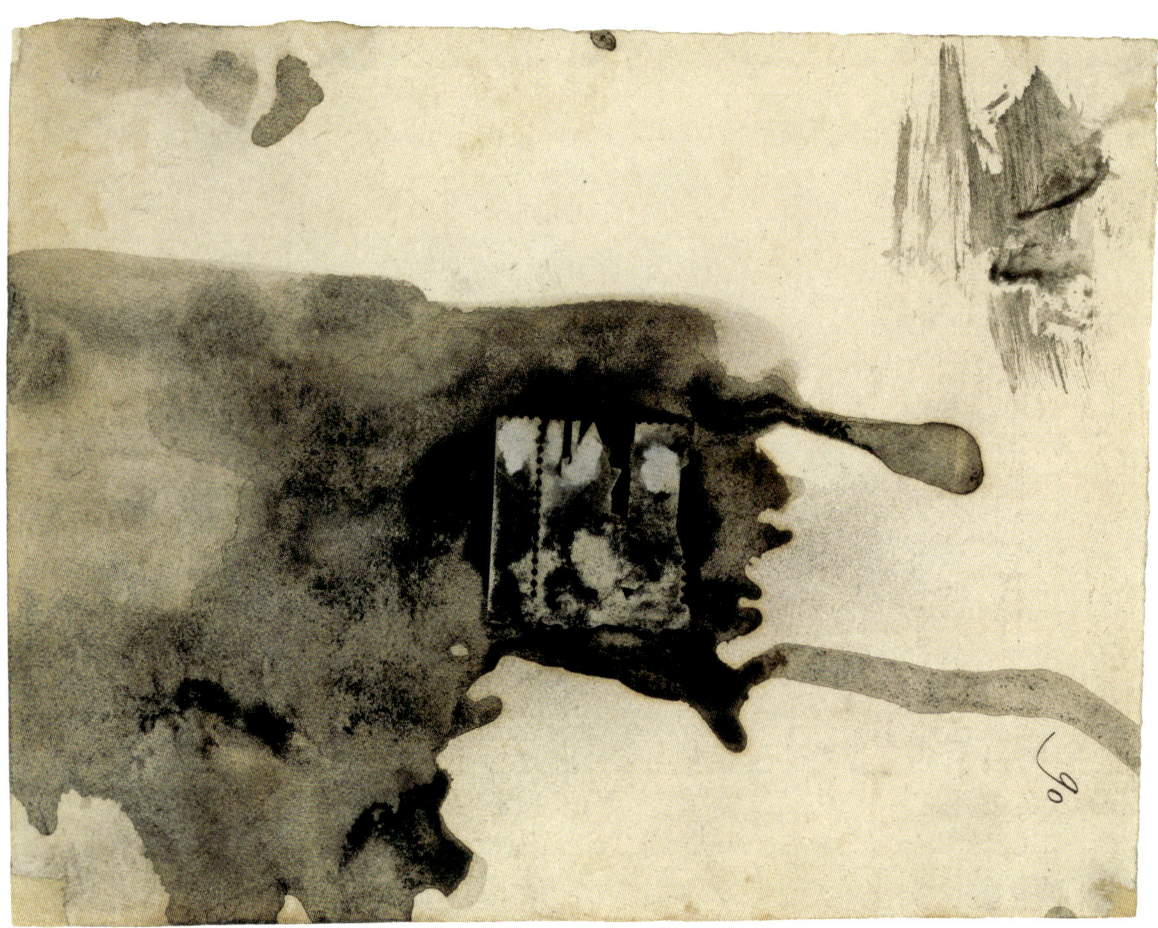

27

Taches and Silhouette of a Castle, 1856
Black ink wash and graphite with
collaged postage stamp on paper, 11.8 x 15.4 cm
Bibliothèque nationale de France, Paris,
Département des Manuscrits,
inv. no. NAF 13355, fol. 90

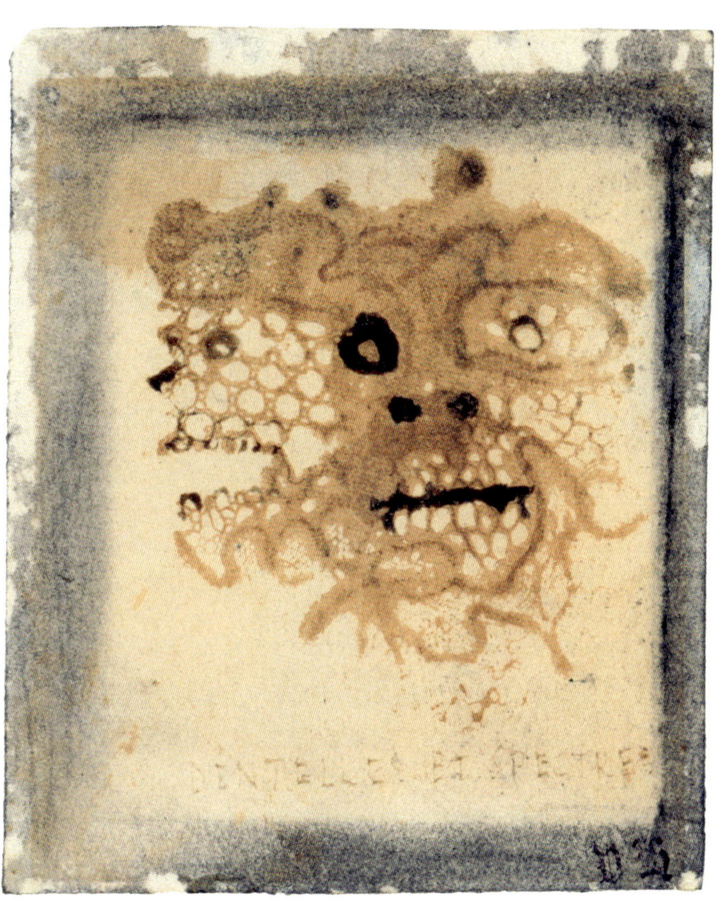

28

Lace and Spectres, c. 1855–56
Pen and brown ink wash, charcoal and
lace imprint on paper, 7.2 x 6.1 cm
Maisons de Victor Hugo, Paris / Guernsey,
inv. no. 878

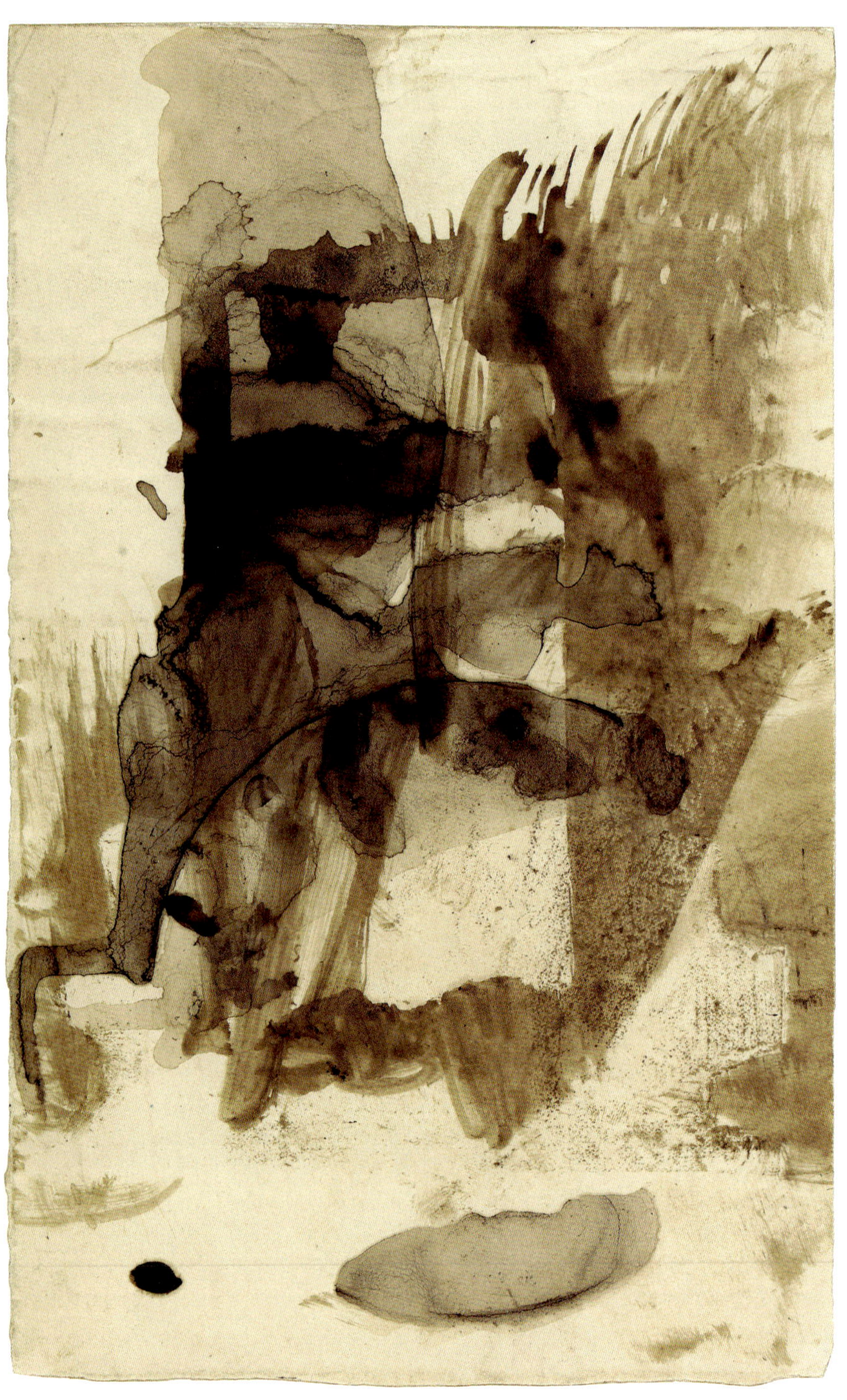

29

Tache with Circular Imprint, c. 1864–69
Wash and brown ink on paper, 22.4 x 14.2 cm
Maisons de Victor Hugo, Paris / Guernsey,
inv. no. 2012.4.1

30

*Ink-blackened Page with Half-moon
and Fingerprints,* 1864–65
Brown ink and wash on paper,
26.5 x 19.5 cm
Bibliothèque nationale de France, Paris,
Département des Manuscrits,
inv. no. NAF 13345, fol. 28

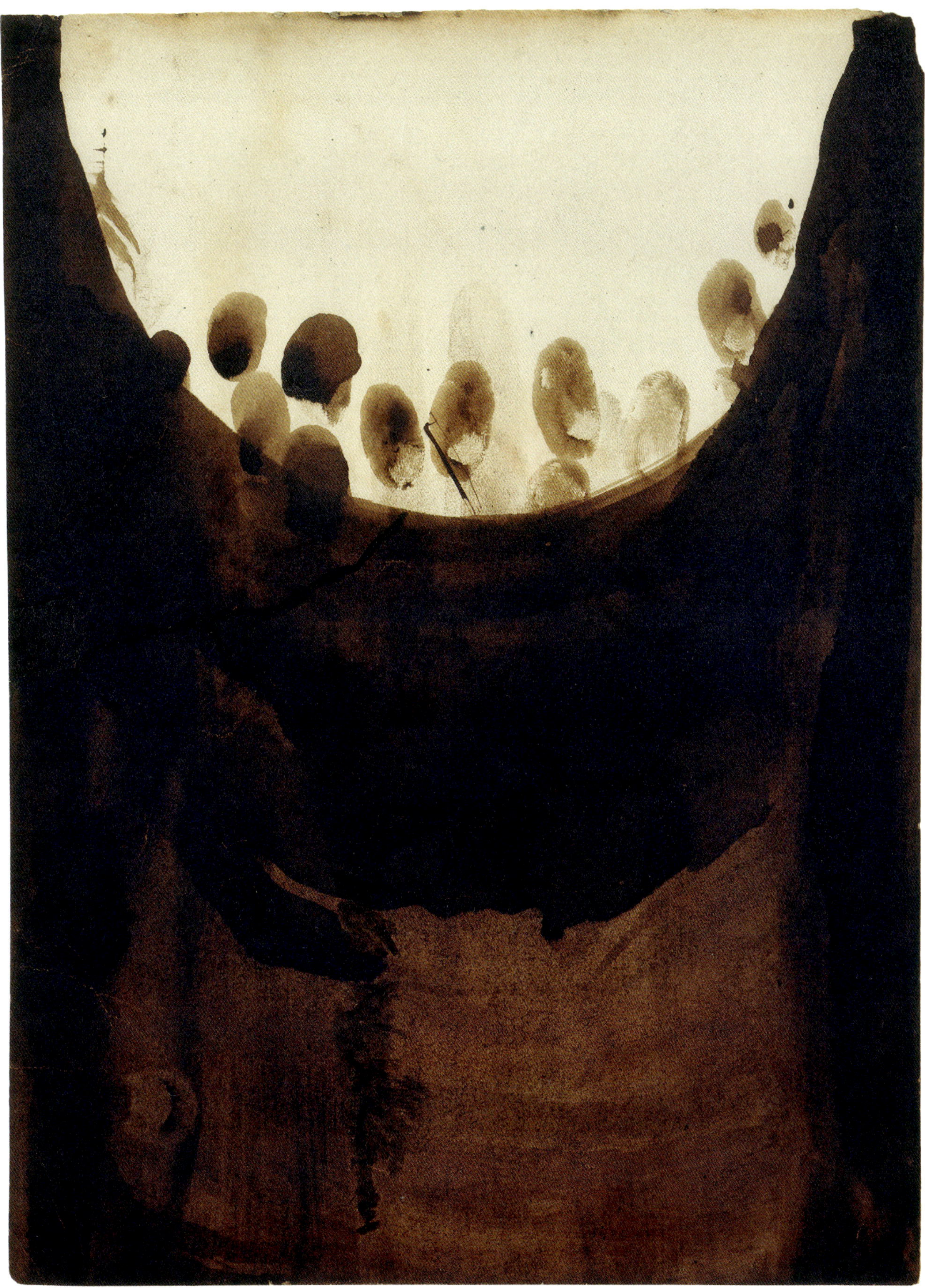

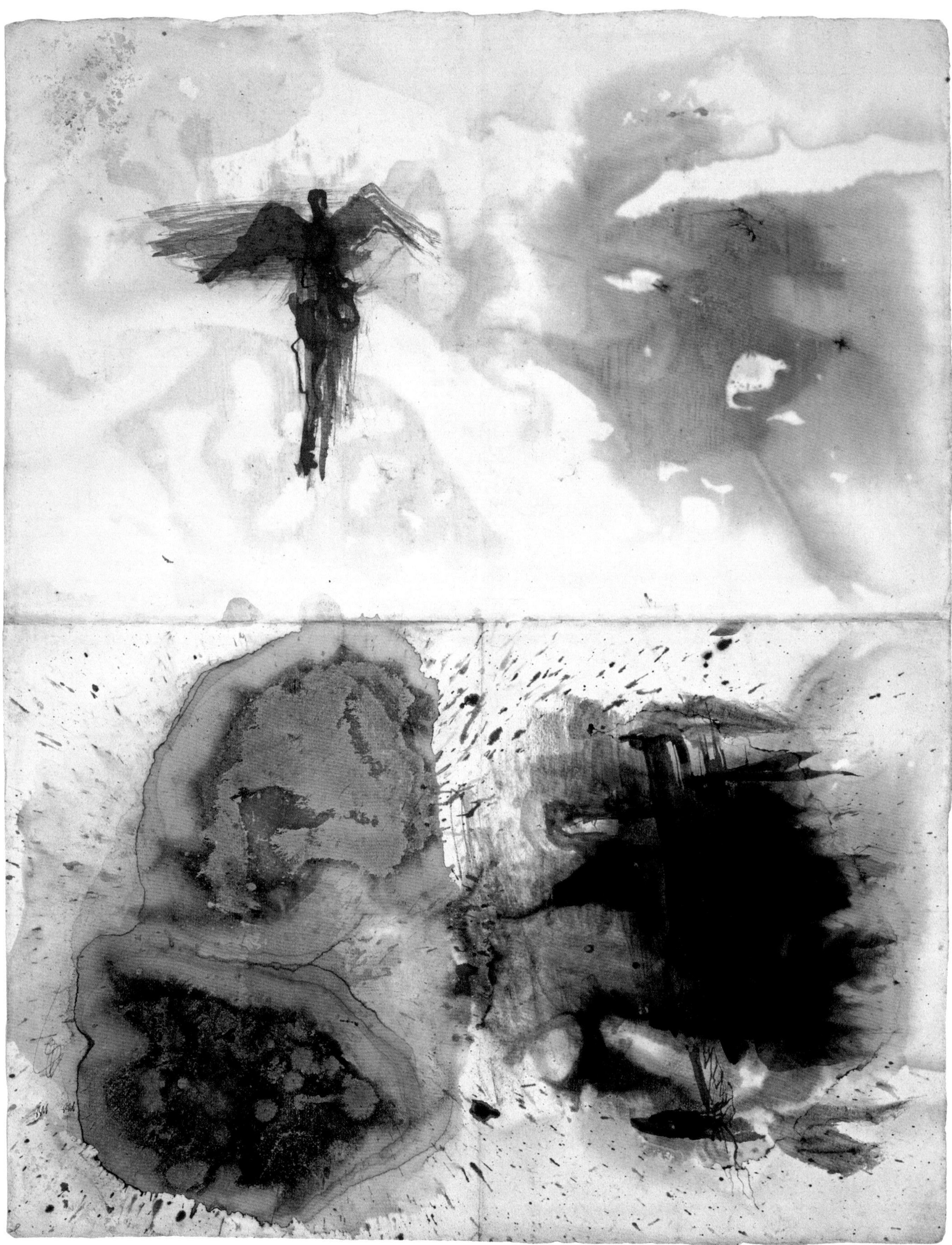

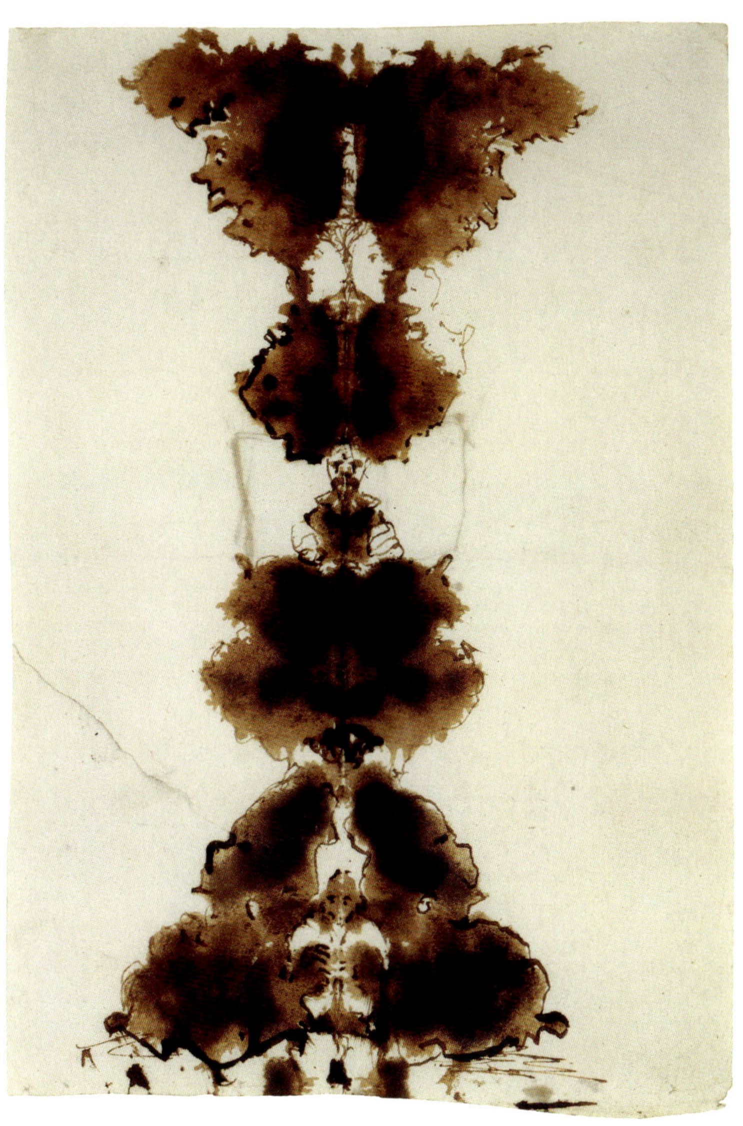

31

Taches, 1875
Black and grey-blue ink and wash
on paper, 54.8 x 44.3 cm
Bibliothèque nationale de France, Paris,
Département des Manuscrits,
inv. no. NAF 24807, fols 41–42

32

*Tache on Folded Paper, Retouched
with a Pen*, 1850–57
Pen and brown ink on paper, 20 x 14.1 cm
Bibliothèque nationale de France, Paris,
Département des Manuscrits,
inv. no. NAF 13351, fol. 28

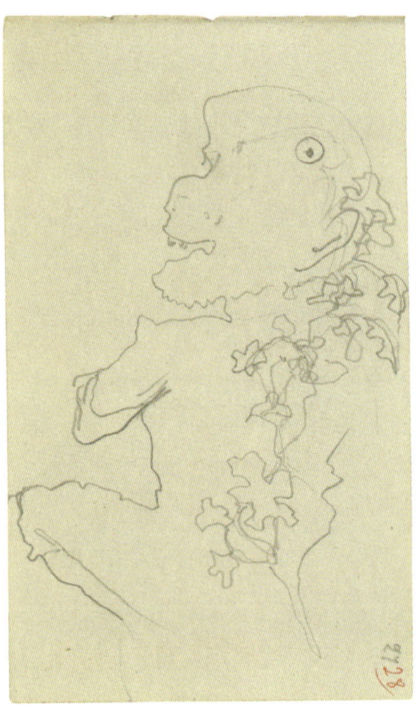

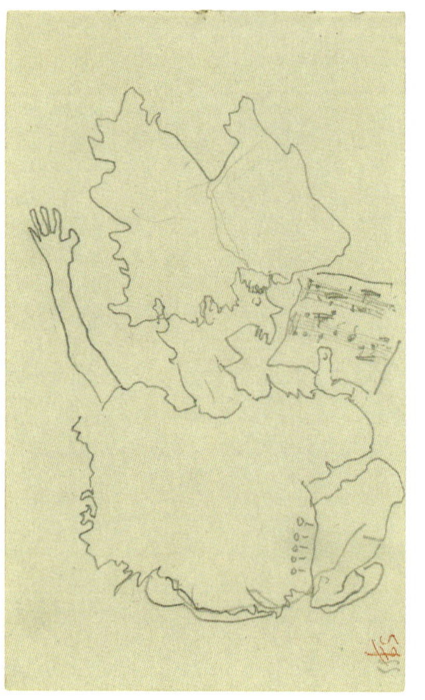

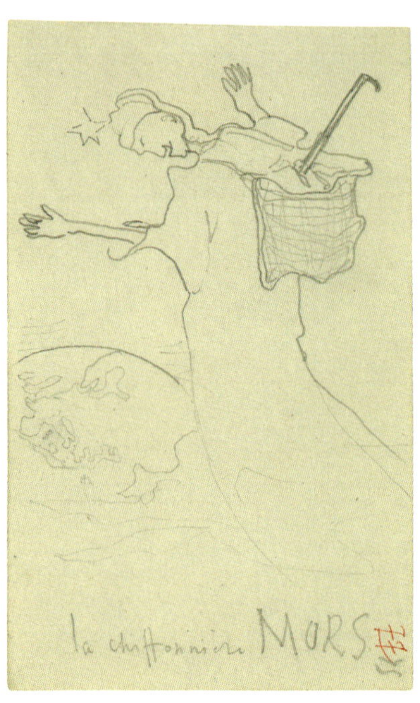

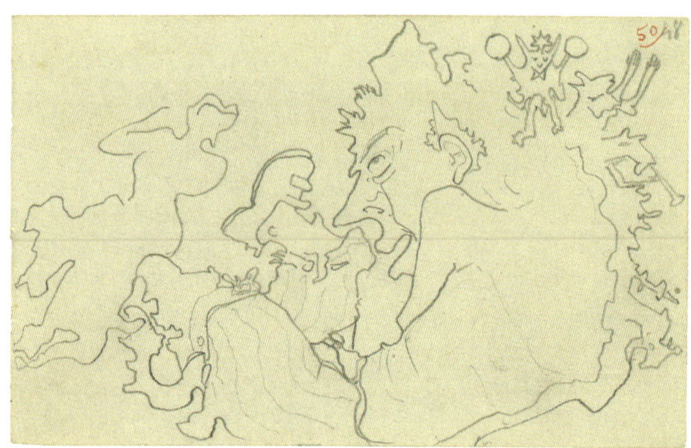

33

*Sketchbook Depicting Imaginary
Creatures (Human, Animal, Plant) and
Musicians*, 15 March – 18 April 1856
Sketchbook, 10 x 16 x 1.5 cm (closed)
Bibliothèque nationale de France, Paris,
Département des Manuscrits,
inv. no. NAF 13447

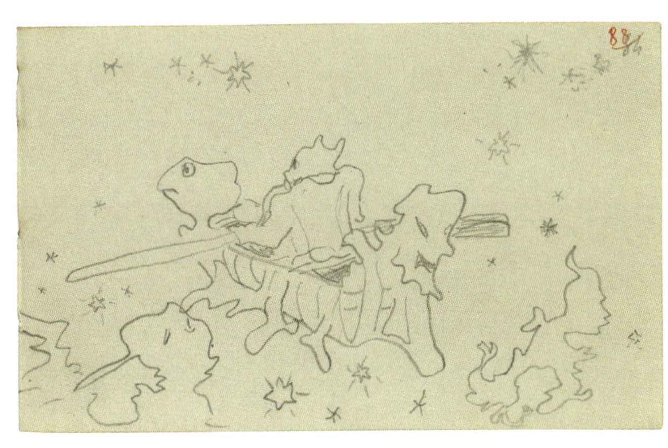

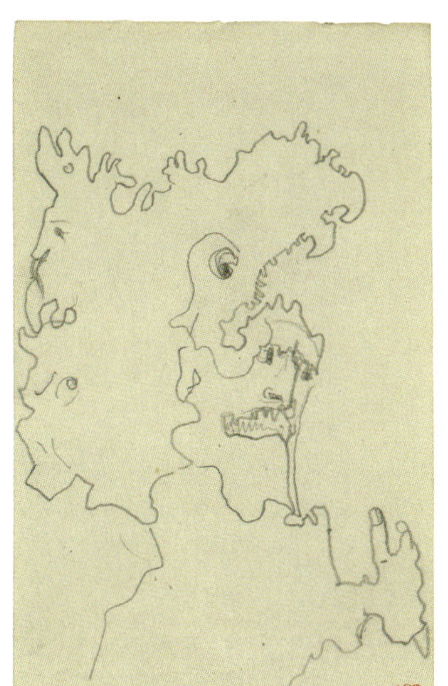

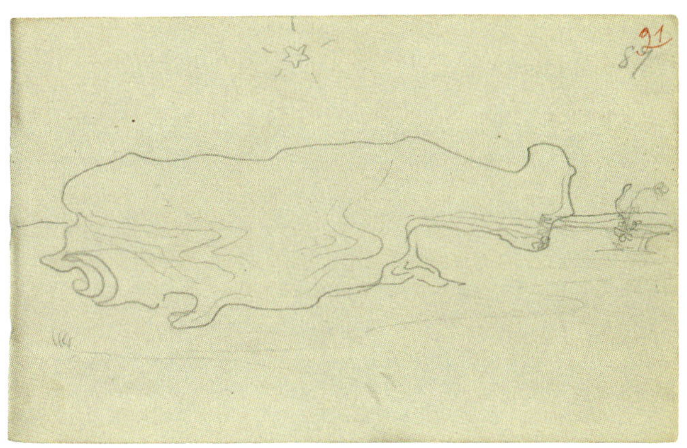

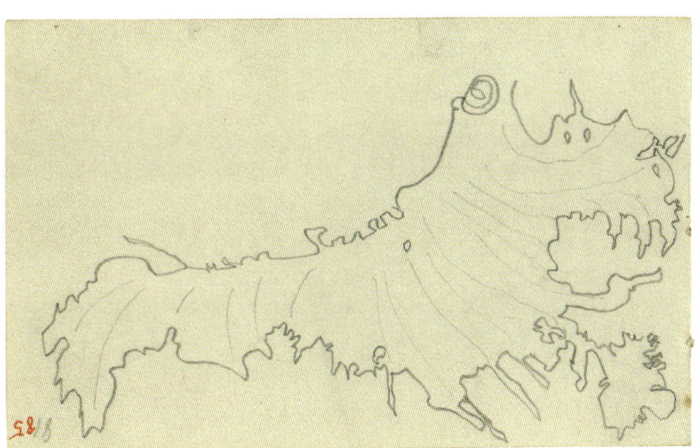

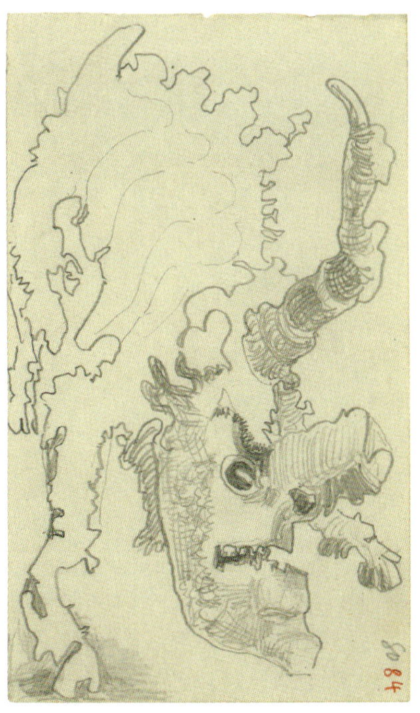

34

Planet-Eye, *c.* 1854
Graphite, black ink and wash
on paper, 29.2 x 20.4 cm
Bibliothèque nationale de France, Paris,
Département des Manuscrits,
inv. no. NAF 13355, fol. 106

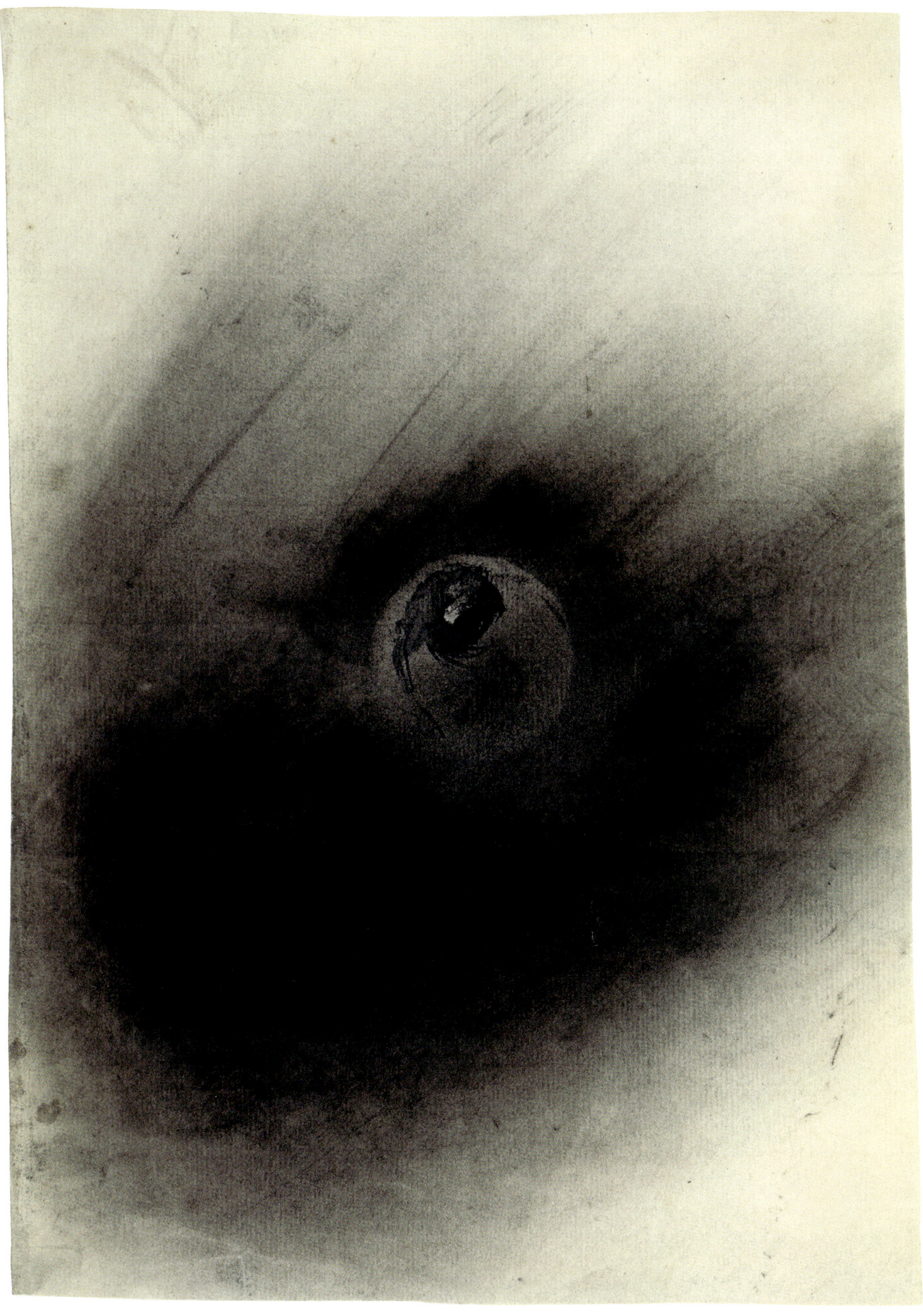

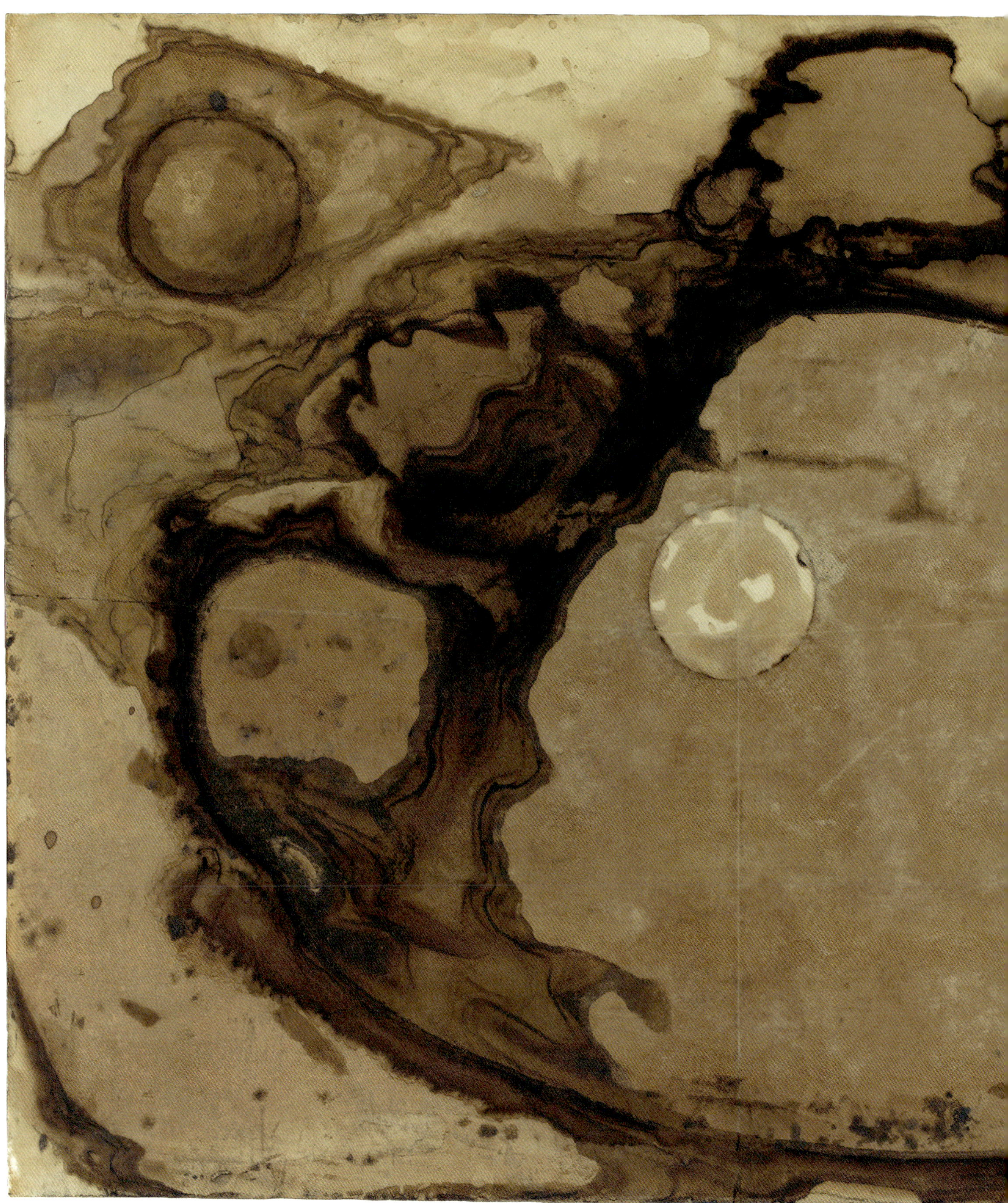

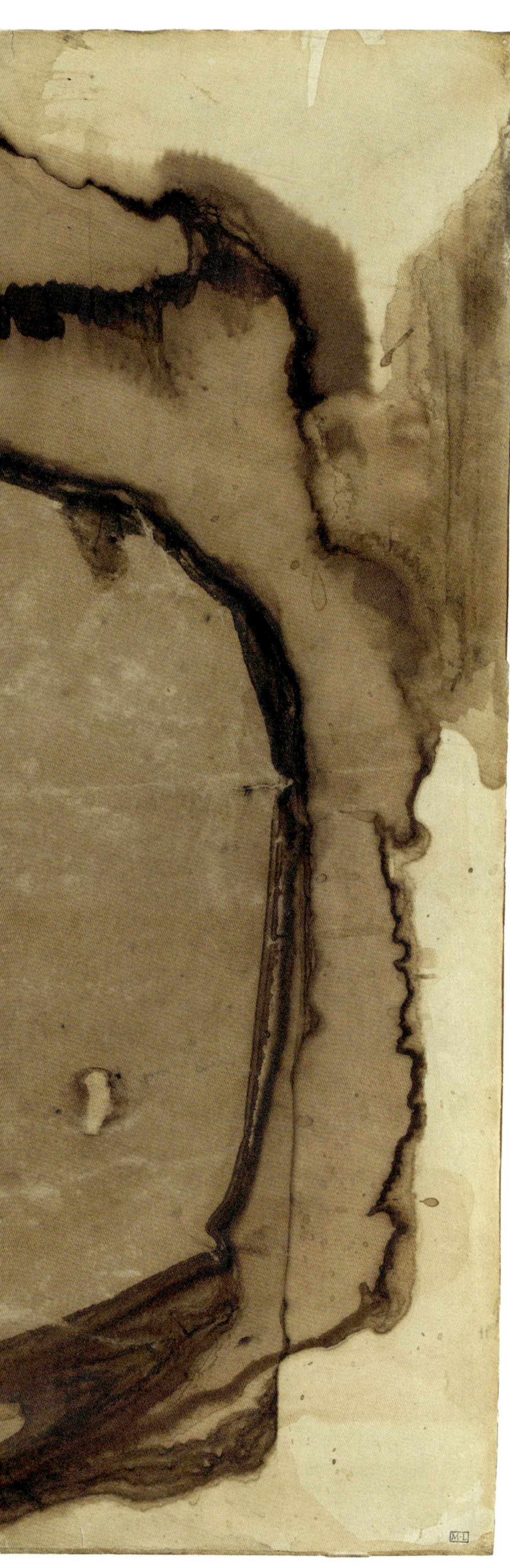

35

Taches-Planètes, c. 1850
Brown ink and wash on paper, 45 x 58.5 cm
Musée du Louvre, Paris, Département des
arts graphiques, inv. no. RF 54787, recto

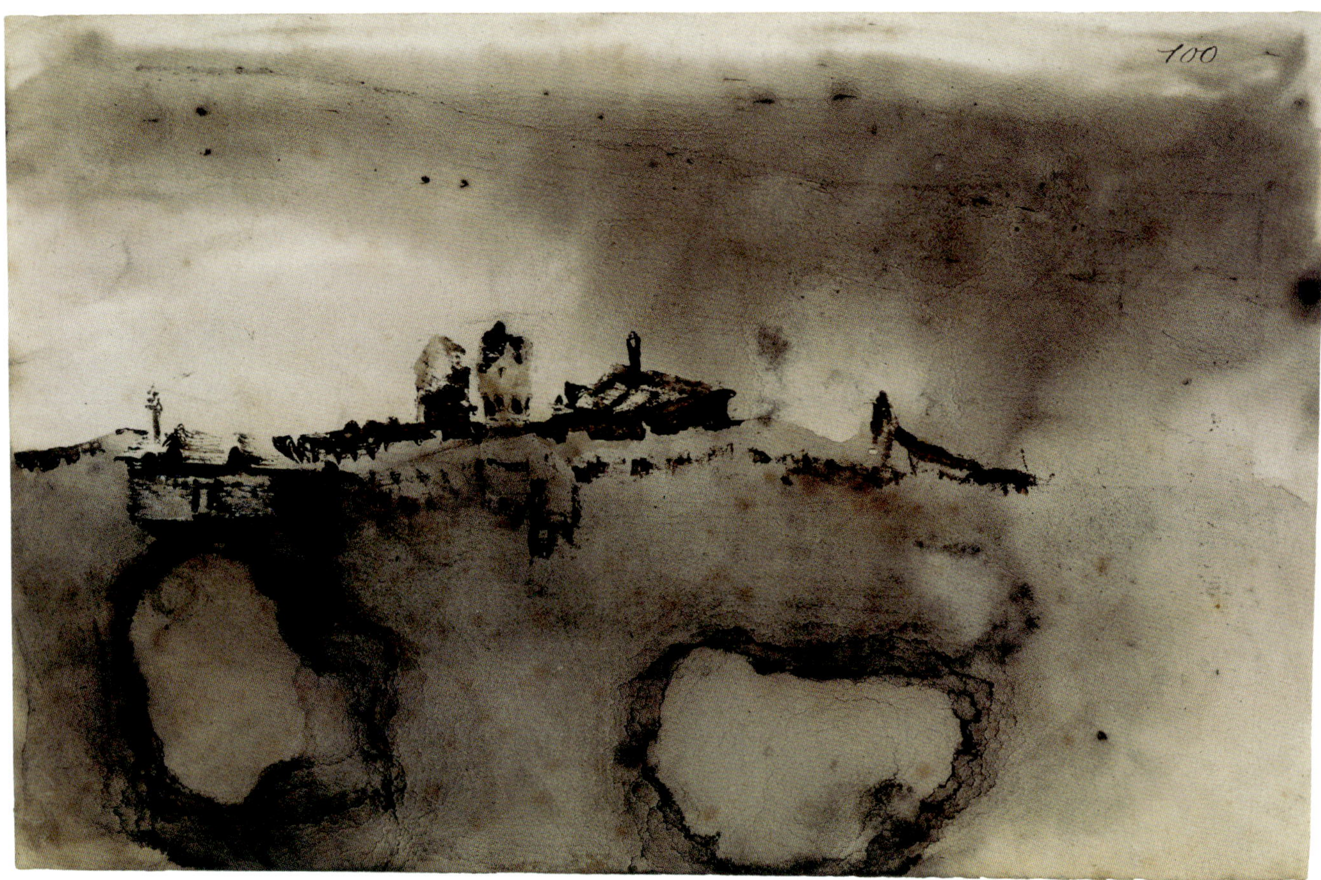

36

*Landscape: Town and Towers
on the Horizon*, 1856
Pen, brown ink, wash and gouache
on paper, 14.1 x 22.2 cm
Bibliothèque nationale de France, Paris,
Département des Manuscrits,
inv. no. NAF 13355, fol. 100

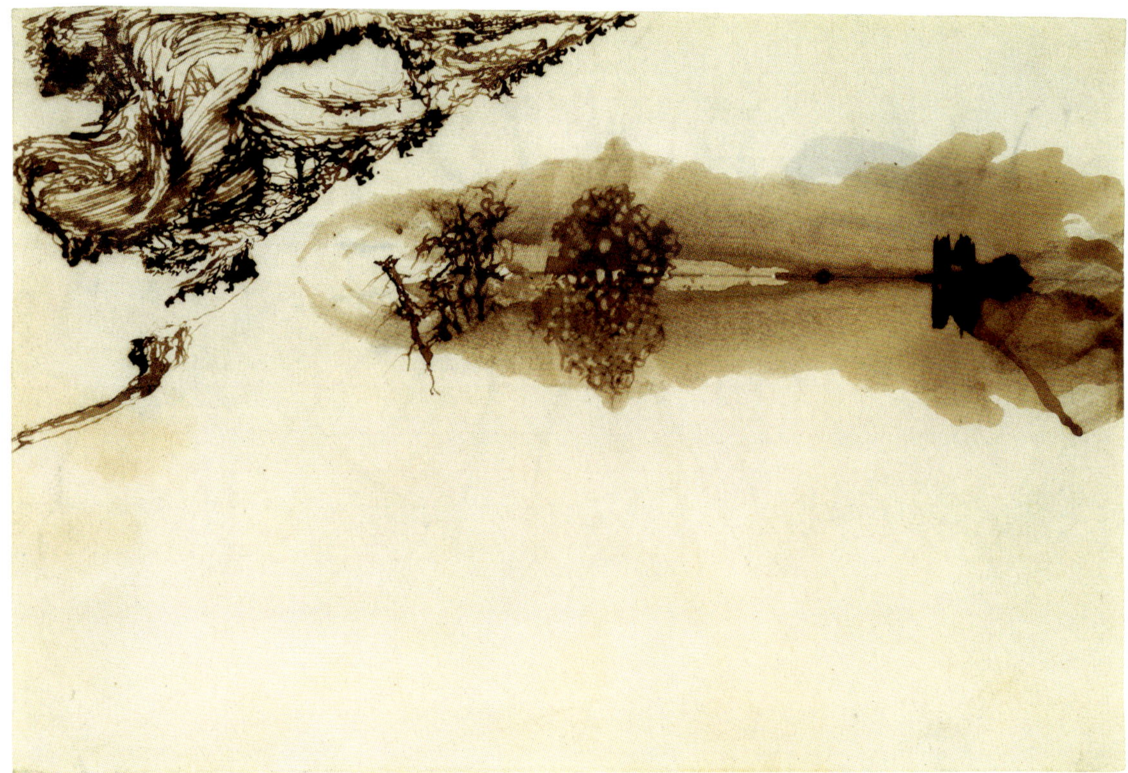

37

Landscape Reflected in Water, 1850
Pen and brown ink on paper, 11.8 x 17.9 cm
Bibliothèque nationale de France, Paris,
Département des Manuscrits,
NAF 13355, fol. 61

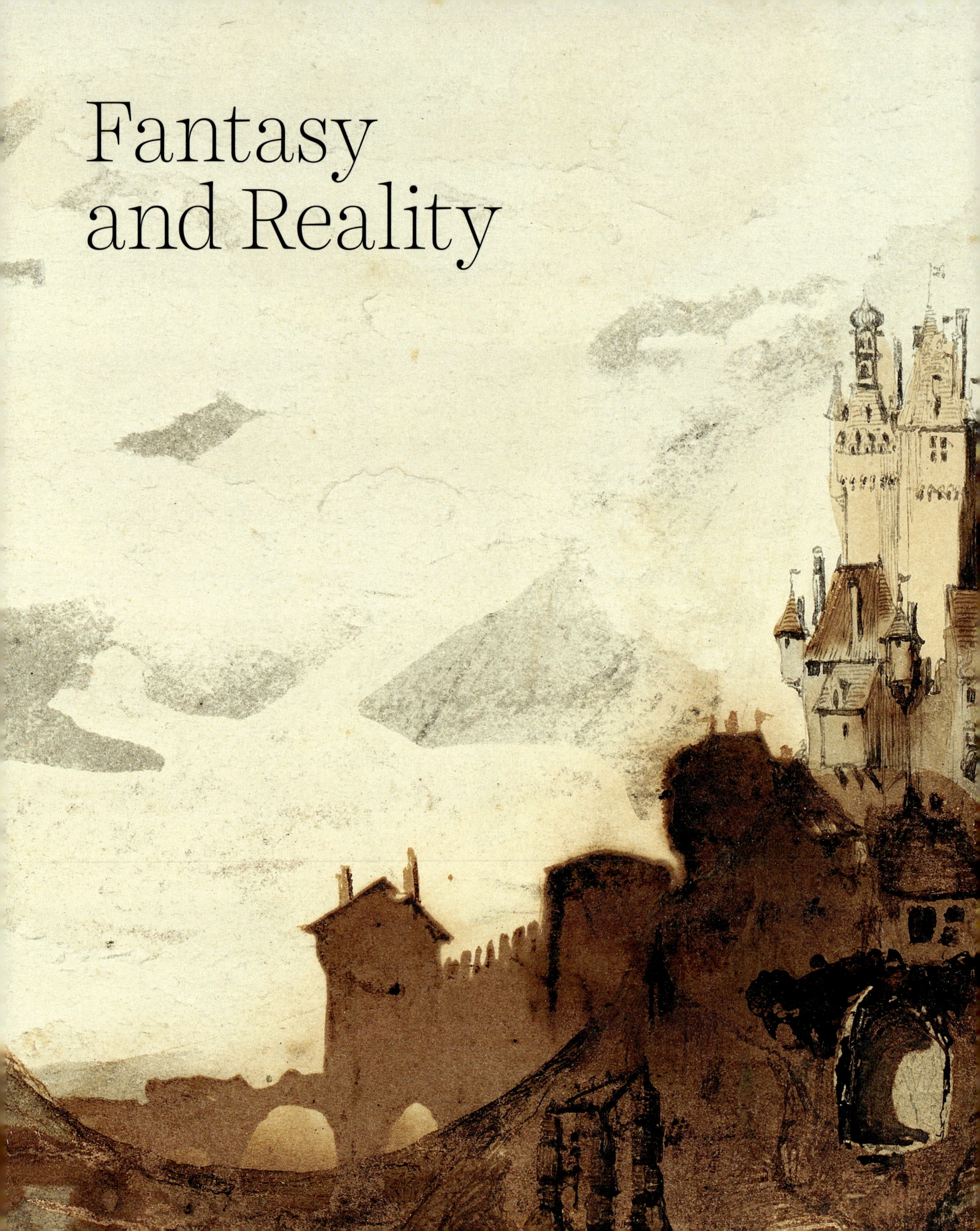

Fantasy
and Reality

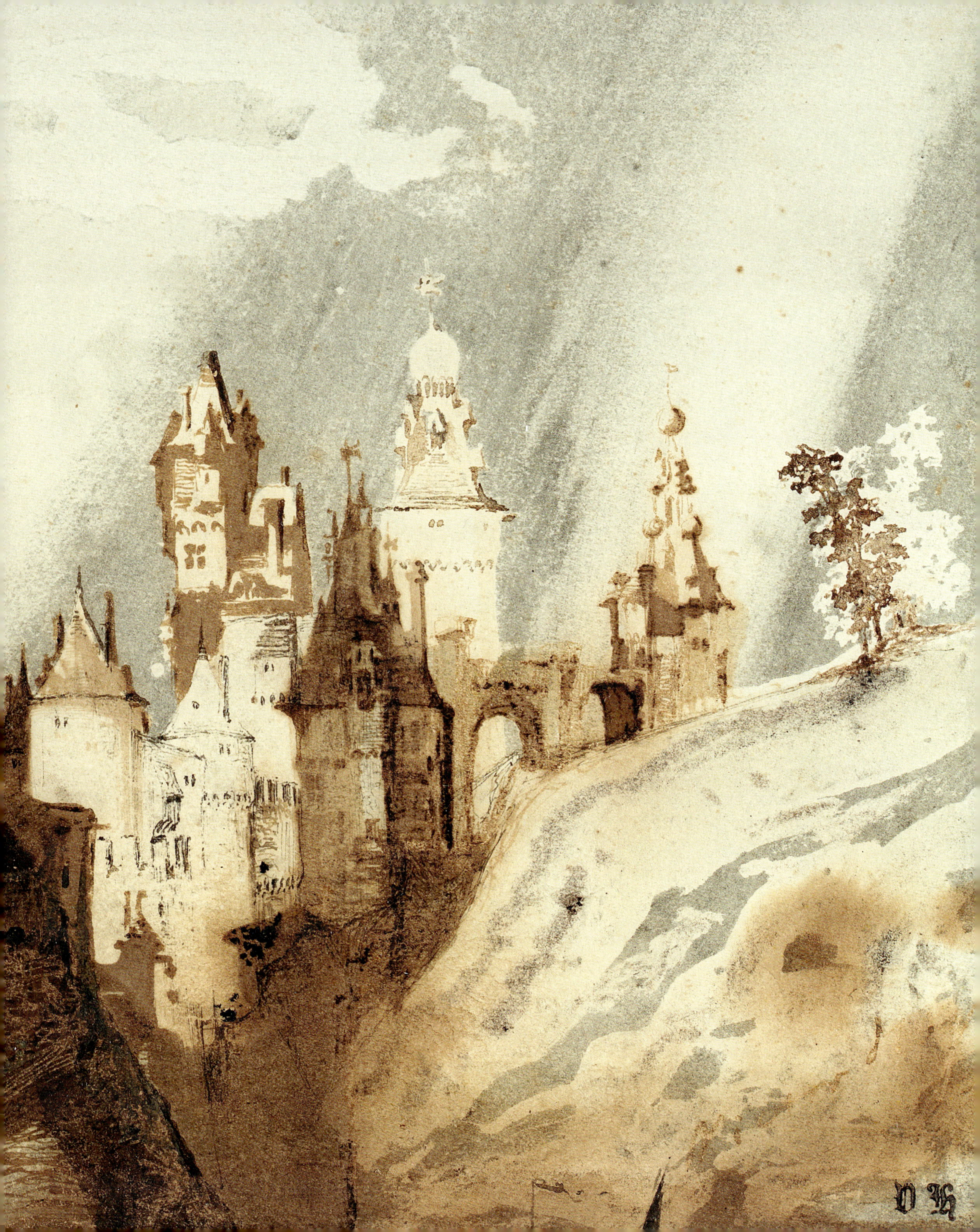

Castles

Hugo had a lifelong obsession with castles. The motif of the 'burg' (a term he used, taken from the German for castle, fortress or walled town) stemmed from his interest in the Middle Ages, and it featured in many of his writings. Perhaps also his fervent opposition to Baron Haussmann's modernisation of Paris – the demolition of crowded medieval neighbourhoods, their replacement with wide avenues and parks – might have played its part, consciously or subconsciously, in his habit of archiving aspects of medieval architecture in his work.

Although many are reminiscent of extant buildings seen on his European travels, Hugo particularly enjoyed depicting fictitious castles, from the exquisitely romantic, some of them colourful, to the hauntingly bleak. He routinely used stencils while doing so, selecting positive and negative silhouettes to create tonal contrasts. In *Landscape with a Castle on a Cliff* (cat. 42) he is thought to have used a paper stencil, *Silhouette of Castle with Three Towers* (cat. 40), and applied a background wash over it. He next added architectural details to the negative area, perhaps reshaping the central tower to distinguish the present drawing from others for which he had also used the stencil between 1855 and 1857. The result is a gloomy composition, but one on which he worked with multiple techniques, among them the addition of white gouache and the application of a brown wash with the back of his quill. In other examples he applied colour, as in *The Castle with the Angel* (cat. 39) where flowers grow around an angel carved into a stone. One of his most ambitious drawings, at over a metre wide, is *The Castle with the Cross* (1850; Maisons de Victor Hugo, Paris / Guernsey, inv. no. 40), which was later engraved into a multi-plate print

of the same title (cat. 46) and scale by Fortuné-Louis Méaulle, and was an extraordinary technical feat.[12]

Ecce / John Brown

Hugo strongly opposed the death penalty. He had attempted to intervene in the case of the convicted murderer John Tapner, but to no avail: Tapner was hanged on 10 February 1854 in Guernsey. After the public execution, Hugo made four drawings: *Ecce Lex* (cat.48); *Ecce (Le Pendu)*; *Le Pendu*; and *Ecce.* The word 'Ecce' is taken from the Latin and means 'behold', while 'Le Pendu' translates from the French as 'the hanged man'.

Hugo later appealed to the 'United States of America' in an attempt to obtain a pardon for the American abolitionist John Brown, who had been sentenced to death in Virginia on charges of treason, murder and conspiracy to incite a slave insurrection. In a letter to the 'Editor of the London News' in 1859, on the imminent hanging of Brown, Hugo wrote 'assuredly, if insurrection is ever a sacred duty, it must be when it is directed against Slavery', adding:

> *viewed in a political light, the murder of Brown would be an irreparable fault … viewed in a moral light, it seems to me that a portion of the enlightenment of humanity would be eclipsed, that even the ideas of justice and injustice would be obscured on the day which should witness the assassination of Emancipation by Liberty.*[13]

These drawings made their way into the public spotlight through print reproductions by Hugo's brother-in-law, Paul Chenay. Chenay's engraving, from the version of the drawing held in the Musée du Louvre, Paris, was later published with a new title, *John Brown* (cat. 49), and circulated in protest at Brown's execution.[14]

Hauteville House

Hugo kept the original drawing for *Ecce Lex* close, always on display at Hauteville House, his home in Saint Peter Port, Guernsey, which he decorated to form a work of art in itself, a *Gesamtkunstwerk*. He and his family lived there, from 1856 to 1870, during his political exile from France. Hugo completely renovated the house to his own design, including some major architectural modifications, most famously the top-floor 'Lookout', a conservatory with panoramic views of the sea, which he used for writing and drawing. His wife Adèle wrote to her sister in 1856:

> *My husband is very happy and completely immersed in his house. This house will be a poem. My husband engraves inscriptions, puts his soul on the walls of his house, he picks up the tools himself and puts his sweat into it. Finally it will be a monument erected by the great exile.*[15]

Hugo once said that he had 'missed his true vocation', that he was 'born to be a decorator'.[16] He designed many features of Hauteville House himself and drew and painted directly onto objects he displayed there. He made numerous drawings for the centrepiece of his dining room: a monumental fireplace (cats 53, 57). A floor-to-ceiling wall of mainly blue delftware tiles surrounds the fireplace, a projecting ceramic 'H' for Hugo of his own design at its centre. Throughout the house, Hugo incorporated objects from many countries and cultures: delftware tiles and heavy oak panelling inspired by European trends, alongside Chinese and Japanese styles of porcelain (largely English or French imitations), with tapestries and silks from across East Asia. His design choices and the panels he created himself, some of which include racialised figures, reflect a wider vogue among writers and artists in England and France during the nineteenth century for chinoiserie and European interpretations of East Asian artistic traditions. Hugo's interest in 'Orientalism', a contested, Western-centric term that conflates diverse cultures belonging to the Eastern world, was subsumed into his broad, eclectic aesthetic; it did not represent a deep engagement with the historical specificity of the artworks nor their cultural meanings.

During his exile in Jersey, Hugo became interested in photography. He met the Caen photographer Edmond Bacot, who had travelled to the island in 1853 to bring resources gathered by the Republicans for those in exile. Bacot's photographs of Gothic monuments in Normandy appealed greatly to Hugo, who wrote to him: 'I congratulate the sun for having a collaborator such as you.'[17] Hugo's son Charles had lessons in photography from Bacot, before setting up and running a photographic studio with Auguste Vacquerie on Jersey between 1852 and 1855, and on Guernsey from 1855. In 1862 Bacot visited Hugo on Guernsey and set about documenting Hauteville House through photographs and stereographs. A 'report' of Hauteville House was produced over fifteen days. Twenty-nine of these photographs have been found to date: twelve views of the house (cats 51, 52, 54, 55) and seventeen portraits, including many of Hugo. *Rose Thompson*

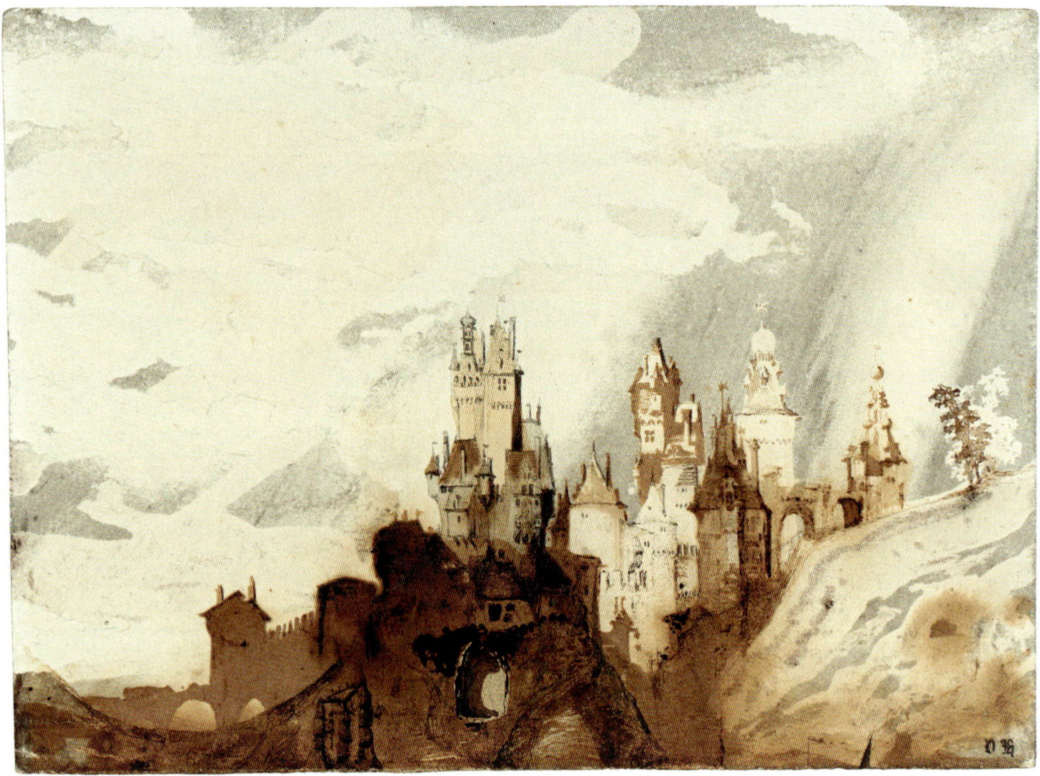

38

The Cheerful Castle, c. 1847
Pen, brown ink and wash, black ink
and wash and crayon on cardboard,
15.8 x 22.2 cm
Maisons de Victor Hugo, Paris / Guernsey,
inv. no. 37

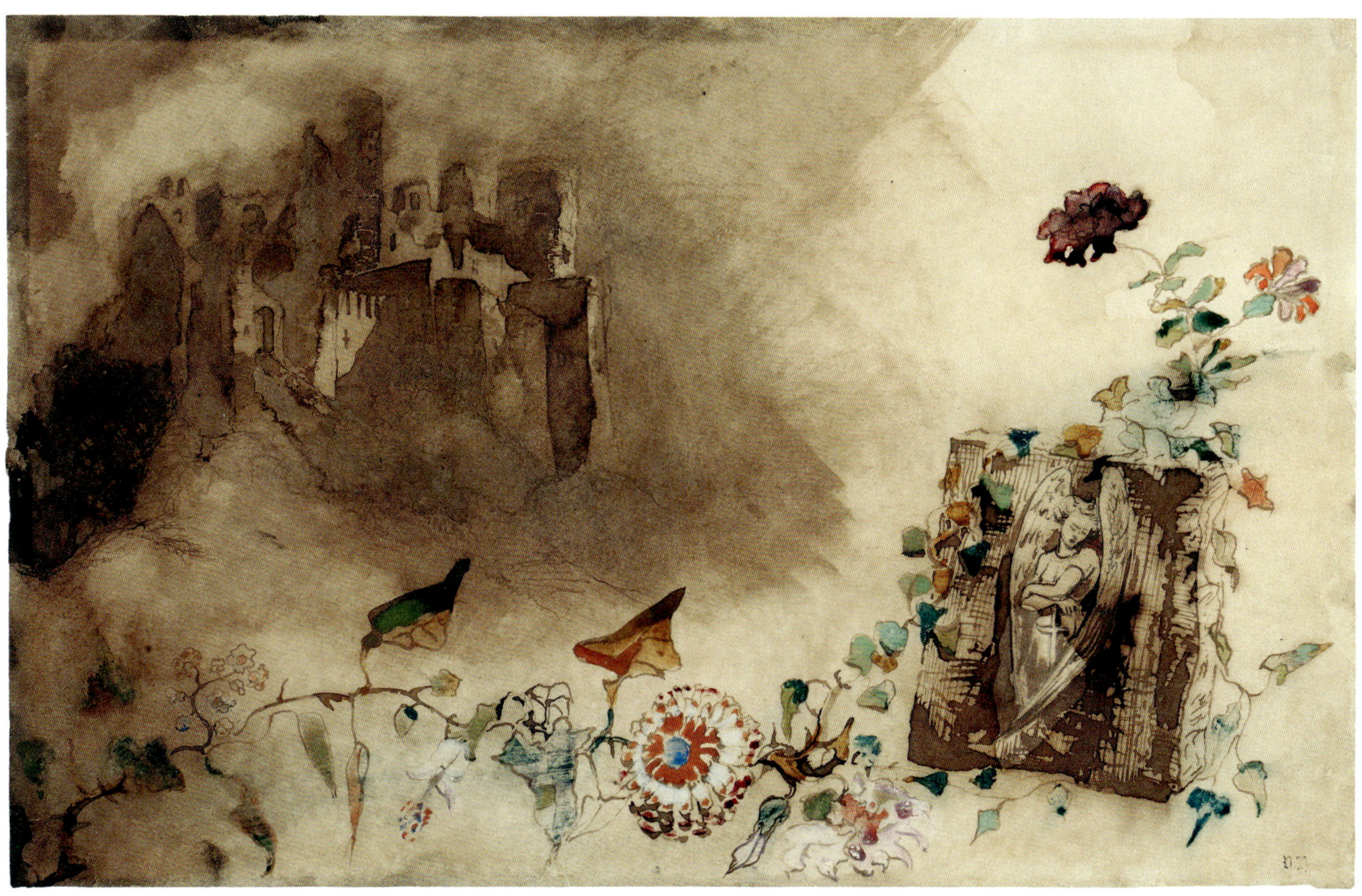

39

The Castle with the Angel, c. 1863
Pen and brown ink wash over graphite
pencil, watercolour, gouache and scrapings
on paper, 21.2 x 34.2 cm
Maisons de Victor Hugo, Paris / Guernsey,
inv. no. 36

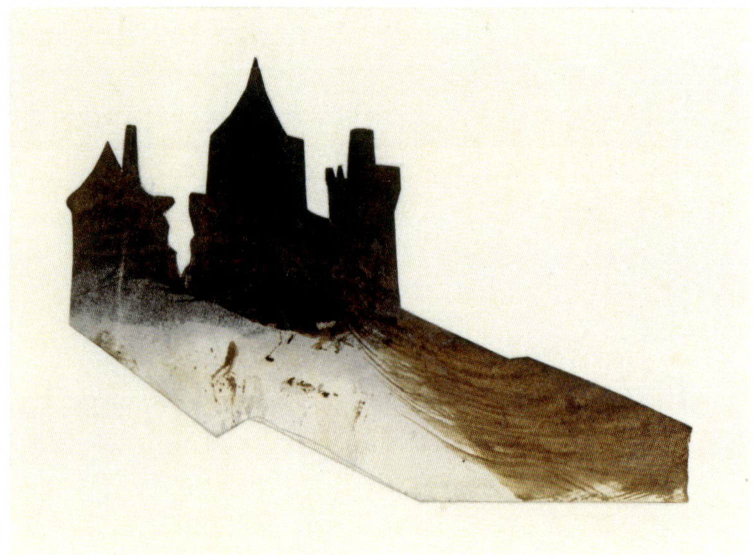

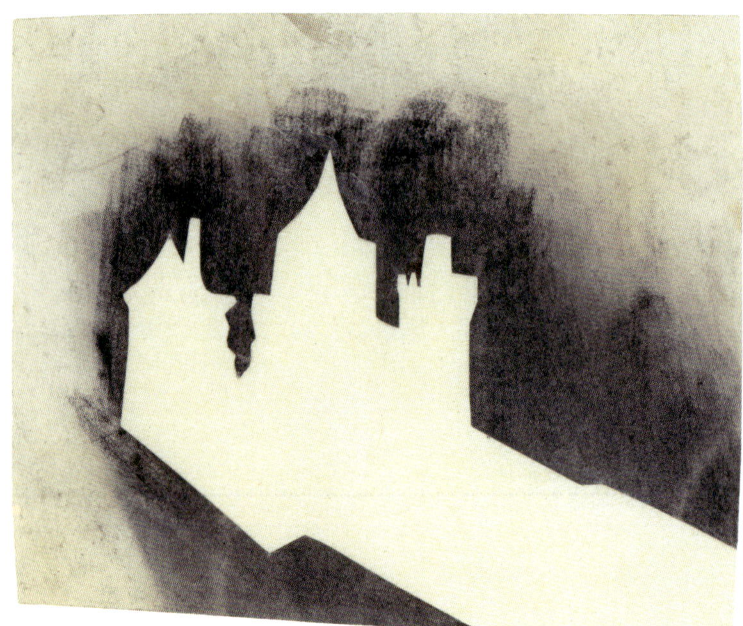

40

Silhouette of Castle with Three Towers, 1855
Charcoal and black ink on paper, 9.5 x 13.5 cm
Bibliothèque nationale de France, Paris,
Département des Manuscrits, inv. no. NAF
13351, fol. 34 (3)

41

Silhouette of Castle with Three Towers, 1856
Charcoal on paper, 12 x 15 cm
Bibliothèque nationale de France, Paris,
Département des Manuscrits,
inv. no. NAF 13351, fol. 34 (2)

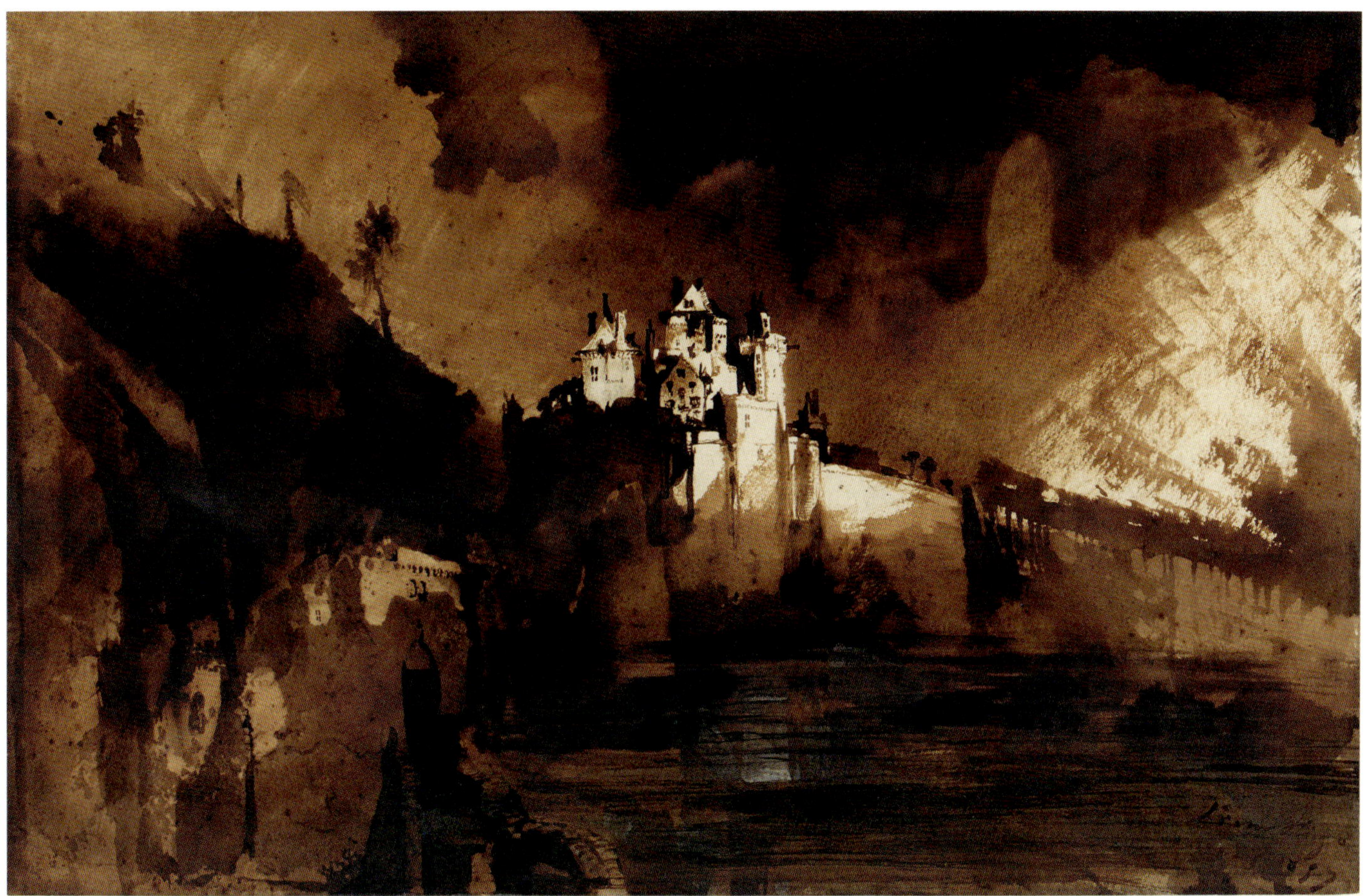

42

Landscape with a Castle on a Cliff, 1857
Brush and brown wash, with stencilling and
white gouache on paper, 31.1 x 49 cm
British Museum, London, inv. no. 1930,0716.3

43

*The Town and Castle of Vianden
by Moonlight*, 1871 (sheet from
an album in the Bibliothèque nationale
de France, Paris [NAF13349])
Pen, brown and purple ink wash on
graphite on paper, 25.7 x 35 cm
Maisons de Victor Hugo, Paris / Guernsey,
inv. no. 5

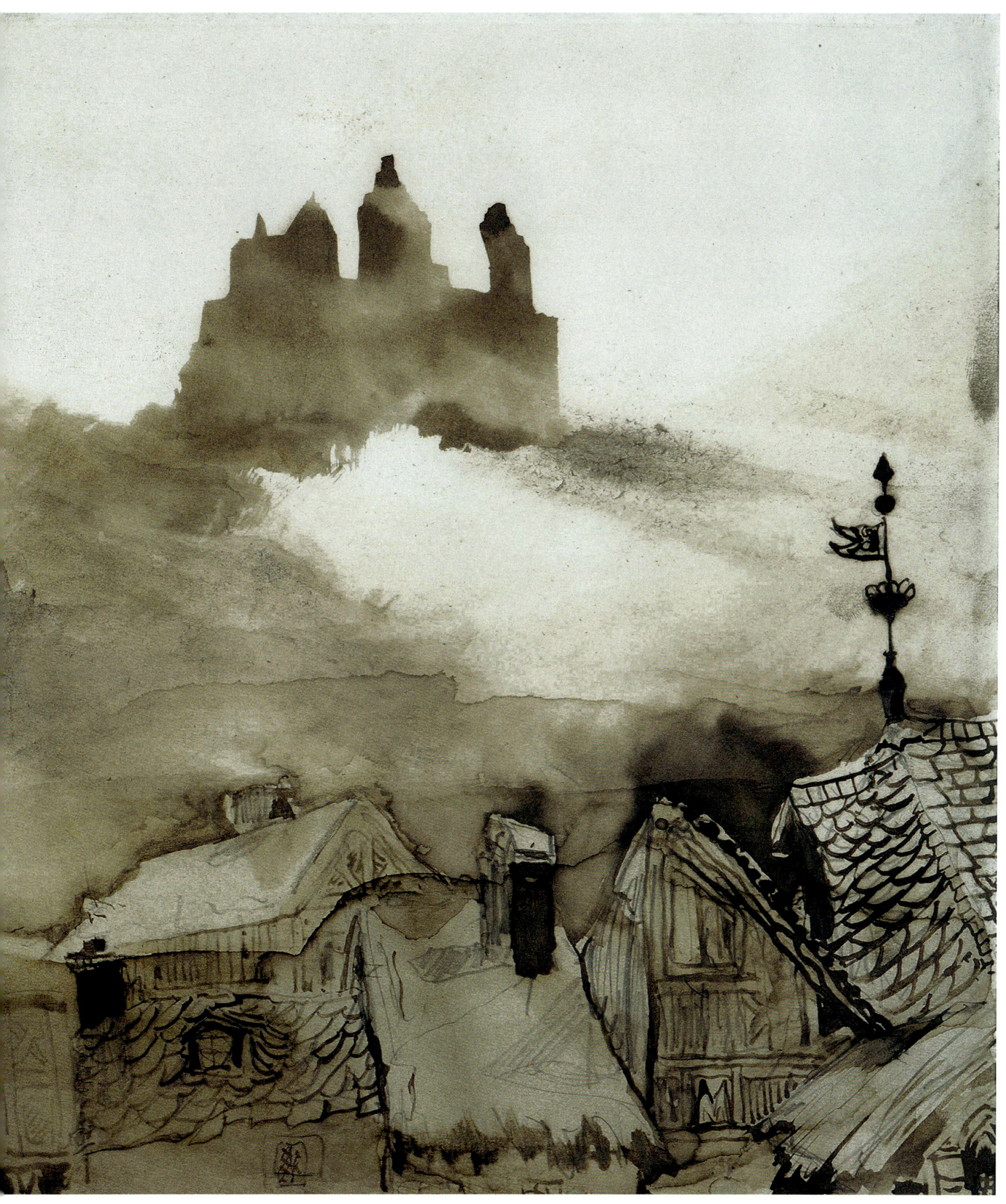

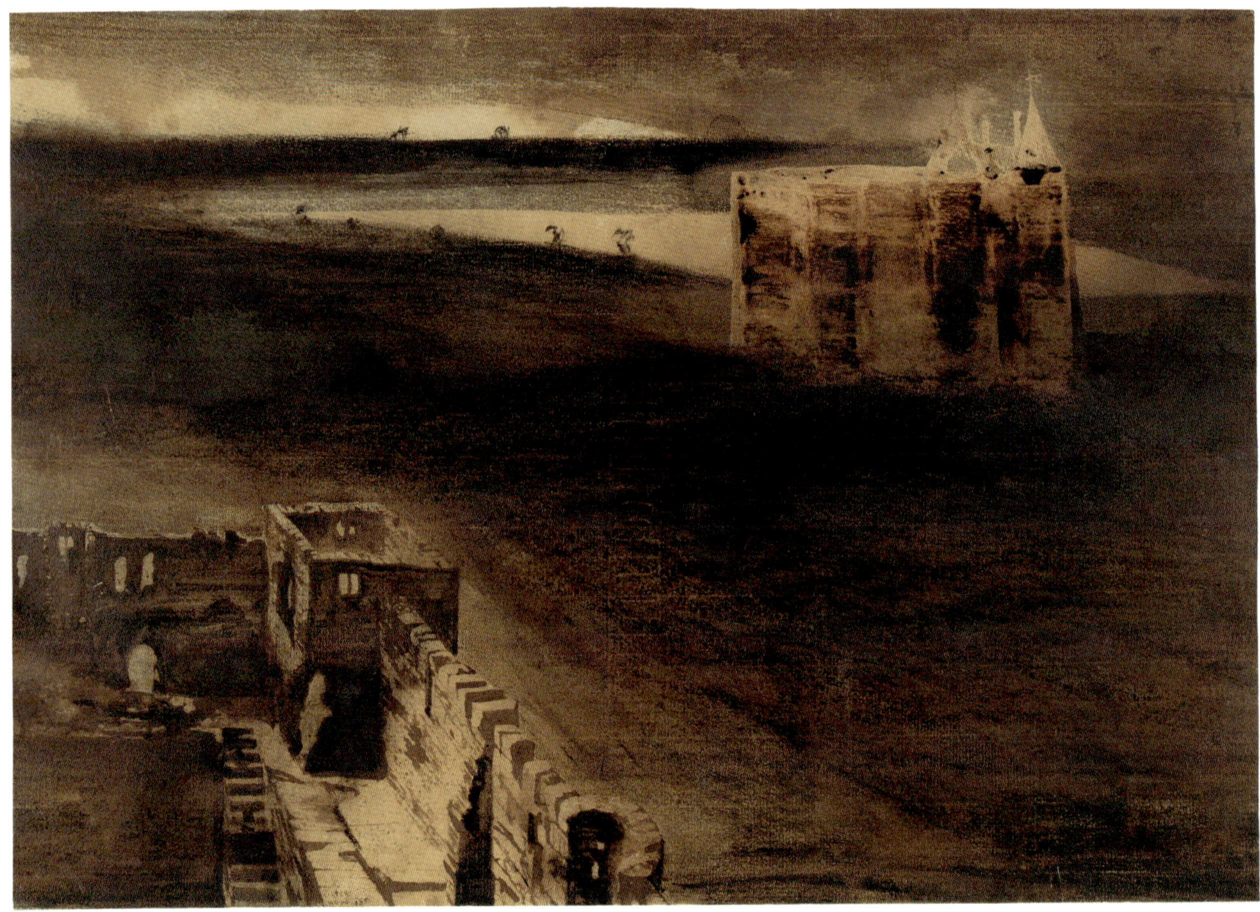

44

The Two Castles, 1850
Pen and brown ink wash, graphite pencil
and charcoal on paper, 34 x 49 cm
Maisons de Victor Hugo, Paris / Guernsey,
inv. no. 16

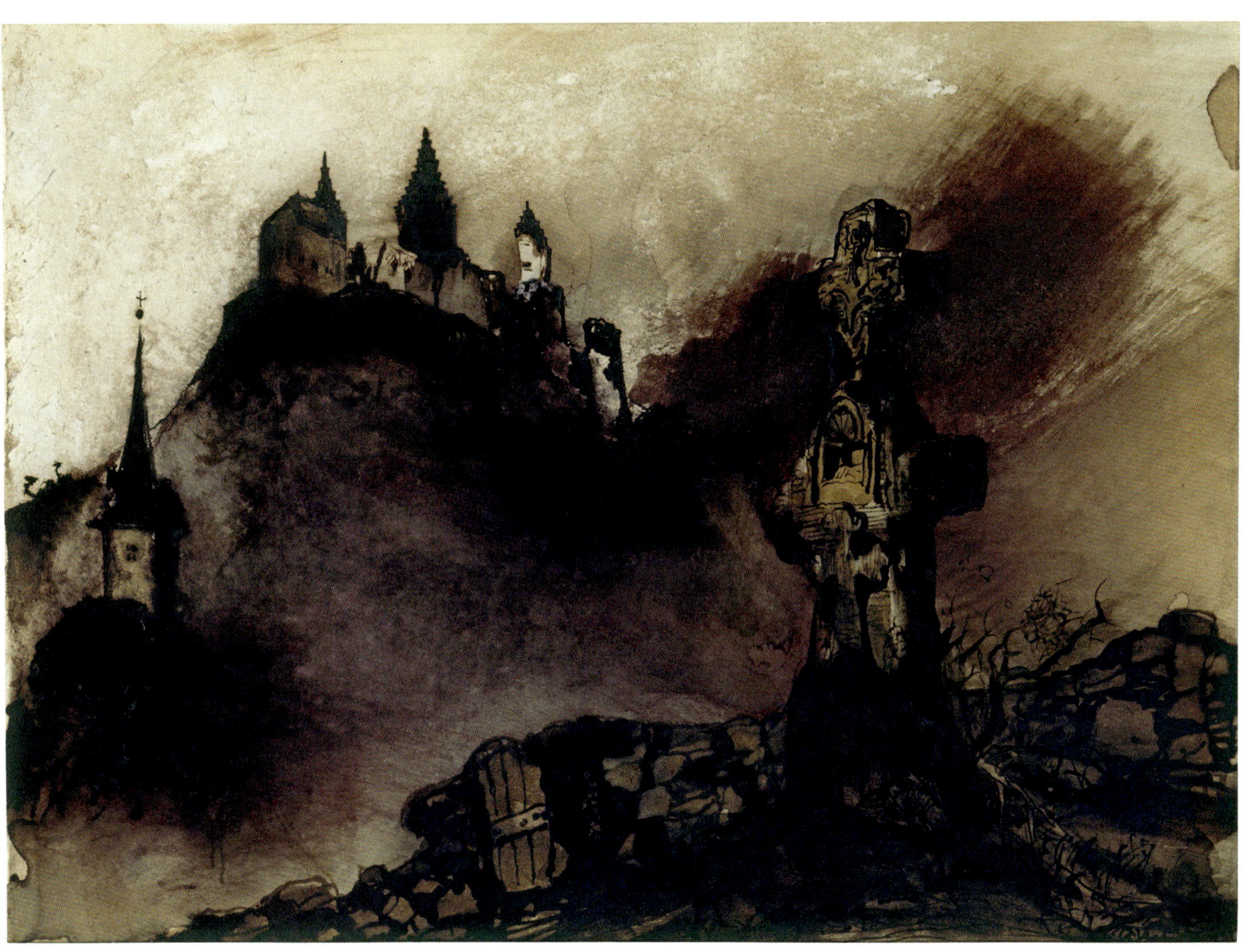

45

The Town of Vianden, with Stone Cross, 1871
Brown and black ink, brown and purple
wash, graphite and varnish on paper,
25 x 34.5 cm
Bibliothèque nationale de France, Paris,
Département des Manuscrits,
inv. no. NAF 13349, fol. 19

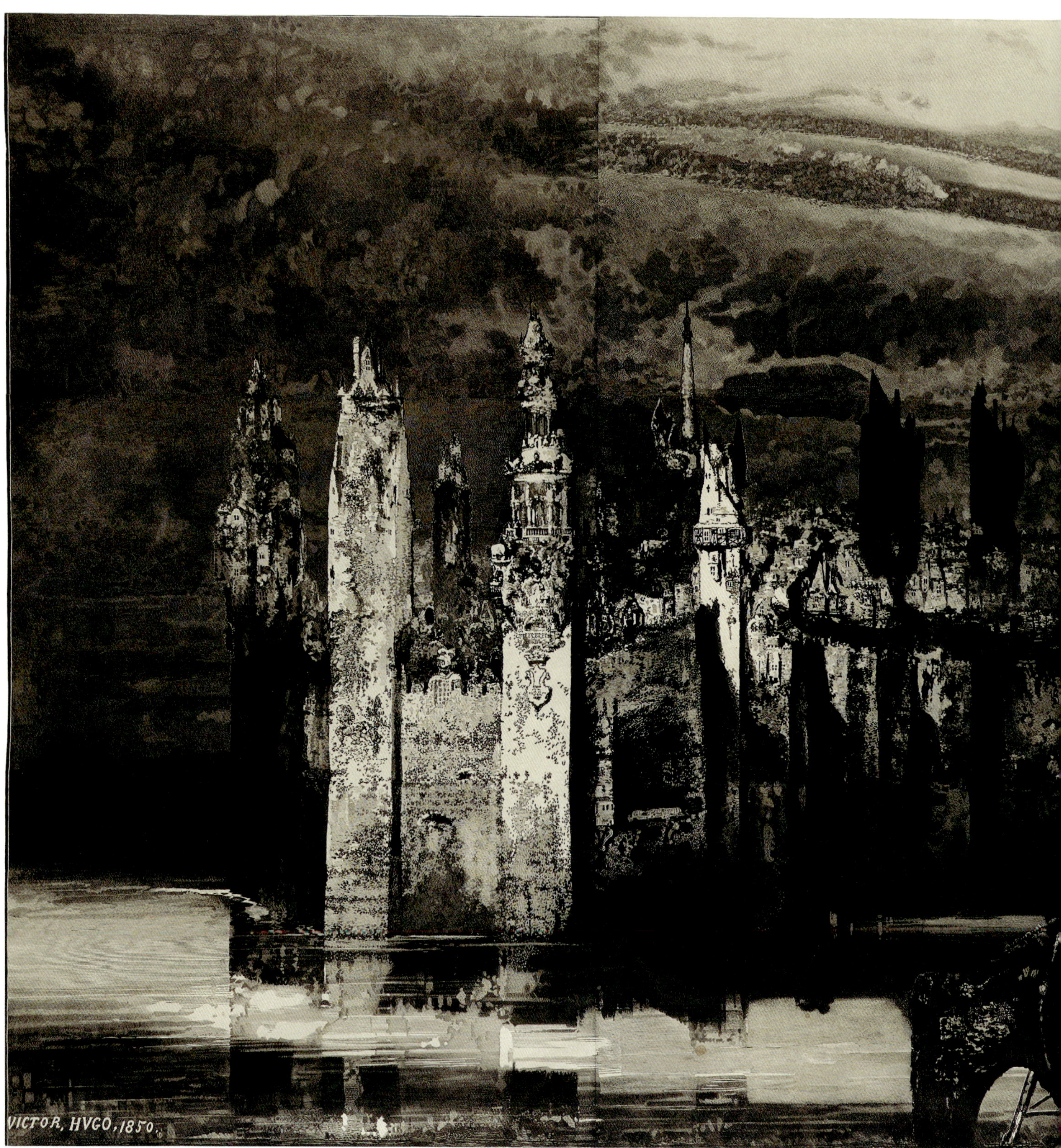

VICTOR, HVGO, 1850.

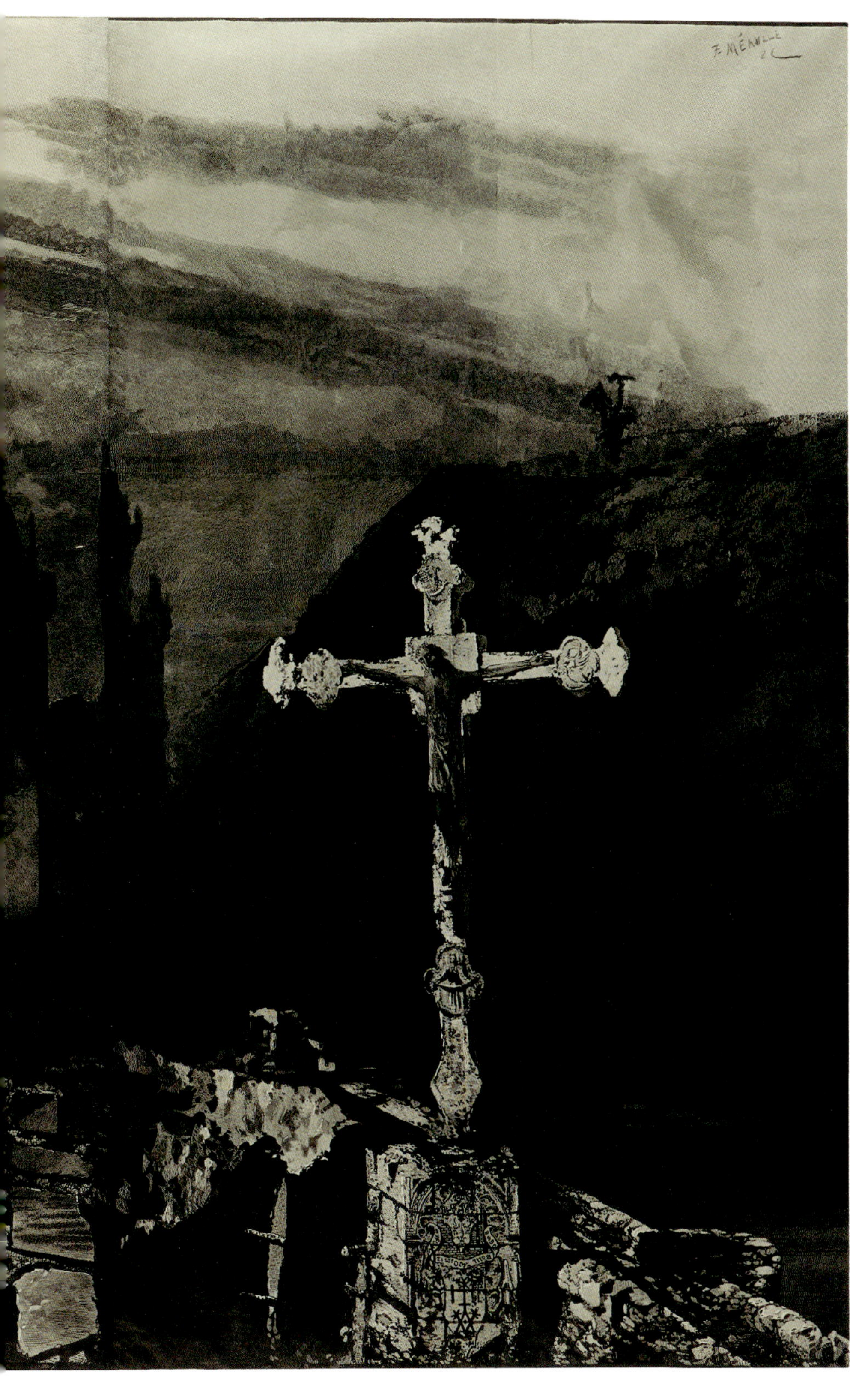

46

Fortuné-Louis Méaulle (1843–1916)
after Victor Hugo
The Castle with the Cross
(*Le Burg à la Croix*), 1875
Etching, 75.9 x 132.2 cm
Maisons de Victor Hugo, Paris / Guernsey,
inv. no. 1498.1

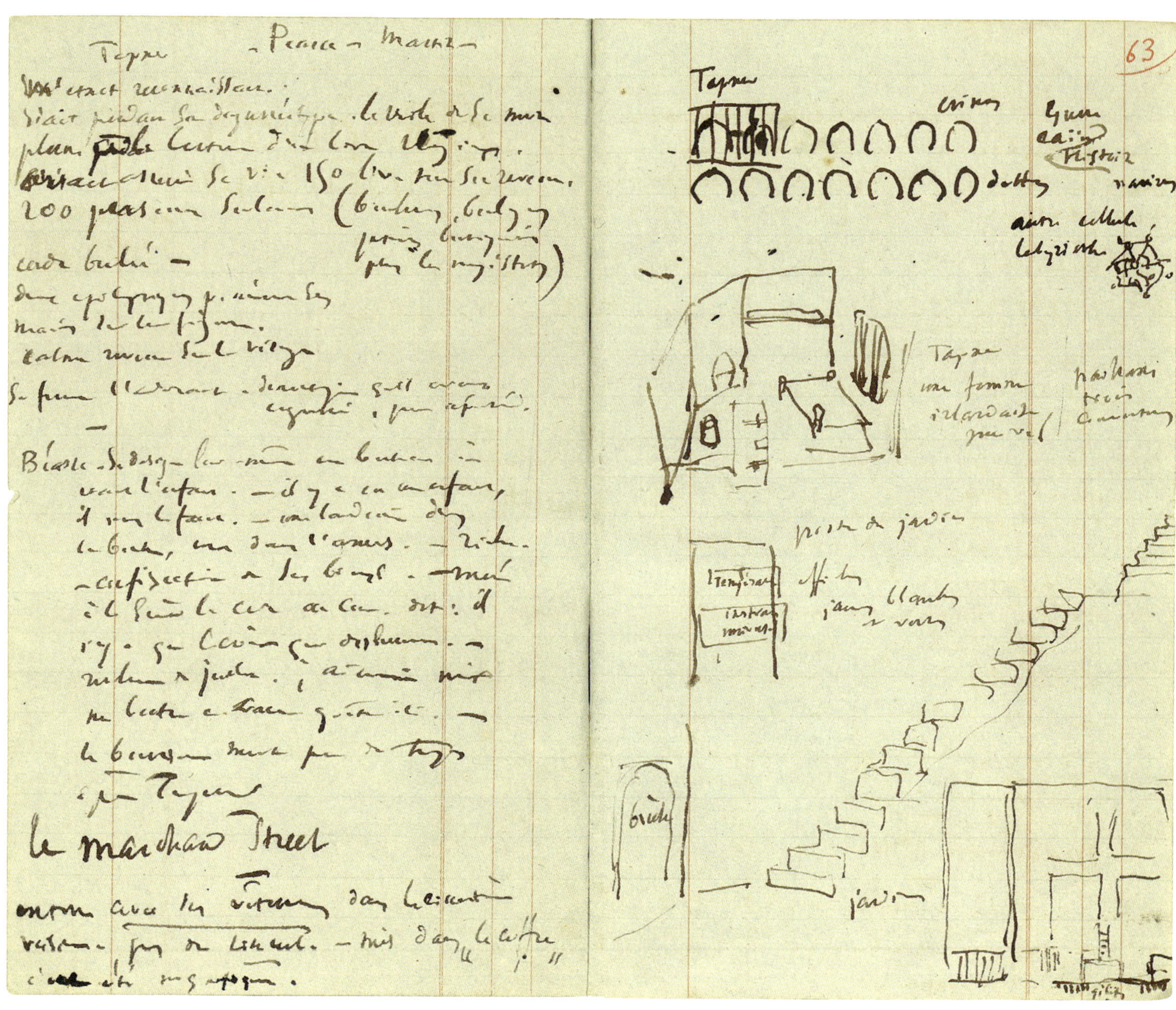

47

Sketchbook Depicting John Tapner's
Prison Cell in Guernsey, 31 October 1855 –
30 September 1857
Sketchbook, 18 x 11.5 x 1.5 cm
Bibliothèque nationale de France,
Paris, Département des Manuscrits,
inv. no. NAF 13446, fols 62–63

48

Ecce Lex, 1854
Pen and brown ink wash, graphite
pencil, black ink and charcoal on paper,
50.8 x 34.9 cm
Maisons de Victor Hugo, Paris / Guernsey,
inv. no. 967

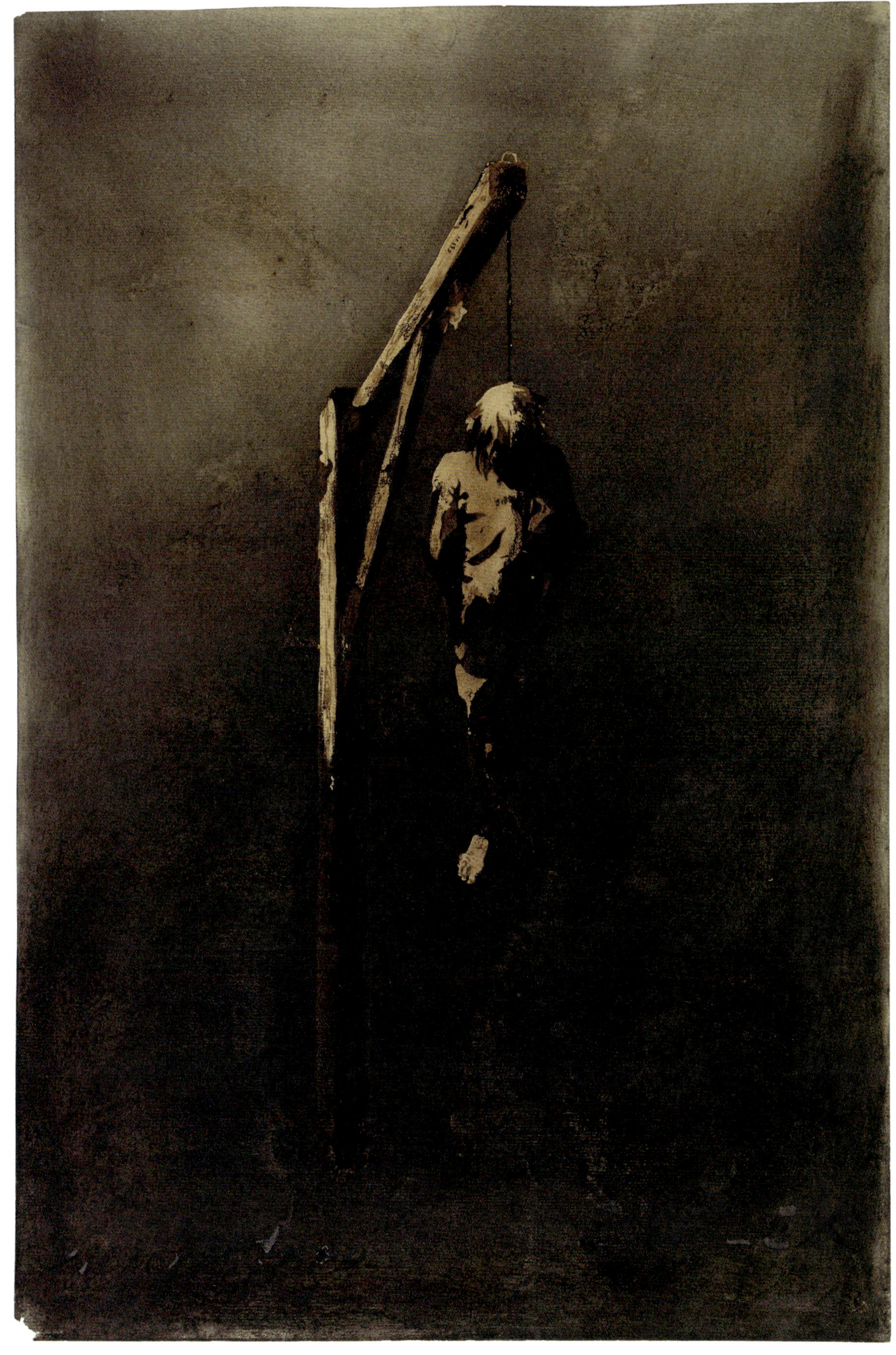

2 décembre 1859 _ Mort de John Brown.
Victor Hugo
1860
VICTOR HUGO DELINEAVIT
PAUL CHENAY SCULPSIT. FAC-SIMILE
JOHN BROWN
A 6302

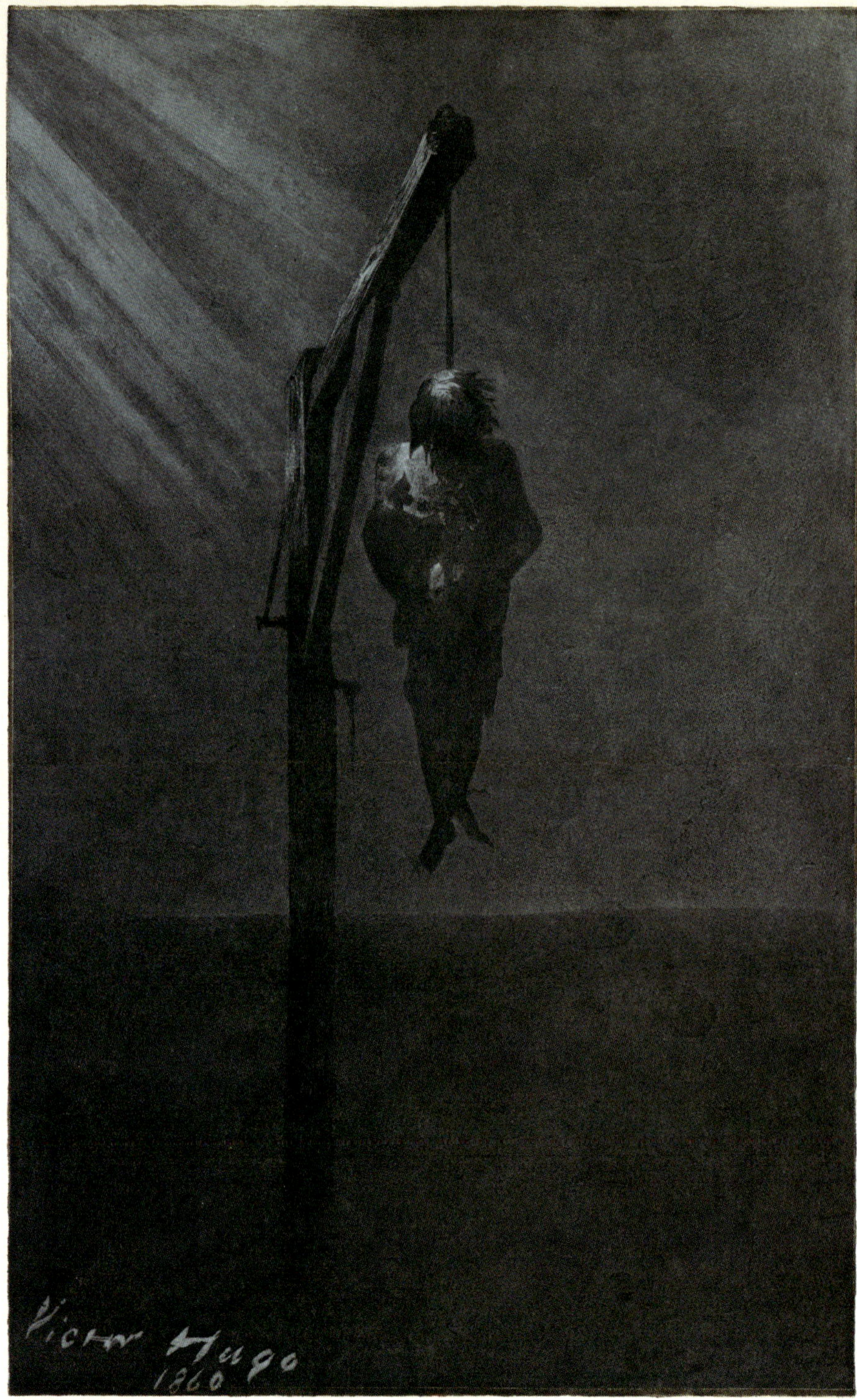

Hauteville house : 21 janvier 1861

Cher M. Chenay, vous avez désiré graver mon dessin de John Brown, vous désirez aujourd'hui le publier ; j'y consens, et j'ajoute que je le trouve utile.

John Brown est un héros et un martyr. Sa mort a été un crime. Son gibet est une croix. Vous vous souvenez que j'avais écrit au bas du dessin : Pro Christo, sicut Christus.

Lorsque, en décembre 1859, avec une profonde douleur, j'annonçais à l'Amérique la rupture de l'Union comme conséquence de l'assassinat de John Brown, je ne pensais pas que l'événement dût suivre de si près mes paroles. À l'heure où nous sommes, tout ce qui était dans l'échafaud de John Brown en sort, les fatalités latentes il y a un an sont maintenant visibles, et l'on peut dès à présent considérer comme consommées la rupture de l'Union américaine, grand malheur, et l'abolition de l'esclavage, immense progrès.

Remettons donc sous les yeux de tous, comme enseignement, le gibet de Charlestown, point de départ de ces graves événements.

Mon dessin, reproduit par votre beau talent avec une fidélité saisissante, n'a d'autre valeur que ce nom, John Brown, nom qu'il faut répéter sans cesse, aux républicains d'Amérique, pour qu'il les ramène au devoir ; aux esclaves, pour qu'il les appelle à la liberté.

Je vous serre la main.

Victor Hugo

A 8202

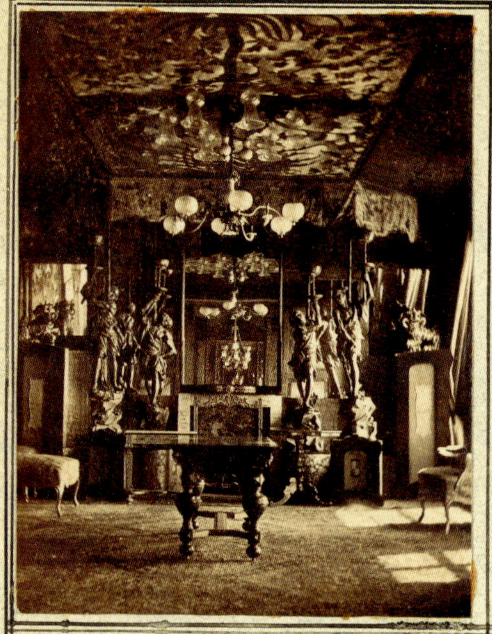

Le Salon Rouge.

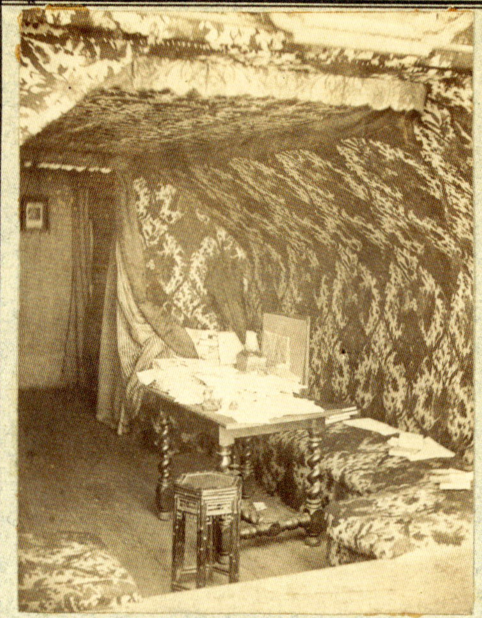

Le lock-out.

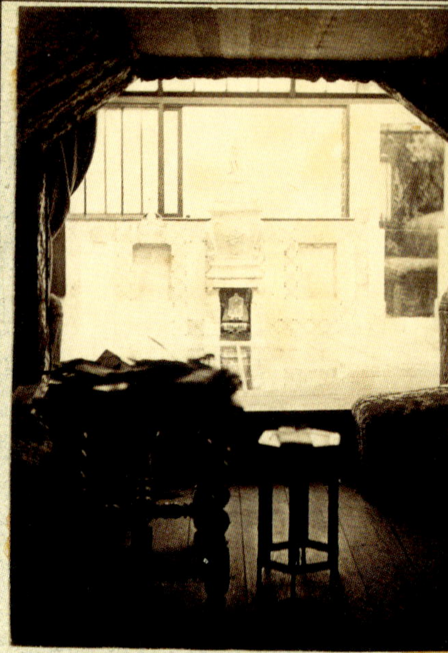

Le lock-out.

La grande cheminée avait un dais supporté par 4 nègres de bois sculpté qui ornaient, à Venise, la poupe du « Bucentaure ». Ils portaient des torchères.

Le lock-out, pièce vitrée où travaillêt toujours Victor-Hugo et d'où la vue s'éten sur tout le port de Guernesey et même, par temps clair, jusqu'aux côtes de Fran
V. Hugo y travaillait toujours debout.

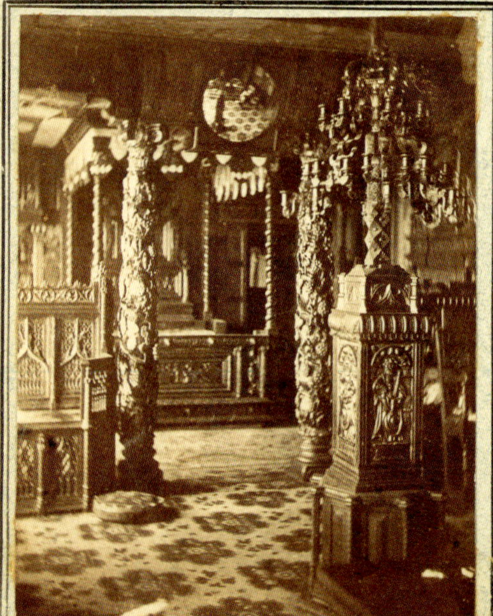

Galerie de Chêne.

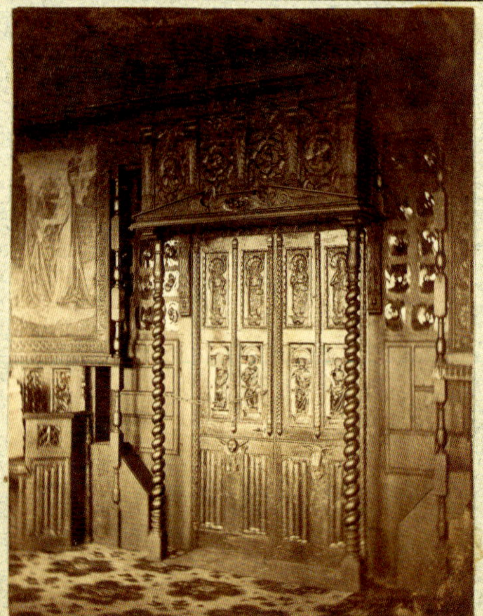

Porte de la Galerie de Chêne.

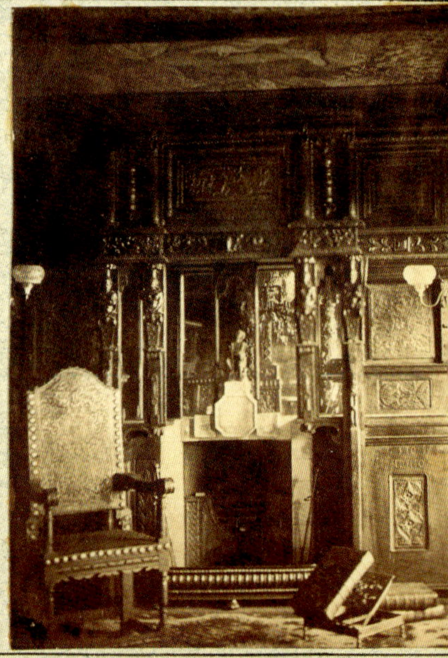

Cheminée de la Galerie de Chê

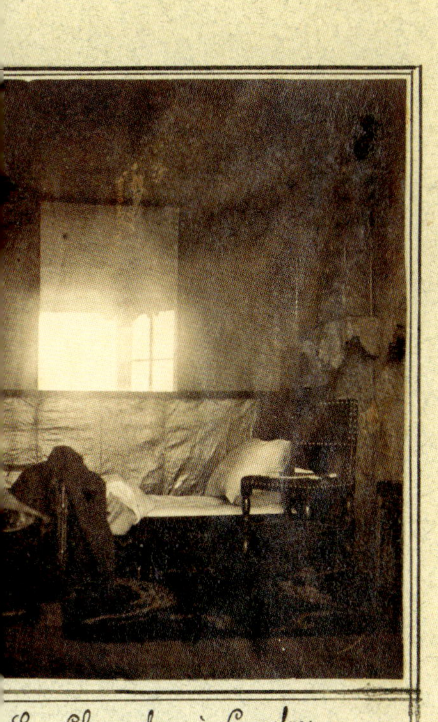

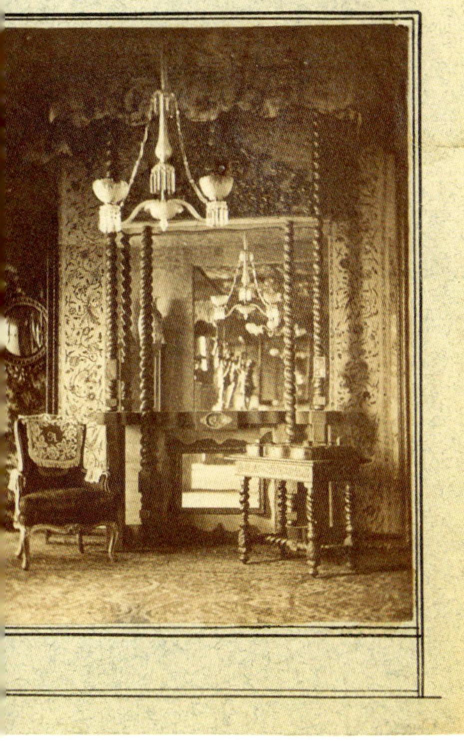

51

Edmond Bacot (1814–1875)
Eight Views of Hauteville House, 1862
Prints on albumen paper, each 9.3 x 7.2 cm
Maisons de Victor Hugo, Paris / Guernsey,
inv. no. 2576

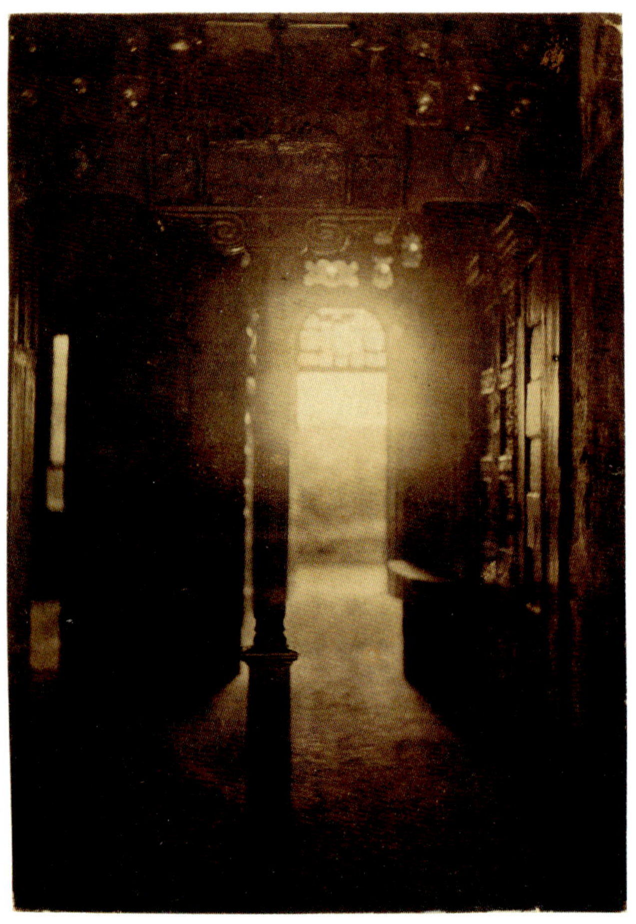

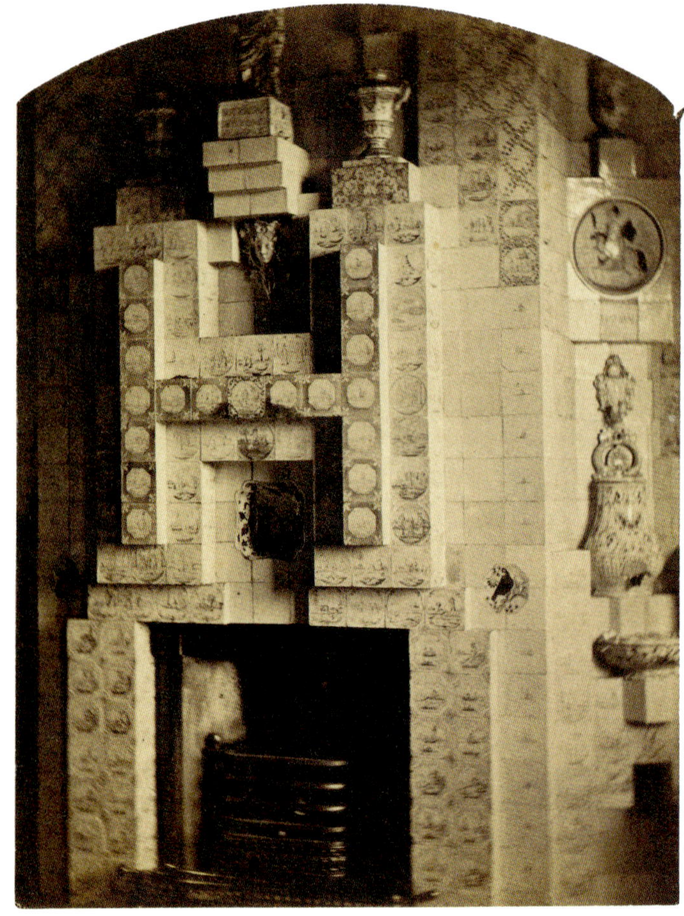

52

Edmond Bacot (1814–1875)
The Vestibule at Hauteville House, 1862
Print on albumen paper, 8.1 x 6.4 cm
Maisons de Victor Hugo, Paris / Guernsey,
inv. no. 3233

53

Edmond Bacot (1814–1875)
*The Fireplace in the Dining Room
at Hauteville House*, 1862
Print on albumen paper, 8.2 x 6.2 cm
Maisons de Victor Hugo, Paris / Guernsey,
inv. no. 3230

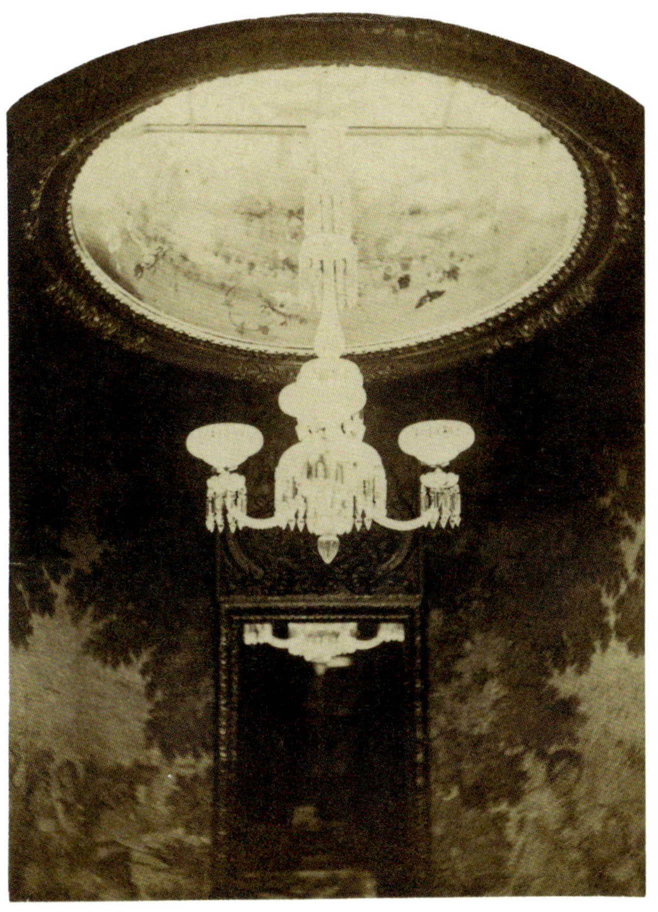

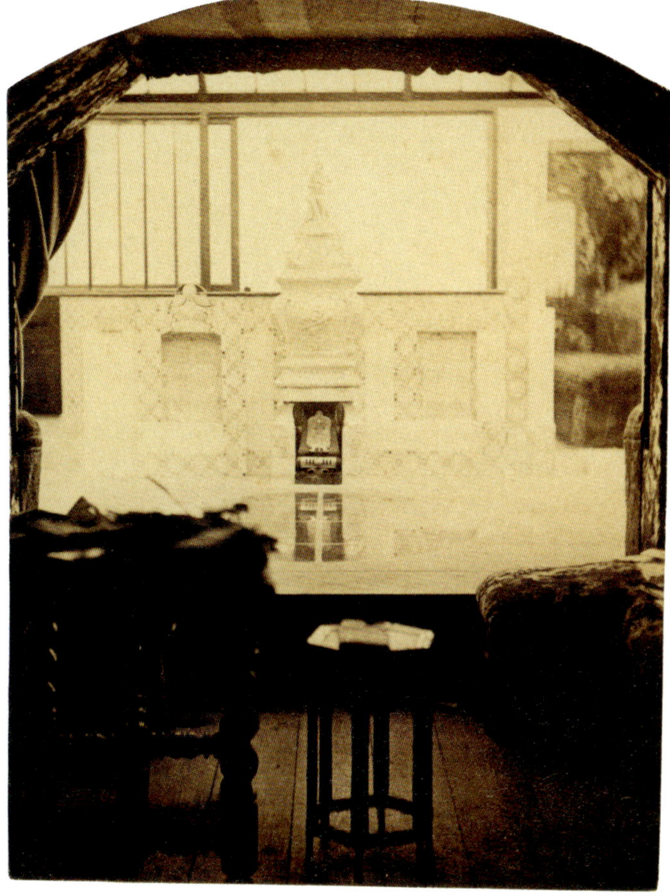

54

Edmond Bacot (1814–1875)
*The Dome and Chandelier on
the Staircase of Hauteville House*, 1862
Print on albumen paper, 8.4 x 6.2 cm
Maisons de Victor Hugo, Paris / Guernsey,
inv. no. 3754

55

Edmond Bacot (1814–1875)
*The Study and the 'Lookout'
at Hauteville House*, 1862
Print on albumen paper, 8.6 x 6.3 cm
Maisons de Victor Hugo, Paris / Guernsey,
inv. no. 3762

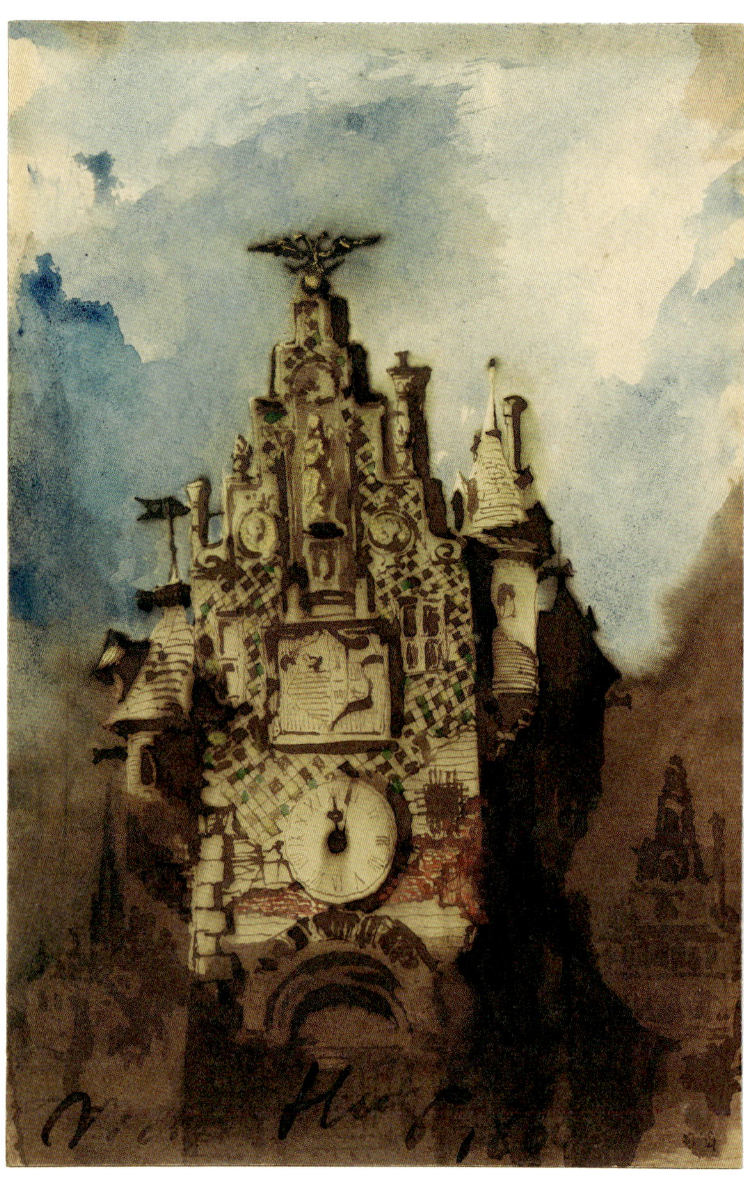

57

*The Fireplace in the Dining Room
at Hauteville House*, 1857
Graphite pencil, pen and brush, brown
ink and wash, black ink wash, charcoal,
blue ink and blue, purple and white
gouache on paper, 47.7 x 34.7 cm
Maisons de Victor Hugo, Paris / Guernsey,
inv. no. 86

56

The Home of 'Hugo-Tête-d'Aigle', 1860
Pen and brown ink wash, blue ink, gouache
and gold ink on cardboard, 21.3 x 14.3 cm
Maisons de Victor Hugo, Paris / Guernsey,
inv. no. 32

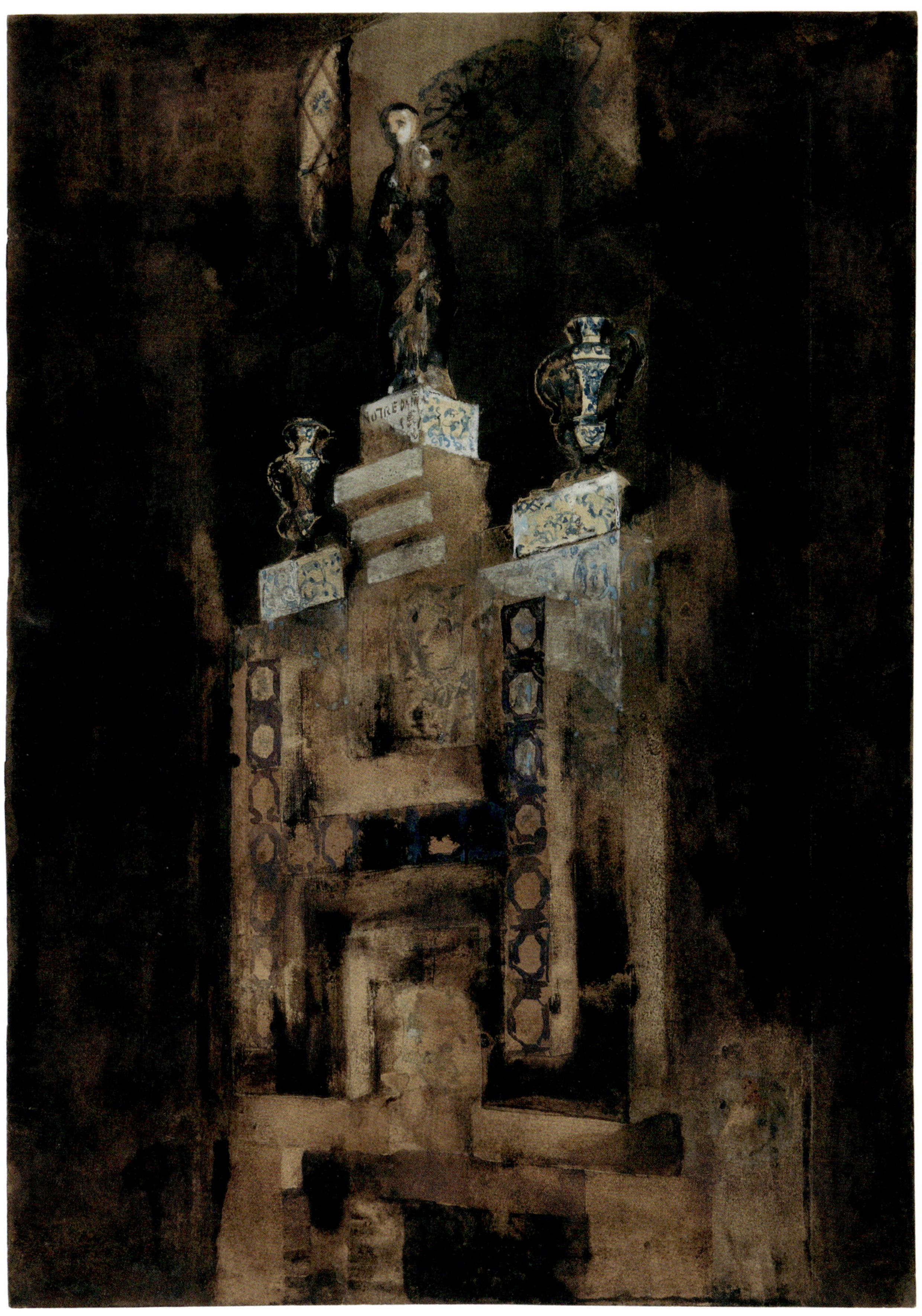

NOTRE DAME

58

Mirror with Birds, 1870
Hand-painted and inscribed wooden
frame, oil paint and varnish, 70 x 65 cm
Maisons de Victor Hugo, Paris / Guernsey,
inv. no. 1017

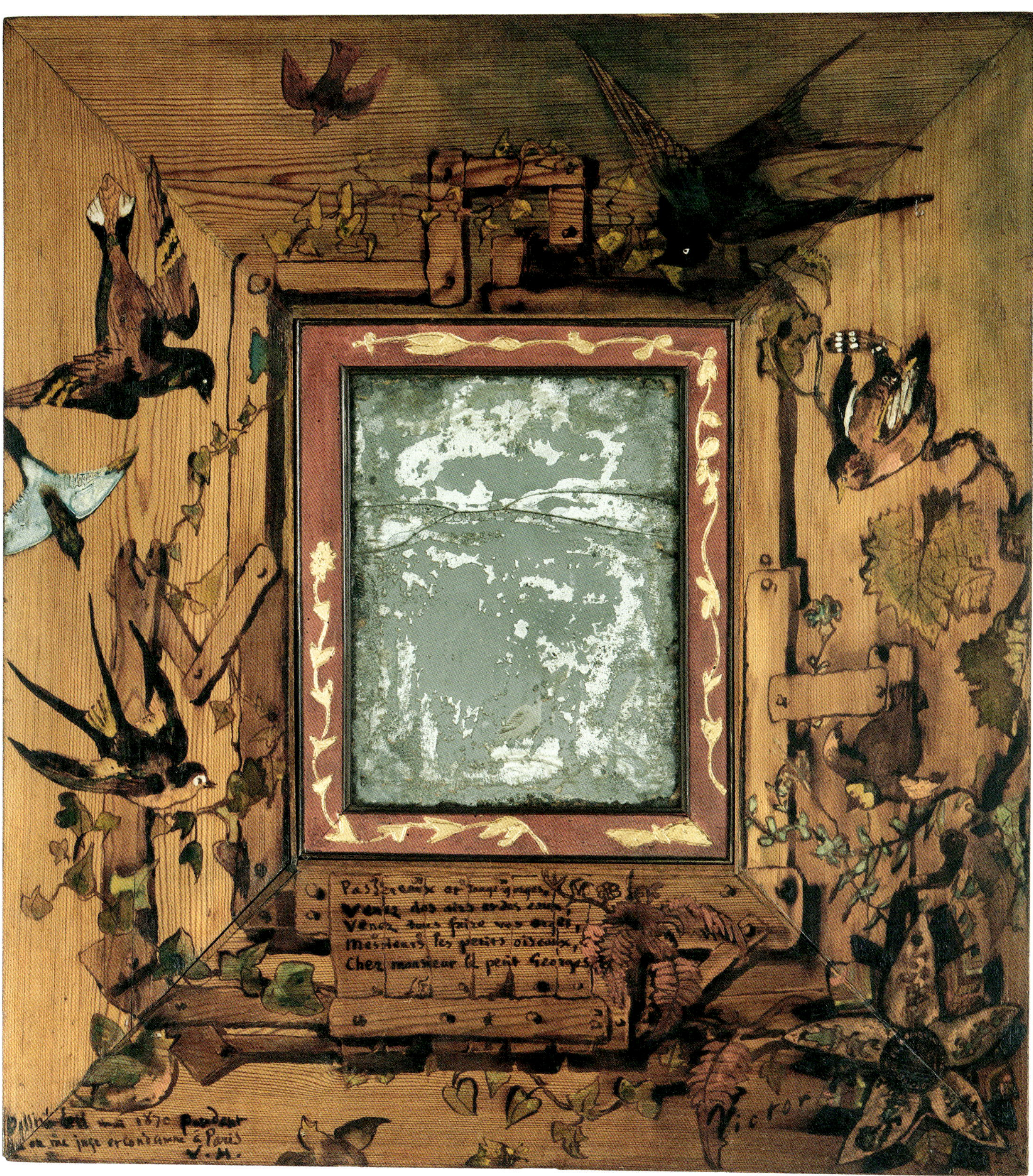
Passereaux et tout-z-oyseaux,
Venez des airs et des eaux;
Venez tous faire vos orges,
Messieurs les petits oiseaux,
Chez monsieur le petit Georges.
Dessiné à ... mai 1870 pendant
qu'on me juge et condamne à Paris
V.H.
Victor

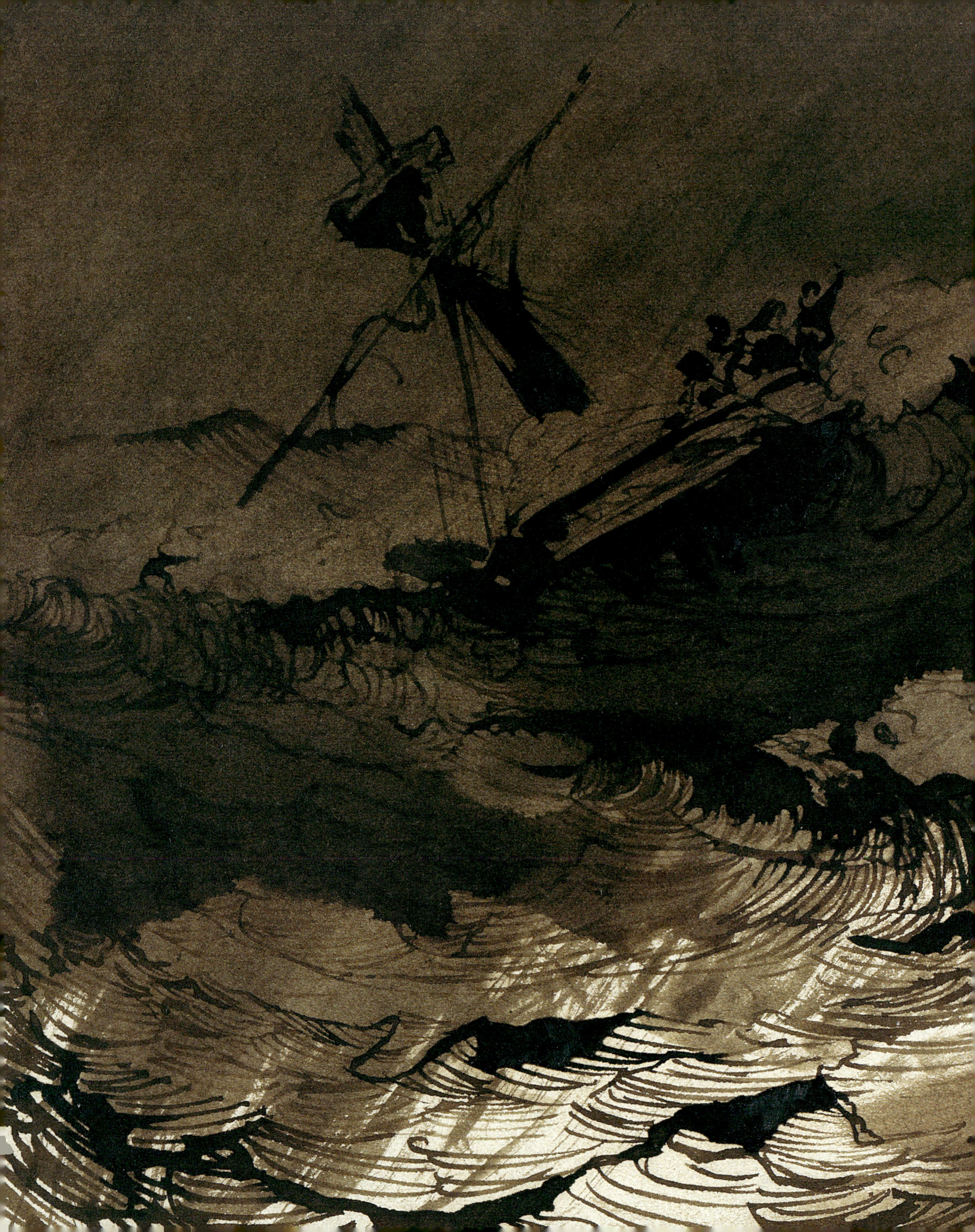

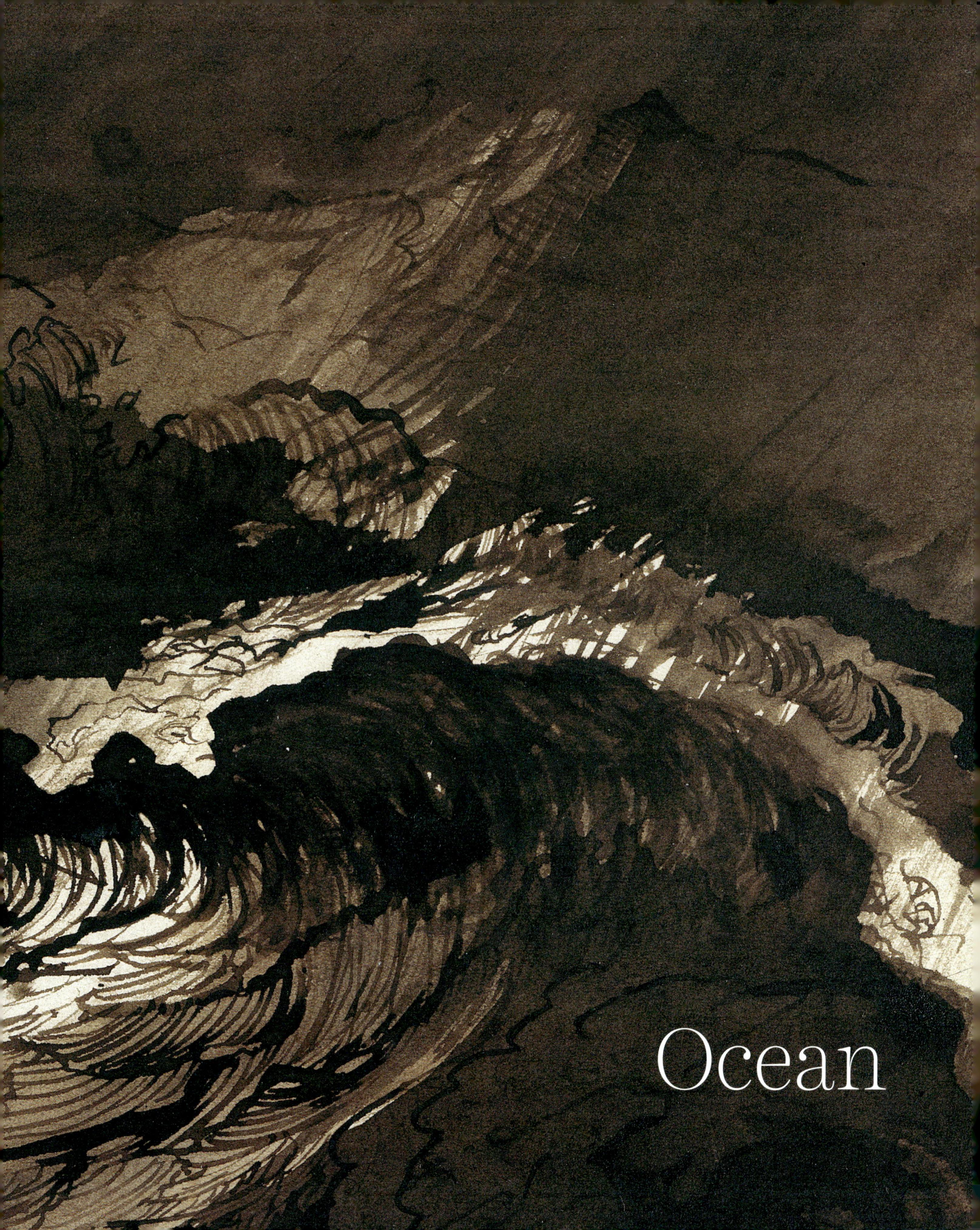
Ocean

*The work ahead of me is like a sea –
a whole immense expanse of partly
glimpsed ideas ... an accumulation
of drifting works into which my thoughts
plunge without knowing whether
they will come back again. If I die with
the task unfinished, my children will
discover ... a considerable quantity
of things partly or completely written,
verse, prose, etc. They are to publish
all of this under the title: Ocean.*[18]

This group of works returns to the opening theme of nature with Hugo's leitmotif of the ocean, a major source of inspiration for his writings and drawings. His work has justly been described as an ocean 'of shifting surfaces and immeasurable depths that only imagination could fathom'.[19] The influence of the sea on Hugo's work was particularly apparent during his exile on Guernsey between 1855 and 1870. In 1861–62 he built the 'Lookout' at Hauteville House, a conservatory on the roof with unobstructed views over Saint Peter Port and out to sea, with the French coast sometimes visible in the distance. This became a place in which Hugo would write: 'And yet, thoughtfully, I write at my window, I watch the flow being born, expiring, reborn, and the gulls cutting through the air. The ships in the wind open their wingspans, and look in the distance like large figures strolling on the sea.'[20]

While residing at Hauteville House, Hugo published *Les Misérables* (1862), which records the political instability of France in the 1830s. The story takes place during the June Rebellion in Paris in 1832, when an anti-monarchist group of Parisian Republicans attempted to overthrow the establishment of the July Monarchy under Louis Philippe I.

Some drawings are thought to be directly related to *Les Misérables*. For example, *The Bowels of Leviathan* (cat. 67), whose title was a term Hugo used to describe the Parisian sewers, is taken from the book, and yet, as with many of Hugo's drawings, it is dated after the novel's publication. *Chain* (cat. 63) is associated with a similar drawing in a sketchbook spanning May 1864 to July 1865, which shows a chain with a cartouche bearing the title 'Les Misérables' (1864-65; Bibliothèque nationale de France, Paris,

Département des Manuscrits, inv. no. NAF 13345, fol. 7). Again dated after the novel's publication, it was perhaps considered by Hugo a potential illustration for the book, as opposed to an aid for writing.

In 1864 Hugo wrote an essay entitled 'William Shakespeare', intended to be the preface to his son François-Victor's French translation of the complete works of Shakespeare. The text instead became a form of literary criticism of the work of a writer whom Hugo considered to be one of the 'greatest geniuses of his time' and a justification for this opinion. Throughout this essay, writing not only of Shakespeare but also of Homer and Dante, he developed the term 'hommes océan' or 'ocean men' to describe these literary giants; it was also to become his own nickname. In the essay he observed, 'looking at these minds is the same thing as to look at the ocean'.[21]

Hugo's novel *The Toilers of the Sea* (1866) is unusual in that a large number of resolved drawings are related to it (cats 69–72, 75–76) and were integrated into Hugo's personal manuscript.[22] Hugo prefaced the first edition with a dedication to Guernsey, noting, 'I dedicate this book to the rock of hospitality and liberty, to that portion of old Norman ground inhabited by the noble little island nation of the sea, to the island of Guernsey, severe yet kind, my present asylum, perhaps my tomb.'[23]

The novel tells the story of a boy named Gilliatt, who lives on Guernsey (cat. 74). The protagonist, often considered to be loosely based on the author, is a loner who falls in love with Déruchette, the niece of a local shipowner, Lethierry. When Lethierry's ship, the *Durande*, is wrecked (cats 71, 76) on a dangerous reef off the coast of Guernsey, known as the Roches-Douvres, Déruchette agrees to marry the man who can salvage the ship's engine. Hugo describes Gilliatt's struggles against the unfathomable sea, battling fierce storms (cat. 72) and a giant octopus (cats 69–70) in the hope of winning Déruchette's hand.

Hugo entrusted his personal copy of the manuscript of *The Toilers of the Sea* to the Guernsey-based bookbinder Henry Turner, requesting that it be bound with 36 original illustrations.[24] Some of these were dated ahead of the book's publication, and can perhaps be considered to have aided Hugo's writing process, thus highlighting the convergence in Hugo's work for writing and drawing as parallel creative processes. *Rose Thompson*

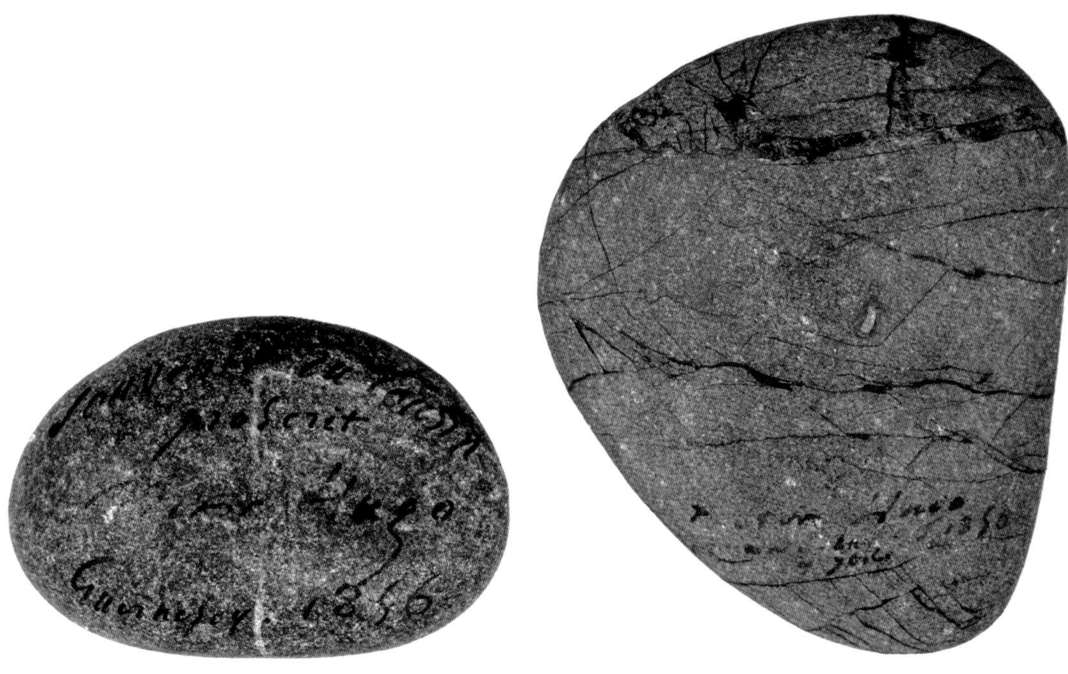

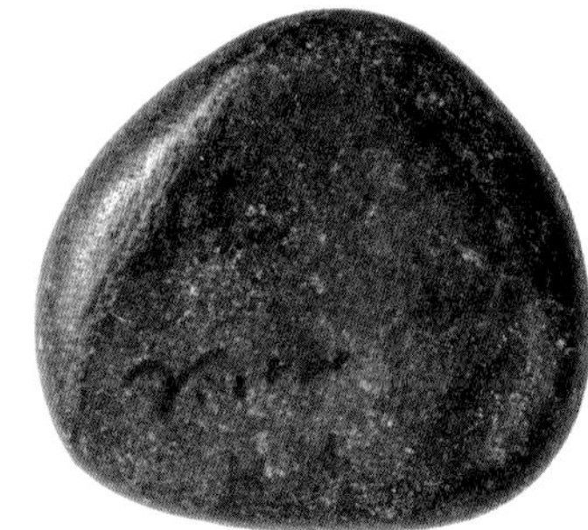

59

Signed Pebble, 1856
Ink on pebble, 7.5 x 11.3 x 5 cm
Maisons de Victor Hugo, Paris / Guernsey,
inv. no. 1179

60

Signed Pebble, 1856
Ink on pebble, 4.7 x 12.5 x 11 cm
Maisons de Victor Hugo, Paris / Guernsey,
inv. no. 2720

61

Signed Pebble, 1856
Ink on pebble, 10.5 x 11.5 x 5.3 cm
Maisons de Victor Hugo, Paris / Guernsey,
inv. no. 2721

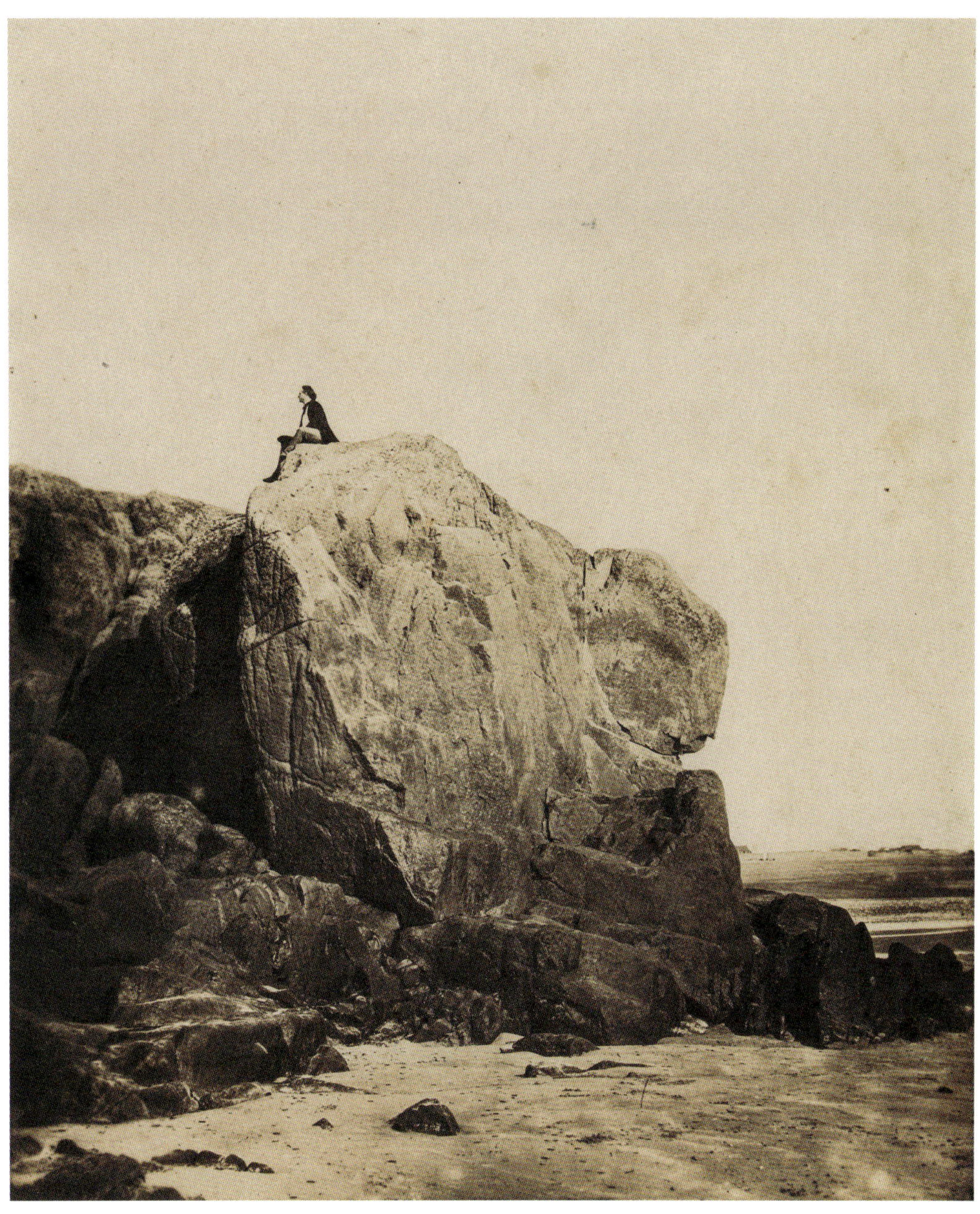

62

Charles Hugo (1826–1871)
Victor Hugo Seated on the Rocher des Proscrits [*Exile's Rock*]*, Jersey*, 1853
Photograph, 21.3 x 18 cm
Maisons de Victor Hugo, Paris / Guernsey,
inv. no. 2119

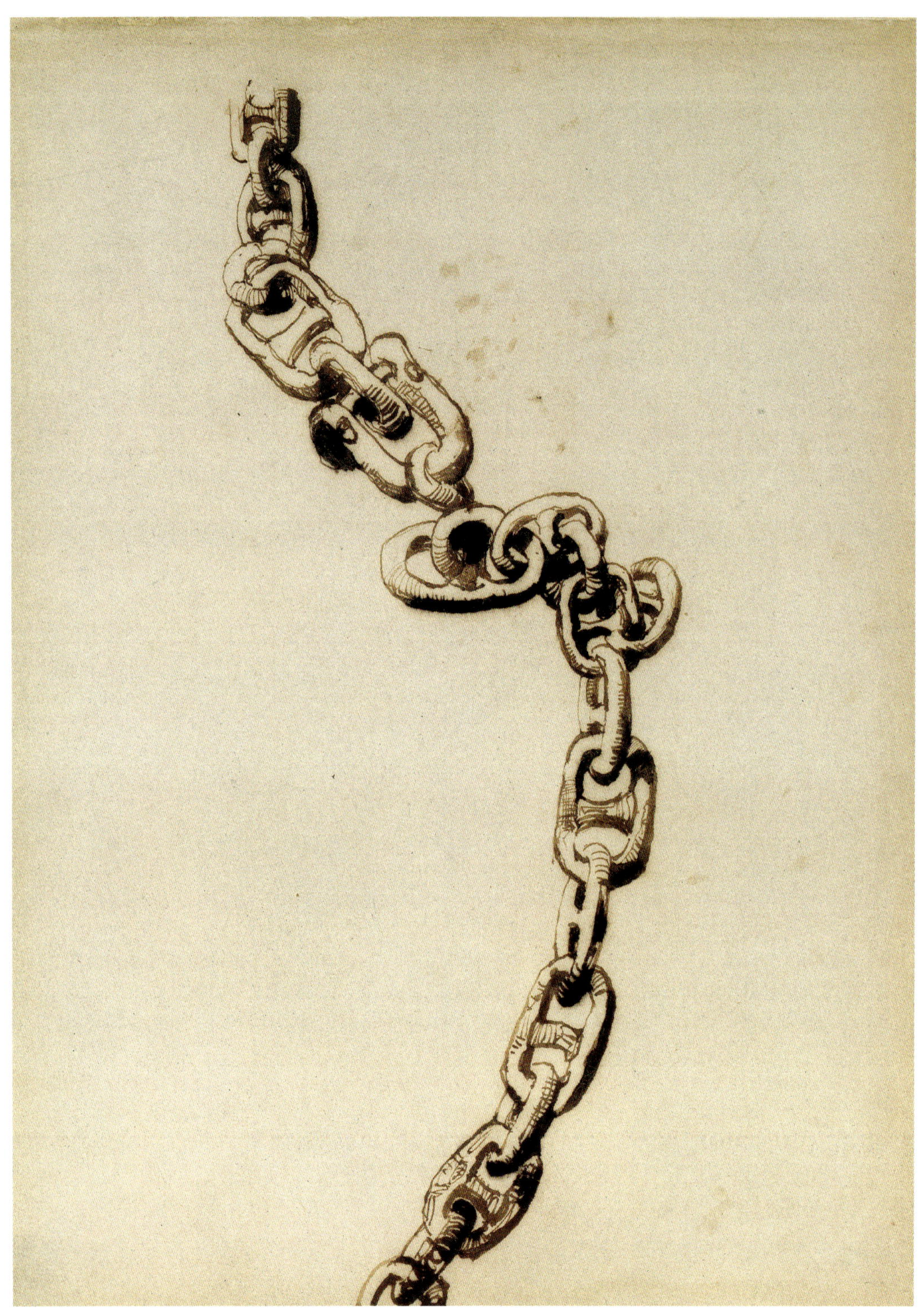

63

Chain, 1864
Pen and brown ink on paper, 19.2 x 26 cm
Bibliothèque nationale de France, Paris,
Département des Manuscrits,
inv. no. NAF 13345, fol. 7

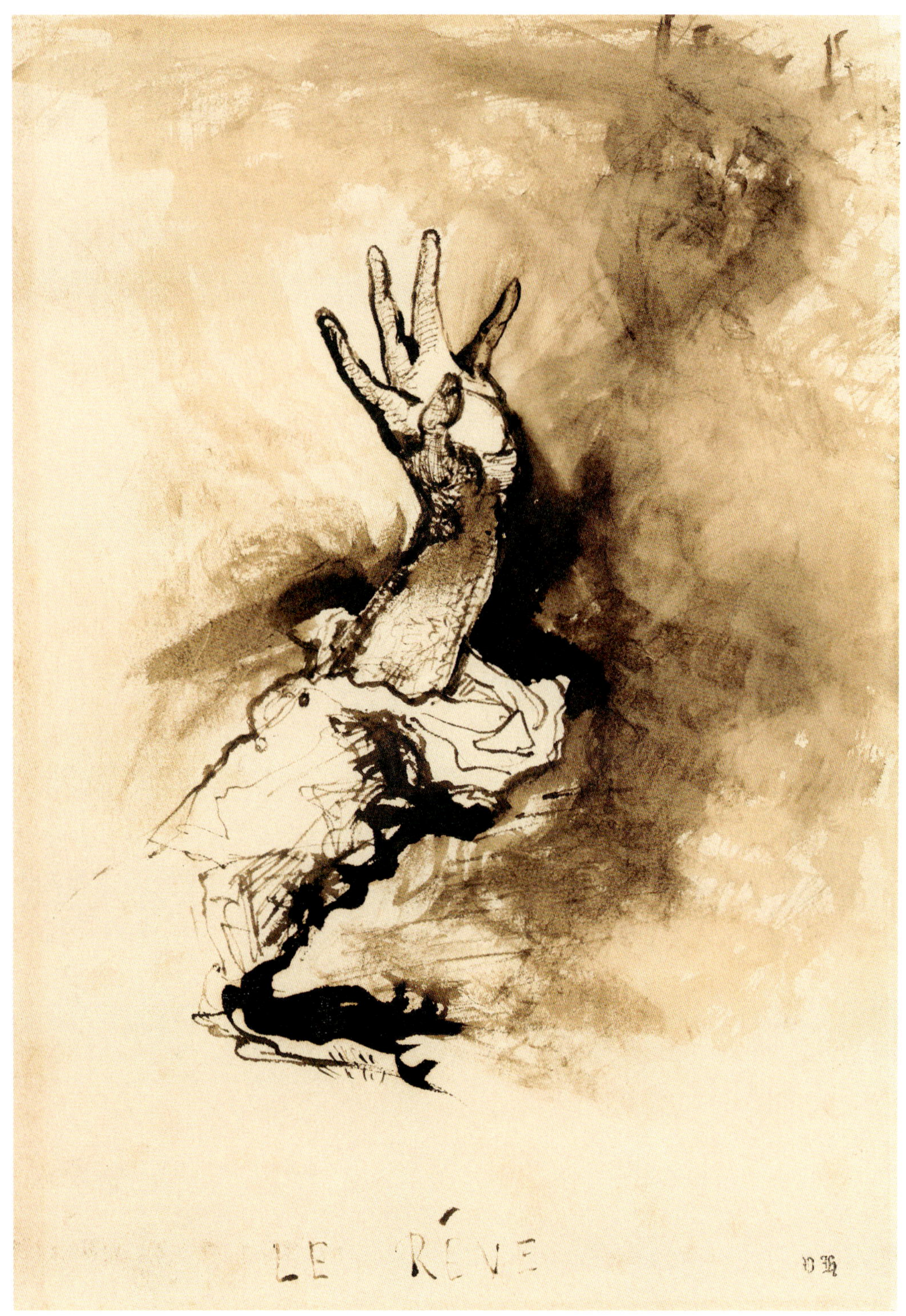

64

The Dream, 1866
Pen, brown ink and wash on paper
with gold edge, 27 x 17.3 cm
Maisons de Victor Hugo, Paris / Guernsey,
inv. no. 179

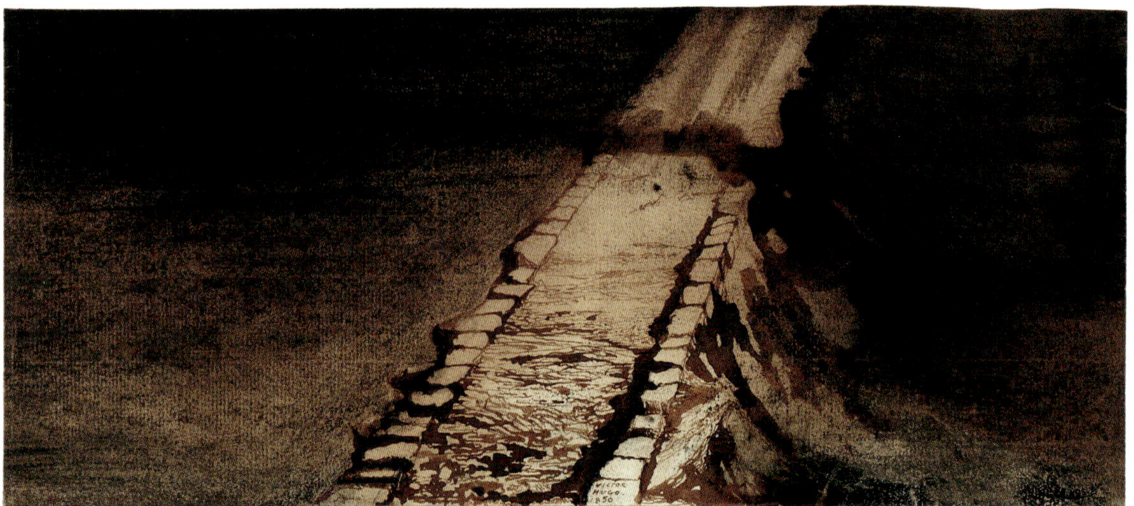

65

Causeway, 1850
Pen and brown ink wash over graphite
pencil, black ink, charcoal, black chalk
and gold on paper, 16 x 36.4 cm
Maisons de Victor Hugo, Paris / Guernsey,
inv. no. 943

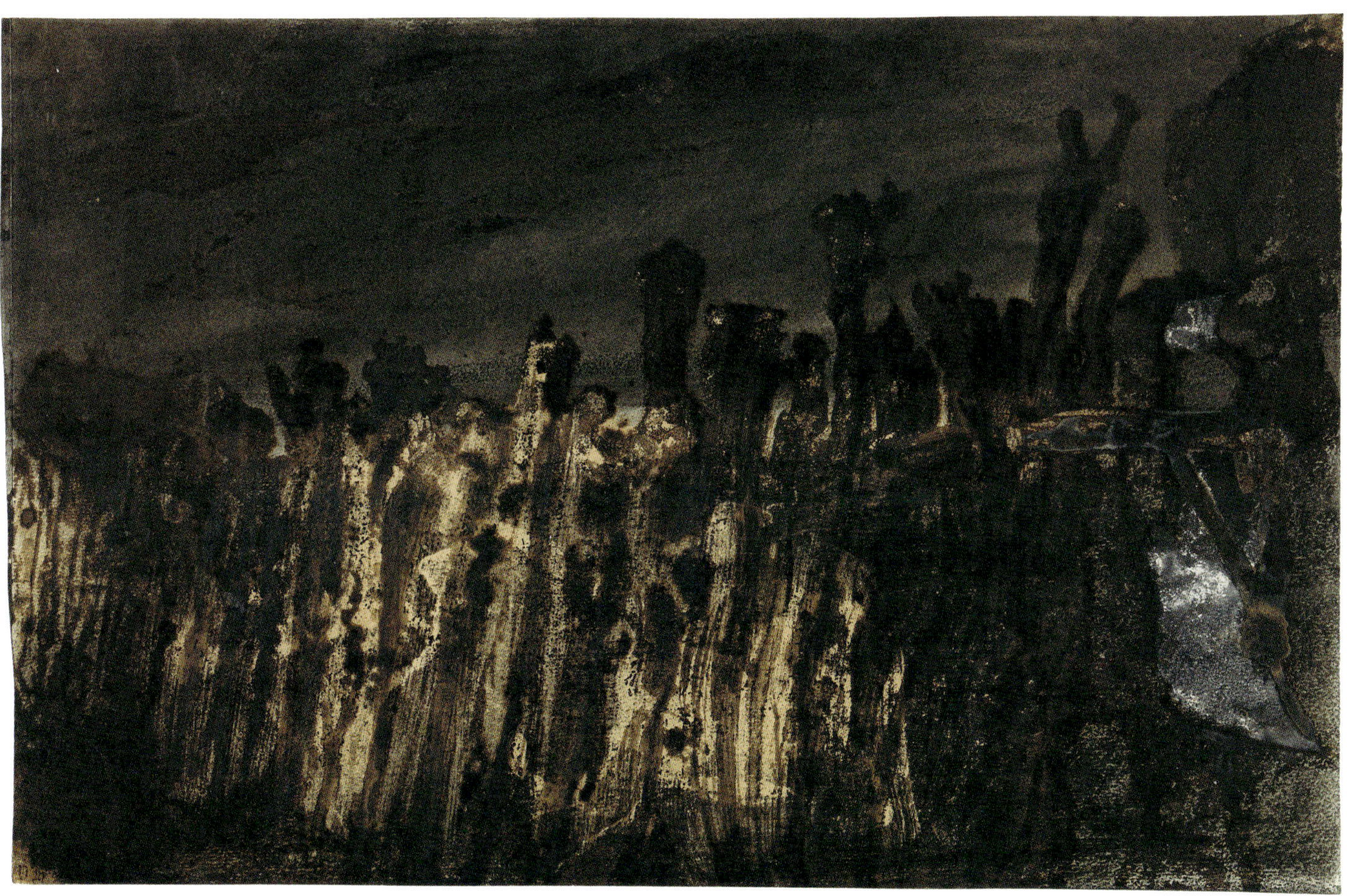

66

Breakwater on Jersey, 1854–55
Brown and black ink, charcoal and
gouache on paper, 28.9 x 45.7 cm
Maisons de Victor Hugo, Paris / Guernsey,
inv. no. 127

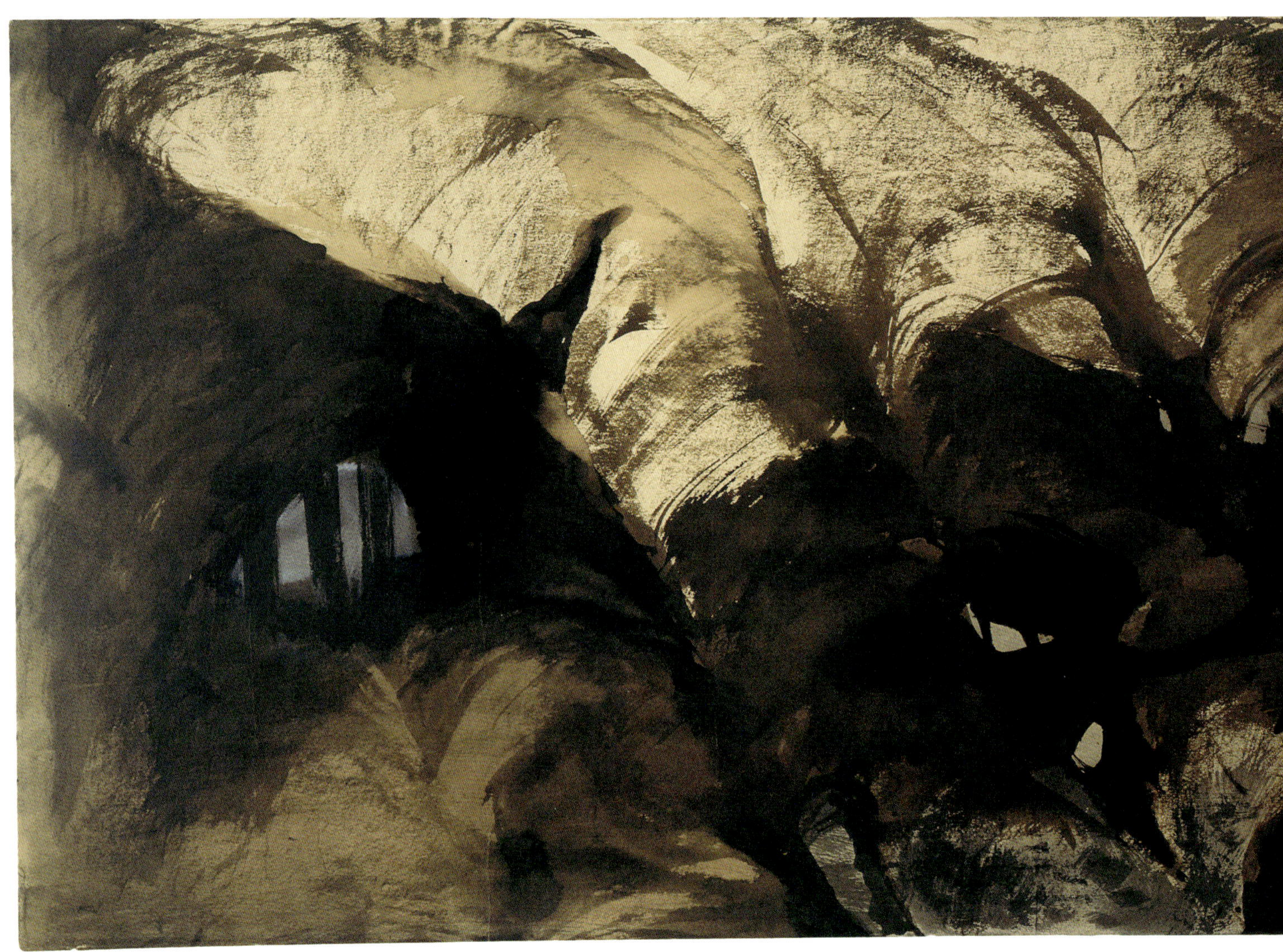

67

The Bowels of Leviathan, 1866
Pen, brush, use of feather, brown ink
and wash, black ink wash, crayon and
white gouache on paper, 48.9 x 90.4 cm
Maisons de Victor Hugo, Paris / Guernsey,
inv. no. 808

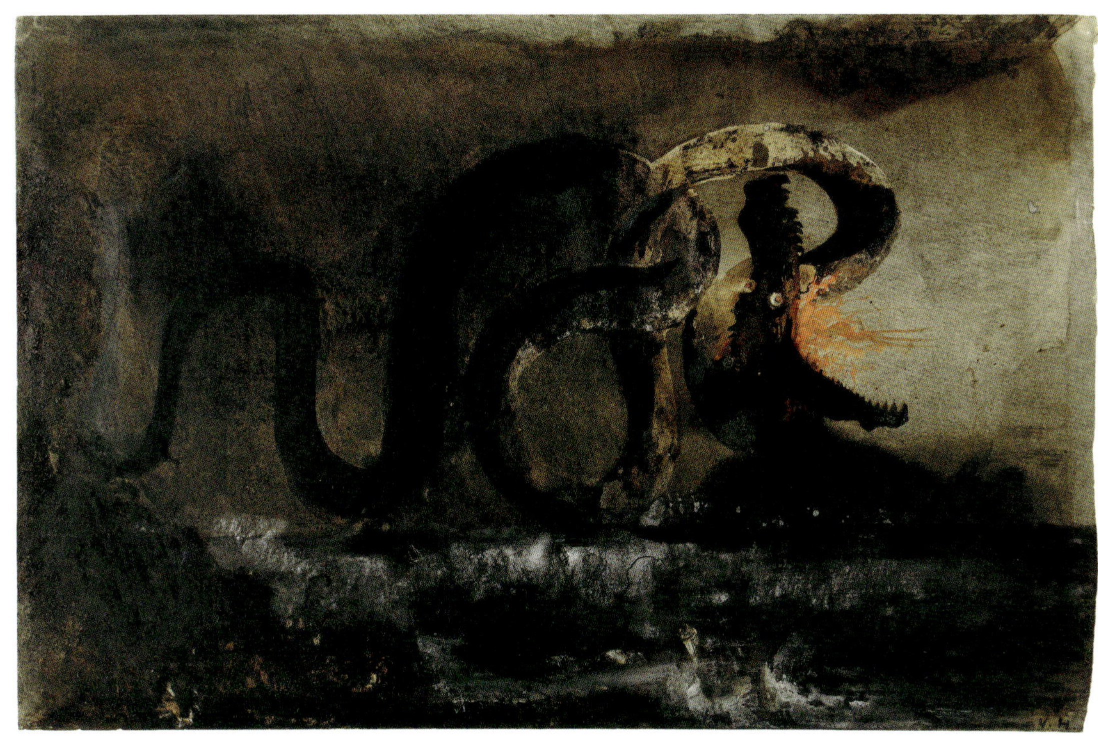

68

The Serpent, c. 1856
Pen, brown ink and wash, black ink wash,
charcoal, red and white gouache and
lace imprint on paper, 31.5 x 49.1 cm
Maisons de Victor Hugo, Paris / Guernsey,
inv. no. 818

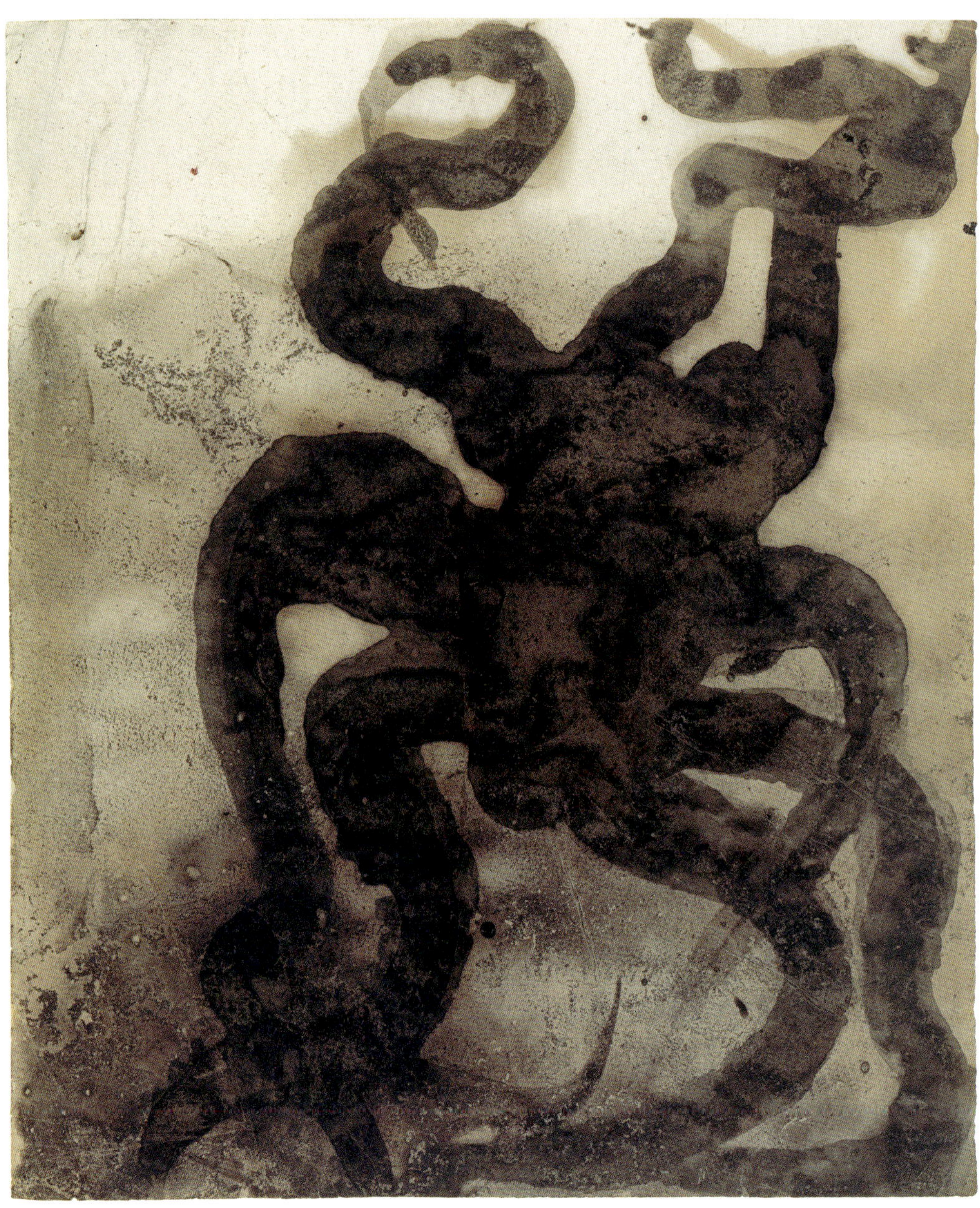

69

Octopus, 1866–69
Brown ink and wash and graphite
on paper, 24 x 20.7 cm
Bibliothèque nationale de France, Paris,
Département des Manuscrits,
inv. no. NAF 24807, fol. 3

70

Octopus, 1864–66
Pen, brown ink and wash on paper,
35.8 x 25.8 cm
Bibliothèque nationale de France, Paris,
Département des Manuscrits,
inv. no. NAF 24745, fol. 382

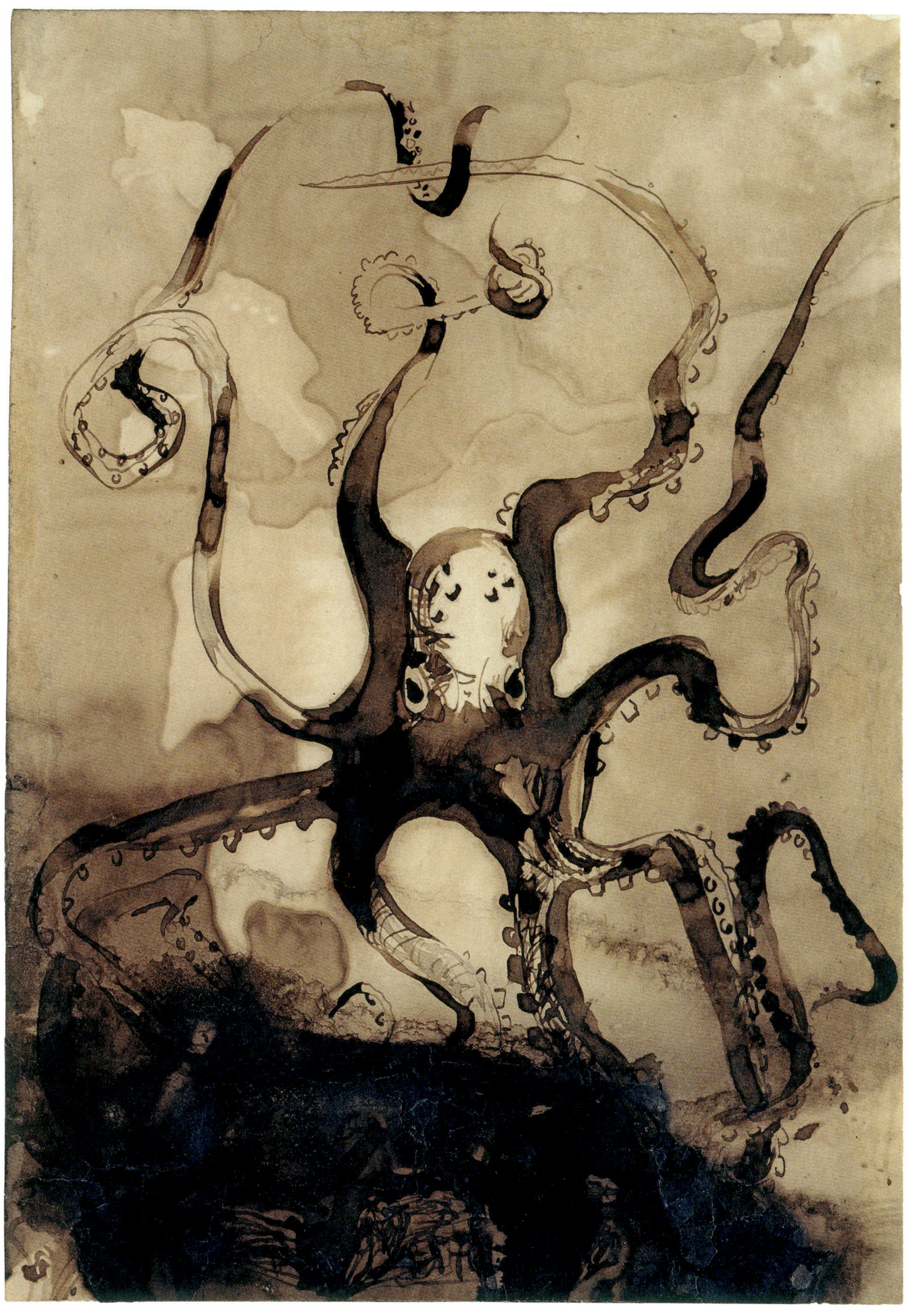

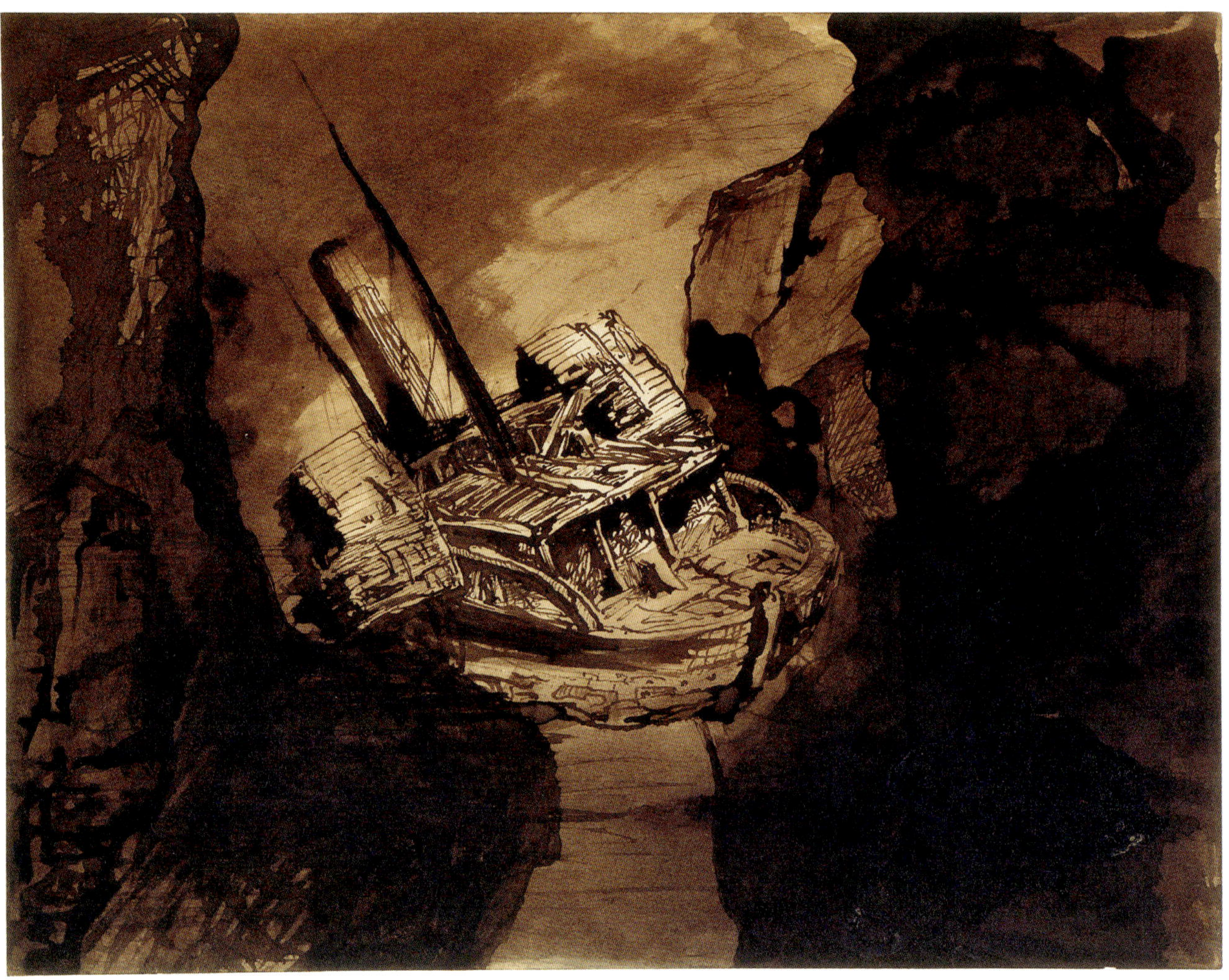

71

'The Durande' Ship after Sinking, 1864–66
Pen, brown ink and wash on paper,
19.2 x 25.3 cm
Bibliothèque nationale de France, Paris,
Département des Manuscrits,
inv. no. NAF 24745, fol. 222

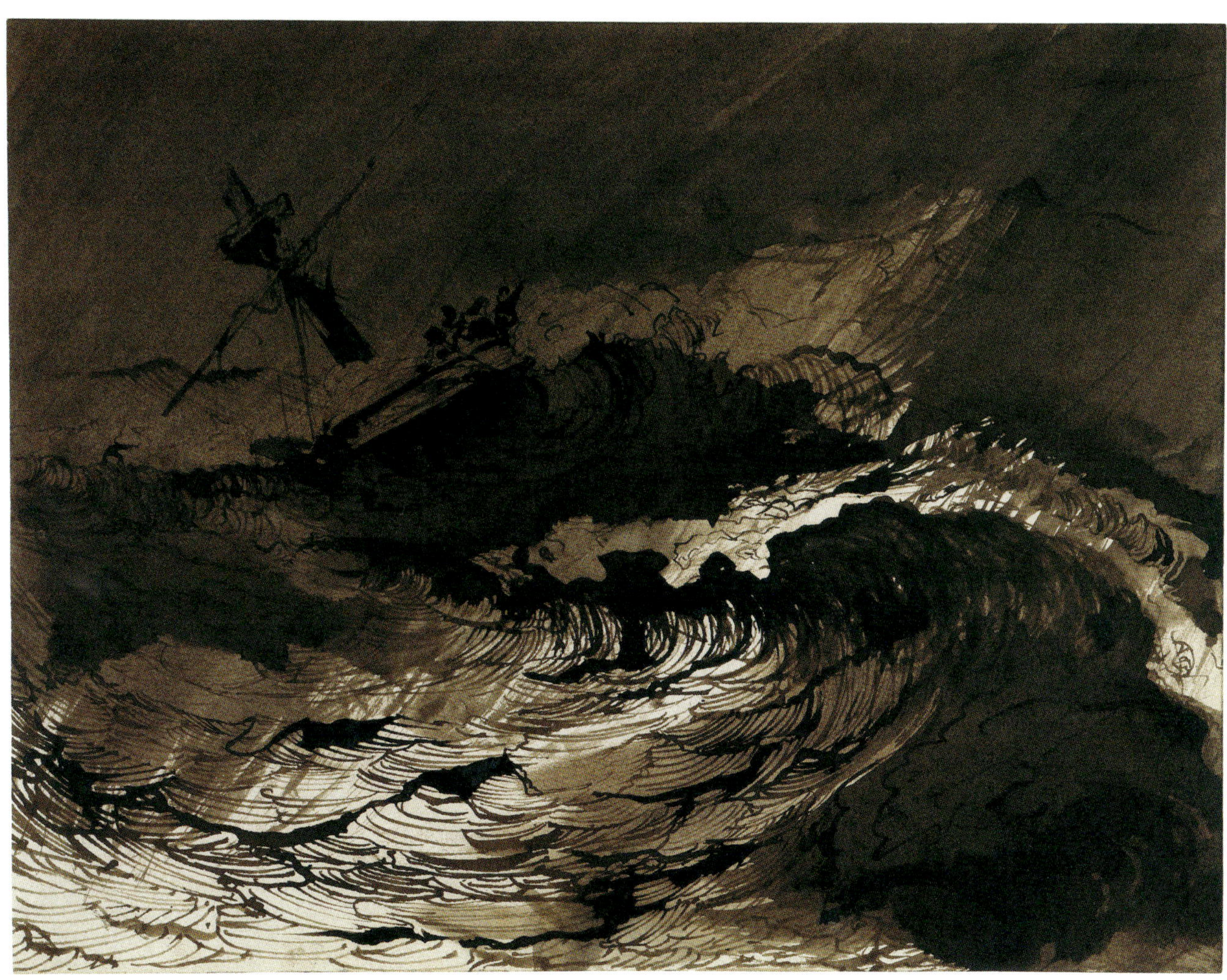

72

The Vision Ship or The Last Struggle,
1864–66
Pen, brown ink and wash
on paper, 19.2 x 25.3 cm
Bibliothèque nationale de France, Paris,
Département des Manuscrits,
inv. no. NAF 24745, fol. 111

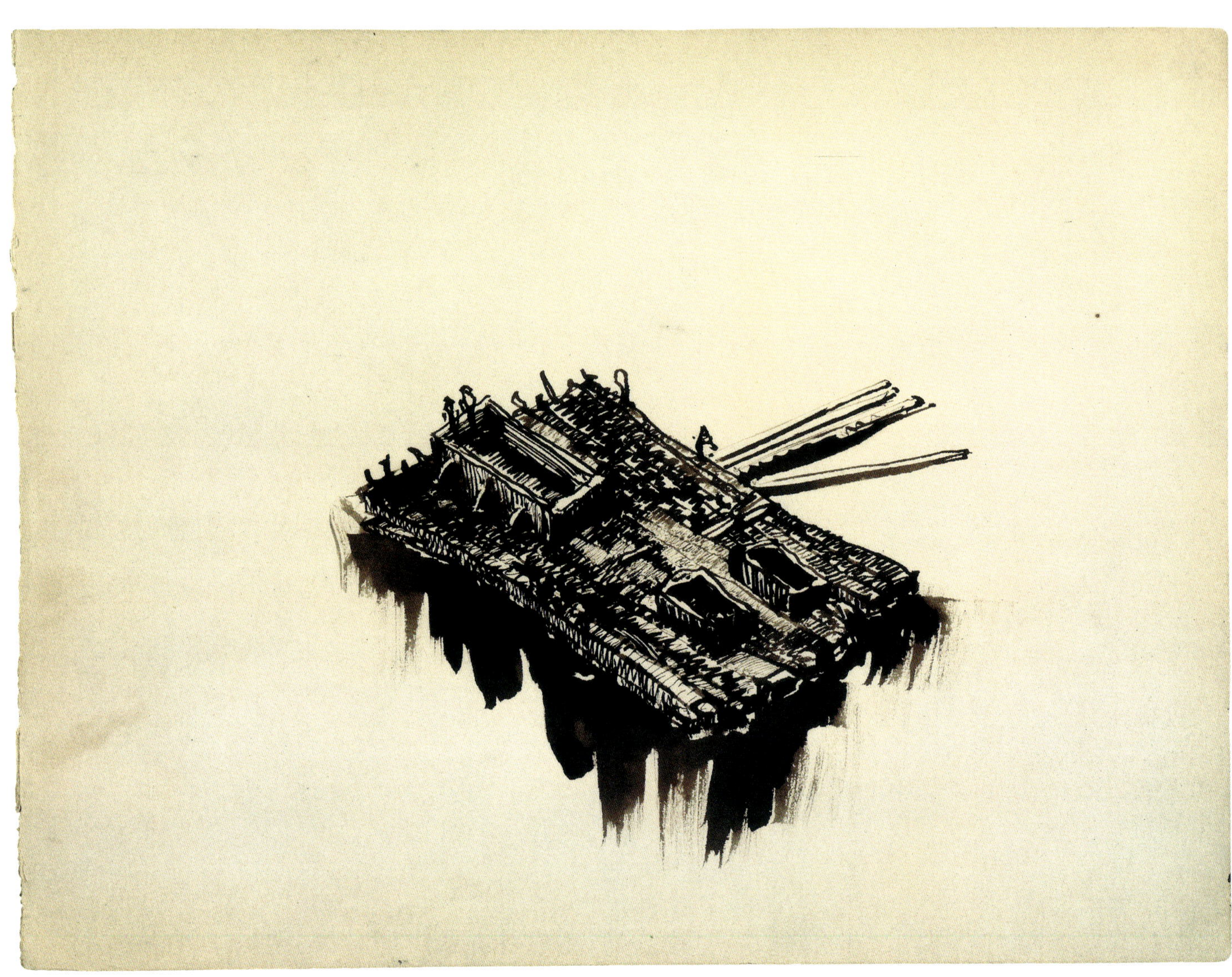

73

Boat without Sails, 1864
Pen, brown ink and wash
on paper, 19.3 x 25.7 cm
Bibliothèque nationale de France, Paris,
Département des Manuscrits,
inv. no. NAF 13345, fol. 30

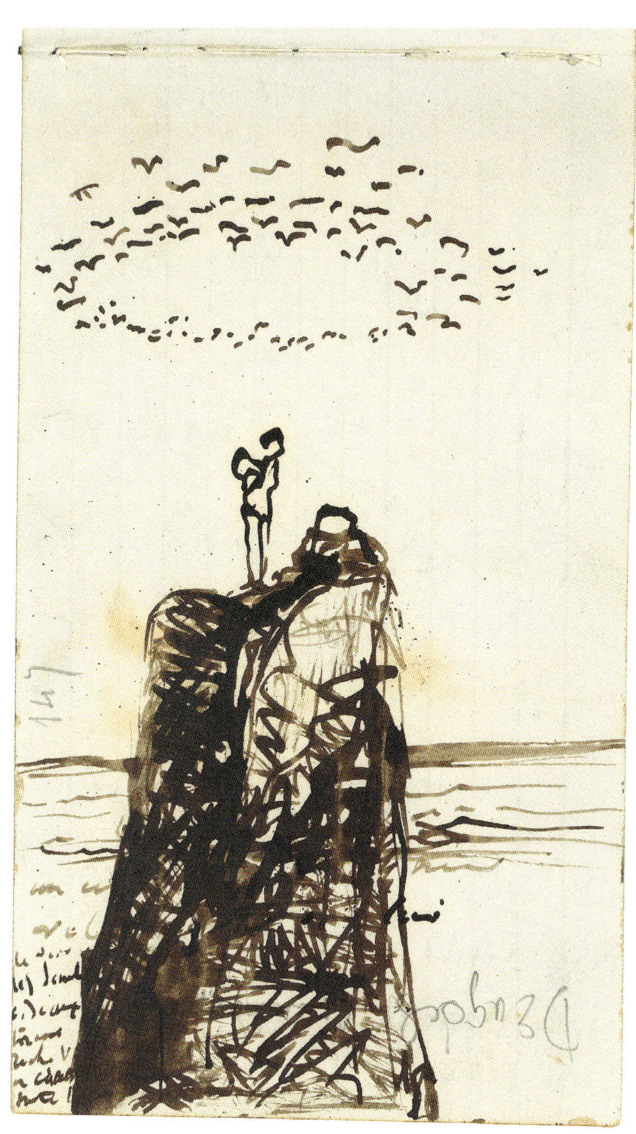

74

Gilliatt at the Grande Douvre,
May 1864 – July 1865
Sketchbook, 11.8 x 18.5 cm
Bibliothèque nationale de France, Paris,
Département des Manuscrits,
inv. no. NAF 13459, fol. 73

75

The Lighthouse at Casquets, Guernsey, 1866
Brown ink and wash, black crayon,
black chalk and white gouache on paper,
89.8 x 48 cm
Maisons de Victor Hugo, Paris / Guernsey,
inv. no. 185

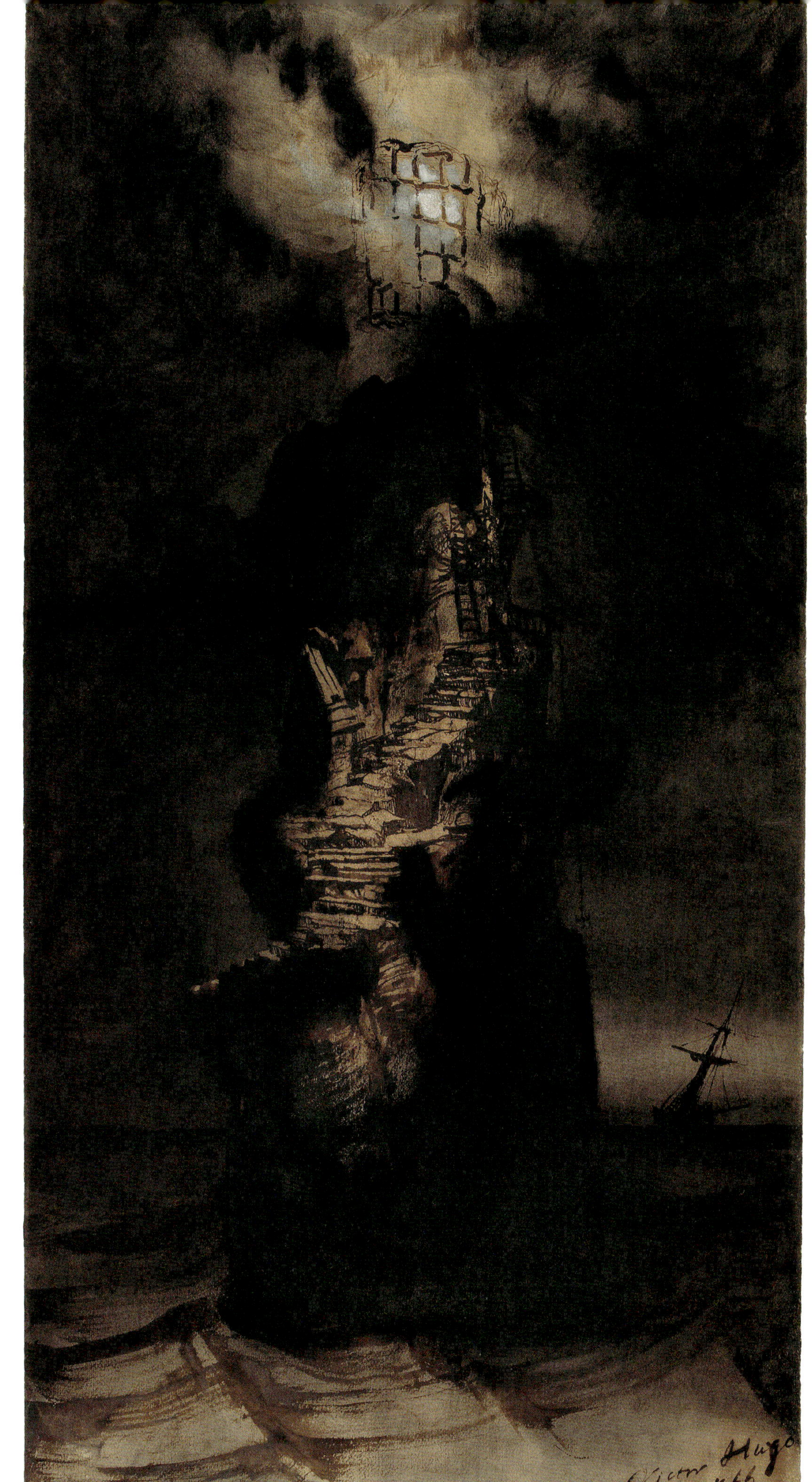

Victor Hugo

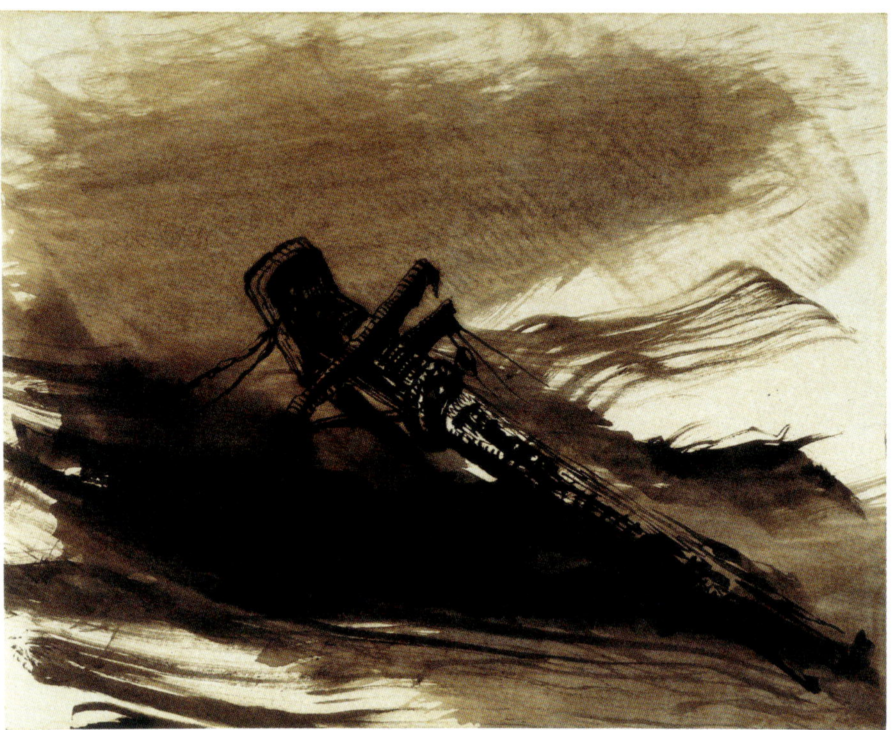

76

The Wreck, 1864–66
Pen, brown ink and wash on paper,
19.2 x 24.6 cm
Bibliothèque nationale de France, Paris,
Département des Manuscrits,
inv. no. NAF 24745, fol. 314

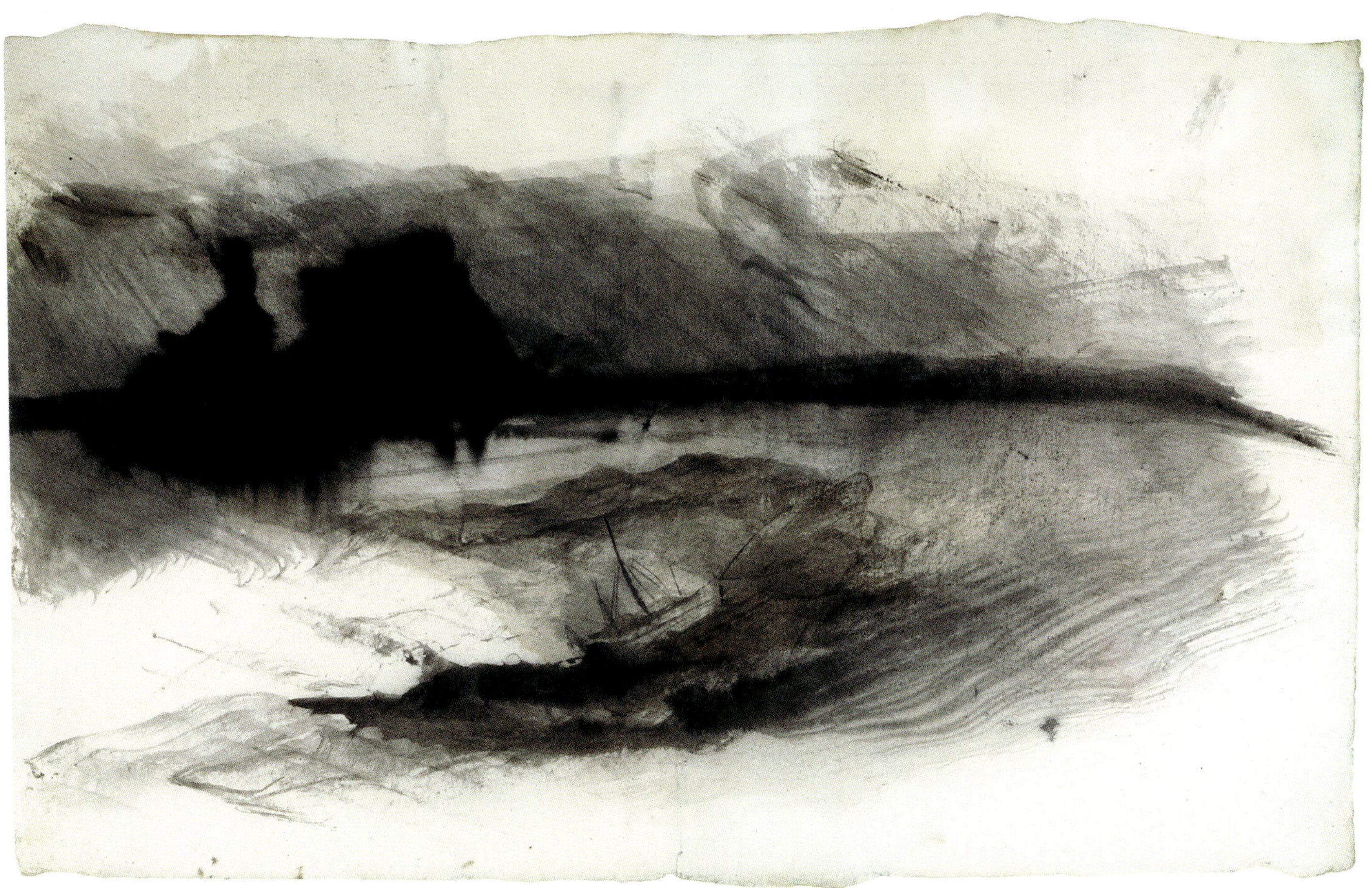

77

Ship in a Storm, 1875
Pen, black ink and wash
on paper, 26.4 x 43.8 cm
Bibliothèque nationale de France, Paris,
Département des Manuscrits,
inv. no. NAF 24807, fol. 40

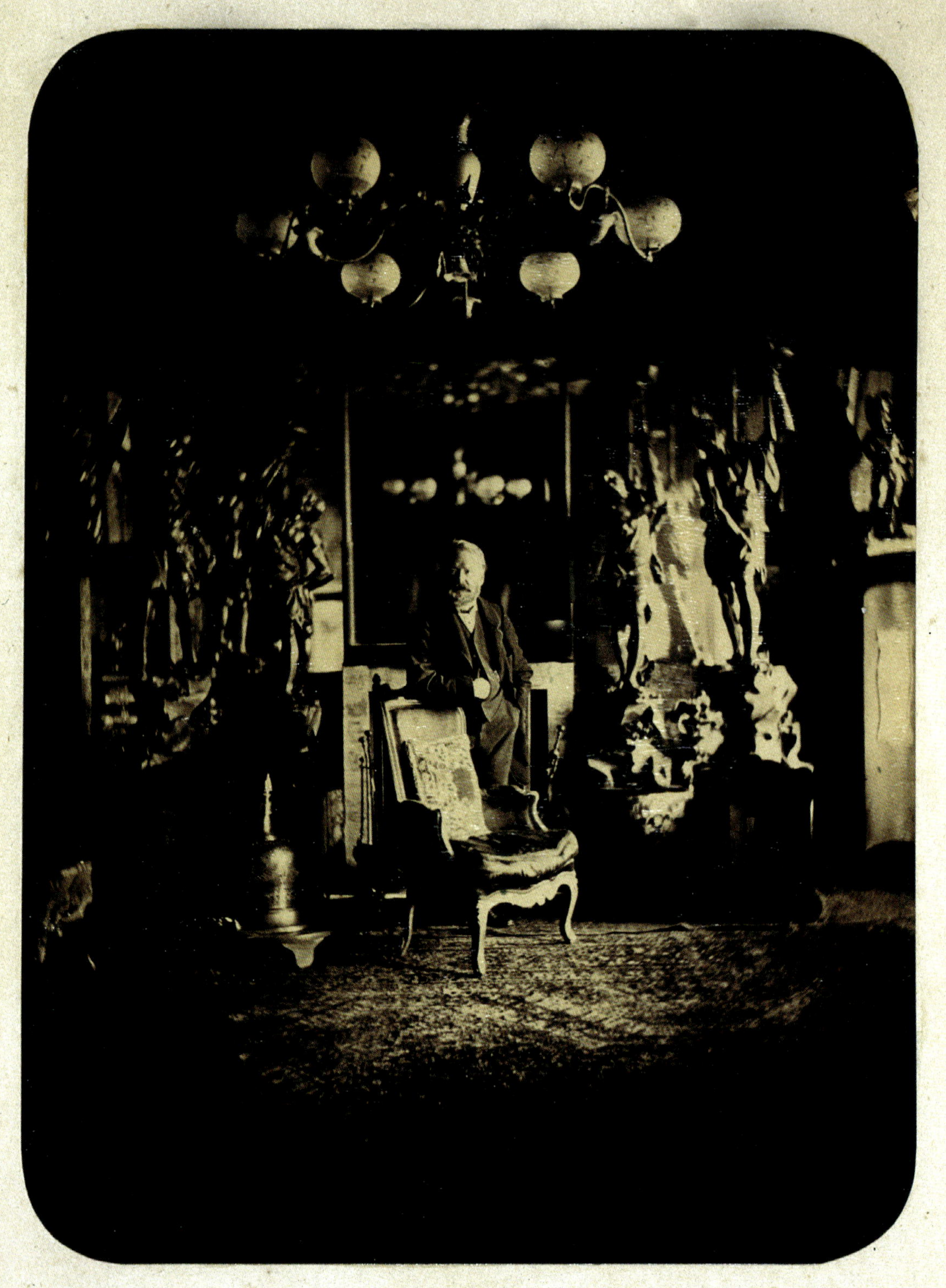

D'un humble artiste
Au plus grand des poètes -
à Victor Hugo.
A. de Garnier
Guernesey, Avril, 1868

Chronology

ROSE THOMPSON

1802

26 FEBRUARY   Birth of Victor-Marie Hugo in Besançon in eastern France, youngest son of Sophie Trébuchet and Joseph Léopold Sigisbert Hugo.

1809–13

As the children of a commander in Napoléon I's army, Hugo and his brothers Abel and Eugène move frequently during childhood, often returning to Paris with their mother, where they settle between 1809 and 1813 in the old Feuillantines Convent near the Latin Quarter.

1811

The family is reunited for a year in Madrid, following Léopold's promotion to general and his ennoblement by the King of Spain, Joseph Bonaparte, as Count Hugo de Cogolludo y Sigüenza. However, he and Sophie, a committed royalist whose views Hugo adopted during his younger years, gradually become estranged.

1815

During their parents' tumultuous separation, Hugo and his brother Eugène board at the Pension Cordier in Paris, where they learn Latin and write plays that are performed at the school, and the Lycée Louis-le-Grand in the Rue Saint-Jacques, where Hugo studies philosophy.

1817

One of Hugo's schoolmasters, Félix Biscarrat, submits a poem to the annual poetry competition of the Académie française on behalf of Hugo, aged fifteen at the time. It receives an honourable mention.

1818

Léopold and Sophie Hugo are legally separated.

1819

Hugo and his brothers found the periodical *Le Conservateur littéraire*, which they publish twice a month between 1819 and 1821. Hugo regularly contributes poetry, translations and critical essays.

1821

Hugo's mother dies aged 49. Later in the year his father marries his long-term mistress, Catherine Thomas.

1822

Hugo publishes his first book of poetry, *Odes et poésies diverses*, which reflects his royalist views at the time. The book earns him a pension of 1,000 francs a year from Louis XVIII and some modest financial stability.
OCTOBER   He marries his childhood love, Adèle Foucher, at Saint-Sulpice in Paris.

Fig. 27

Arsène Garnier (1822–1900), *Victor Hugo in the 'Salon Rouge' at Hauteville House, Guernsey*, 1878. Photograph. Maisons de Victor Hugo, Paris / Guernsey, inv. no. 1319

1823

JULY Hugo and his wife welcome their first child, Léopold, named after Hugo's father, but the boy dies three months later. Hugo publishes his first novel, *Han d'Islande*, and his *Odes*.

1824

AUGUST The couple's daughter Léopoldine is born. Publication of the poems *Nouvelles Odes*.

1825

Aged 23, Hugo is made a *chevalier* of the Légion d'Honneur for his services to literature. He is invited to the coronation of Charles X, following the death of Louis XVIII.

1826

Hugo publishes *Bug-Jargal* (fig. 3), a novel set in the early stages of the Haitian Revolution (1791–1804), which saw enslaved people overthrow the French colonial regime and eventually establish the independent nation of Haiti. He also publishes the poems *Odes et ballades*. Birth of his son Charles.

1827

Publication of the play *Cromwell*.

1828

Hugo's father suffers a stroke and dies, aged 54. Birth of Hugo's son François-Victor. Publication of an expanded version of the poems *Odes et ballades*.

1829

Publication of a collection of poems entitled *Les Orientales*, inspired by the Greek War of Independence (1821–32) and exploring the fashion in nineteenth-century France for art about the 'Orient'; and the novel *Le Dernier Jour d'un condamné*.

1830

The second French Revolution – the July Revolution – leads to the abdication of Charles X and the accession to the throne of Louis Philippe, whose reign is known as the July Monarchy. Birth of Hugo's second daughter Adèle. Premier of Hugo's play *Hernani*.

1831

Hugo publishes the novel *Notre-Dame de Paris*, known in English as *The Hunchback of Notre-Dame*; the play *Marion de Lorme*; and the poems *Les Feuilles d'automne*. Creation of his earliest dated caricature drawing.

1832

Hugo witnesses the fighting of the June Rebellion, also known as the Paris Uprising, and is forced to take cover in Les Halles when he gets too close to the barricades. Publication of his censored play *Le Roi s'amuse*. Hugo and his family move to the Place Royale (now the Place des Vosges, home to the Paris site of the Maisons de Victor Hugo).

1833

About this time Hugo's wife, Adèle, has an affair with the reviewer and writer Charles-Augustin Sainte-Beuve, which lasts until around 1837. Hugo falls in love with the actress Juliette Drouet and remains her close companion until her death in 1883. Drouet writes twice a day to Hugo, sending him some 20,000 letters throughout their 50-year relationship. Publication of the plays *Lucrèce Borgia* and *Marie Tudor*.

1834

Publication of *Littérature et philosophie mêlées* and the short story *Claude Gueux*. Creation of Hugo's earliest dated sketchbook.

1835

Publication of the play *Angelo, Tyran de Padoue* and the poems *Les Chants du crépuscule*.

1836

Publication of the libretto, adapted from his 1831 novel *The Hunchback of Notre-Dame*, for Louise Bertin's opera *La Esmeralda*.

1837

Death, at the age of 36, of Hugo's brother Eugène, who had been secretly in love with Hugo's wife and interned in an asylum at Charenton while suffering from depression in 1822 and 1823. Publication of the poems *Les Voix intérieures*.

1838

Publication of the play *Ruy Blas*.

1840

Publication of the poems *Les Rayons et les ombres*.

1841

Hugo is elected to the Académie française.

1842

Publication of the travel book *The Rhine*.

1843

Marriage of Hugo's daughter Léopoldine to Charles Vacquerie, brother of one of his most steadfast supporters. Tragically, both Léopoldine and Charles drown in a boating accident on the Seine at Villequier a few months later, while Hugo is travelling with Juliette in the Pyrenees. Hugo begins an affair with the author and arctic explorer Léonie d'Aunet, who had been married to the painter François-Auguste Biard. Publication of the play *Les Burgraves*.

1845

Hugo is appointed Pair de France (Peer of the Realm) and sits in the Chambre des Pairs. A few months later, d'Aunet is arrested for her adulterous affair with Hugo, who is immune to arrest due to his seat in the Chambre des Pairs. He begins work on his novel *Les Misérables*.

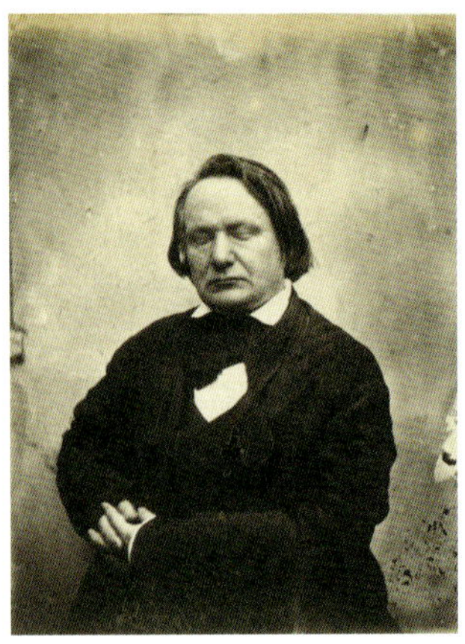

Fig. 28

Auguste Vacquerie (1819–1895), *Victor Hugo Listening to God*, c. 1853. Proof on salt paper, 9.5 x 7.2 cm. Musée d'Orsay, Paris, inv. no. PHO1986-123-107

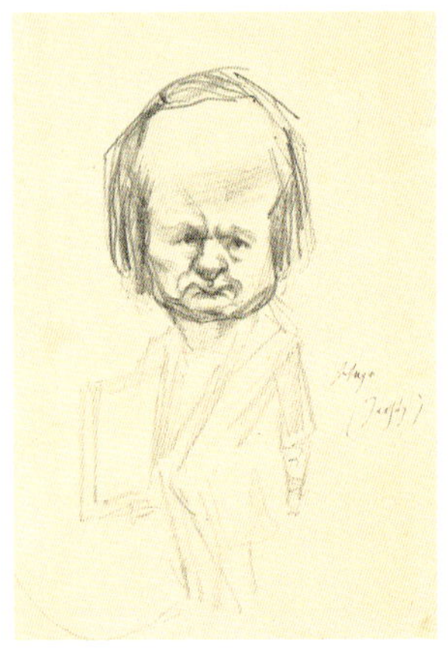

Fig. 29

Félix Nadar (1820–1910), *Victor Hugo on Jersey*, c. 1852–54, a preliminary drawing for Nadar's *Pantheon* (no. 8 in the *Pantheon*). Pencil on paper, 31.1 x 20.4 cm. Bibliothèque nationale de France, Paris, Département Estampes et photographie, inv. no. STORAGE NA-88-ÉCU BOX

1848

The February Revolution leads to the collapse of the July Monarchy and the end of Louis Philippe's reign. The Second Republic is established, with Louis Napoléon Bonaparte (Napoléon III) elected president. Hugo is temporarily elected mayor of the 8th arrondissement in Paris, but his term lasts only a week. In June, he is elected Deputy for Paris in the Constituent Assembly.

1850

Hugo sets up a studio in Juliette Drouet's apartment in Paris. He experiments with drawings in larger formats, including possibly *Mushroom* (cat. 8) and *The Castle with the Cross* (Maisons de Victor Hugo, Paris / Guernsey, inv. no. 40).

1851

Hugo is outspoken against Louis Napoléon Bonaparte, stating in a speech early in the year, 'We had Napoléon le Grand, must we now have Napoléon le Petit?'.[1]

2 DECEMBER   Louis Napoléon Bonaparte seizes power by force after staging a *coup d'état* and dissolving the National Assembly. Hugo organises a resistance committee, but on learning that his home has been under surveillance he goes into hiding at Juliette Drouet's house.

11 DECEMBER   Hugo escapes to Brussels, beginning an exile from France that is to last nineteen years. Publication of *Douze Discours*, *Treize Discours* and *Quatorze Discours*. In Brussels, Hugo writes the critical political pamphlet *Napoléon le Petit*, which is published the following year.

1852

Bonaparte proclaims himself Emperor of France as Napoléon III, establishing the Second Empire. After eight months in Brussels, and with the looming publication of the controversial *Napoléon le Petit*, Hugo moves to Jersey (fig. 28), where he and his family live for three years at Marine Terrace, a large house by the sea in Saint Helier (fig. 30), with Juliette Drouet moving into an apartment nearby. Within months of arriving on Jersey, Hugo sets up a darkroom in his house to enable his son, Charles, to develop his interest in photography; the following year, the photographer Edmond Bacot visits Jersey and provides Charles with lessons in photography.

1853

SEPTEMBER   The writer Delphine de Girardin, a family friend, visits Jersey and introduces the Hugo family to table-turning as a means to communicate with spirits. Séances take place between 1853 and 1855, and many famous figures throughout history, including Shakespeare and Galileo, are contacted, as well as Hugo's daughter Léopoldine, who had died a decade before. First publication of *The Chastisements*, a collection of poems fiercely attacking Napoléon III's Second Republic, and *Oeuvres oratoires*.

1854

Hugo protests unsuccessfully against the execution of the convicted murderer John Tapner, who becomes the last person to be hanged on Guernsey. During this time, Hugo makes drawings entitled *Ecce* (Museum of Fine Arts, Budapest, inv. no. 1913-402), *Le Pendu* (Musée de Louvre, Paris, inv. no. RF 23314), *Ecce (Le Pendu)* (Maisons de Victor Hugo, Paris / Guernsey, inv. no. 124) and *Ecce Lex* (cat. 48).

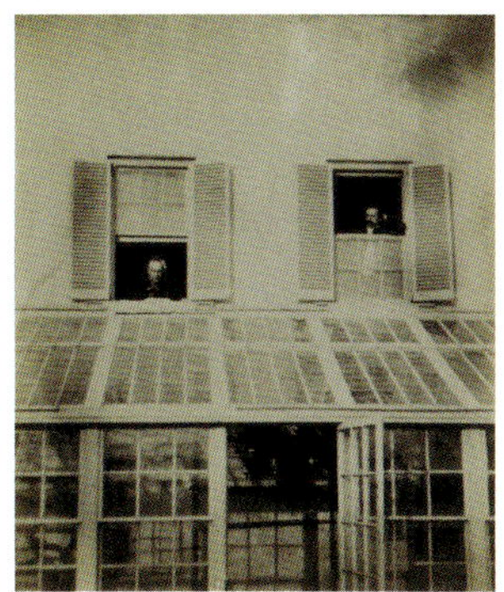

Fig. 30

Auguste Vacquerie
(1819–1895), *Victor Hugo
and Charles Hugo at
the Two Windows of
Marine Terrace, Jersey*,
1853–54. Photograph.
Maisons de Victor Hugo,
Paris / Guernsey, inv. no.
2257FOL60

Fig. 31

Jean-Baptiste Hugo,
'Lookout', Hauteville House,
2015. Photograph.
Courtesy the artist

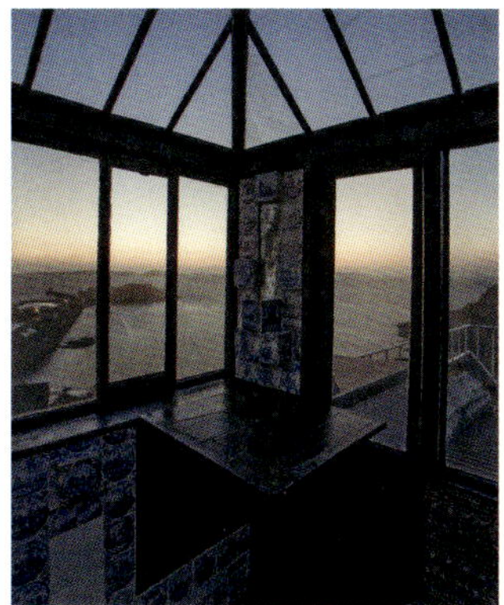

Fig. 32

*Postcard of Victor Hugo on
the Balcony at Hauteville
House, Guernsey*, 1878.
Photograph. Bibliothèque
nationale de France, Paris,
inv. no. 4-ICOPER-13005

1855

After being involved in collective protests against the reconciliation between Queen Victoria and Napoléon III, Hugo is expelled from Jersey and his family move to Guernsey, where he remains until 1870; Juliette Drouet joins them, moving into a house nearby. Publication of *Discours de l'exil, 1851–84*.

1856

16 MAY   Hugo acquires Hauteville House, Saint Peter Port (fig. 32), with the sizeable proceeds from *Les Contemplations*, his biggest commercial success as a poet. He spends the next three years renovating and decorating the house. It becomes clear that his daughter Adèle is suffering from a severe mental illness attuned with schizophrenia (she had become romantically obsessed with a British military officer, Andrew Albert Pinson, who had proposed to her and been rejected; she later changed her mind and pursued him ferociously, following him to various military postings around the world).

1859

Napoléon III announces a full amnesty for exiles but Hugo refuses to return to France, stating 'When liberty returns, I will return.'[2] Publication of the first volume of the poems *La Légende des siècles*, with two further volumes published in 1877 and 1883.

1860

Following a bout of illness, Hugo resumes work on his novel *Les Misérables*. He recommences his travels, visiting the Netherlands and Belgium with Drouet. Hugo allows his brother-in-law Paul Chenay to produce an aquatint of his drawing of the hanged man from 1854. Entitled *John Brown* (cat. 49), the print is circulated as a protest against the execution of the American abolitionist in 1859.

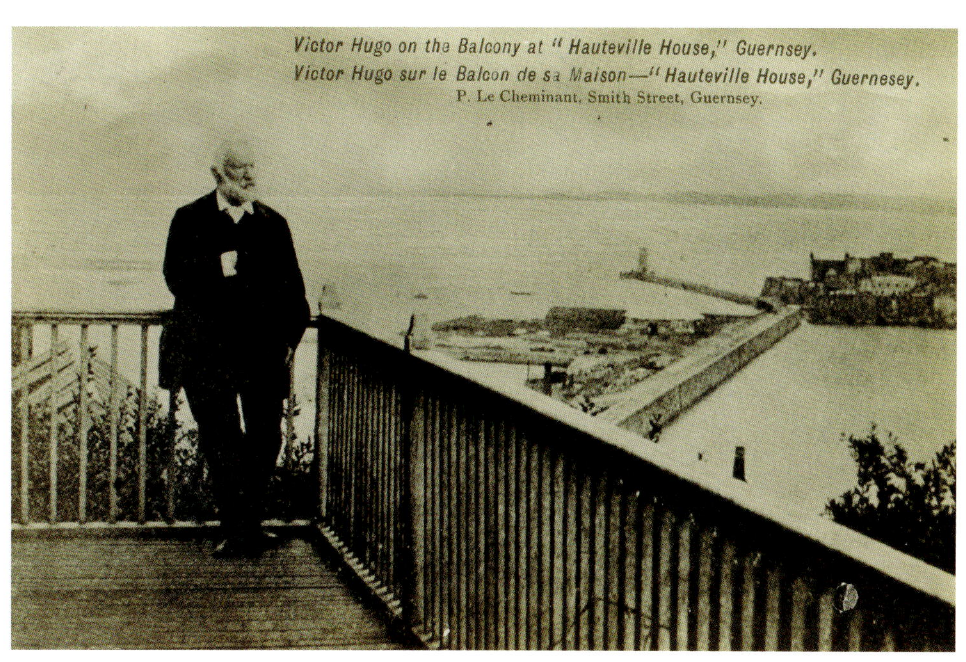

156

1861

Hugo finishes the interior design of Hauteville House, complete with a glass 'Lookout' on the top floor (figs 31, 34), where he can write. He also resumes his summer travels around north-western Europe.

1862

Hugo begins to invite local children from poor families to lunch at Hauteville House (fig. 33). The photographer Edmond Bacot stays with Hugo's family on Guernsey, where he photographs Hauteville House (cats 51–55). Publication of *Les Misérables*.

1863

Encouraged by his brother-in-law Paul Chenay, Hugo produces a portfolio of etchings of his work, entitled *Drawings of Victor Hugo*, which includes twelve etchings and aquatints by Chenay. Proceeds from the sale of the book benefit poor families on Guernsey, although the book is not a commercial success.

1864

Publication of an essay entitled 'William Shakespeare'. Intended to introduce Hugo's son François-Victor's translation of the playwright's works, this becomes a long-format essay about 'one of the greatest geniuses of his time'.[3]

1865

Publication of the poems *Songs of the Streets and Woods*.

1866

Publication of the novel *The Toilers of the Sea*.

1867

Publication of the poem *La Voix de Guernesey*.

1868

Death in Brussels of Hugo's wife Adèle, aged 64.

Fig. 33

Edmond Bacot (1814–1875), *Dining with the Children of the Poor at Hauteville House*, 1862. Photograph. Collection Pierre-Marc Richard, inv. no. 1321.6

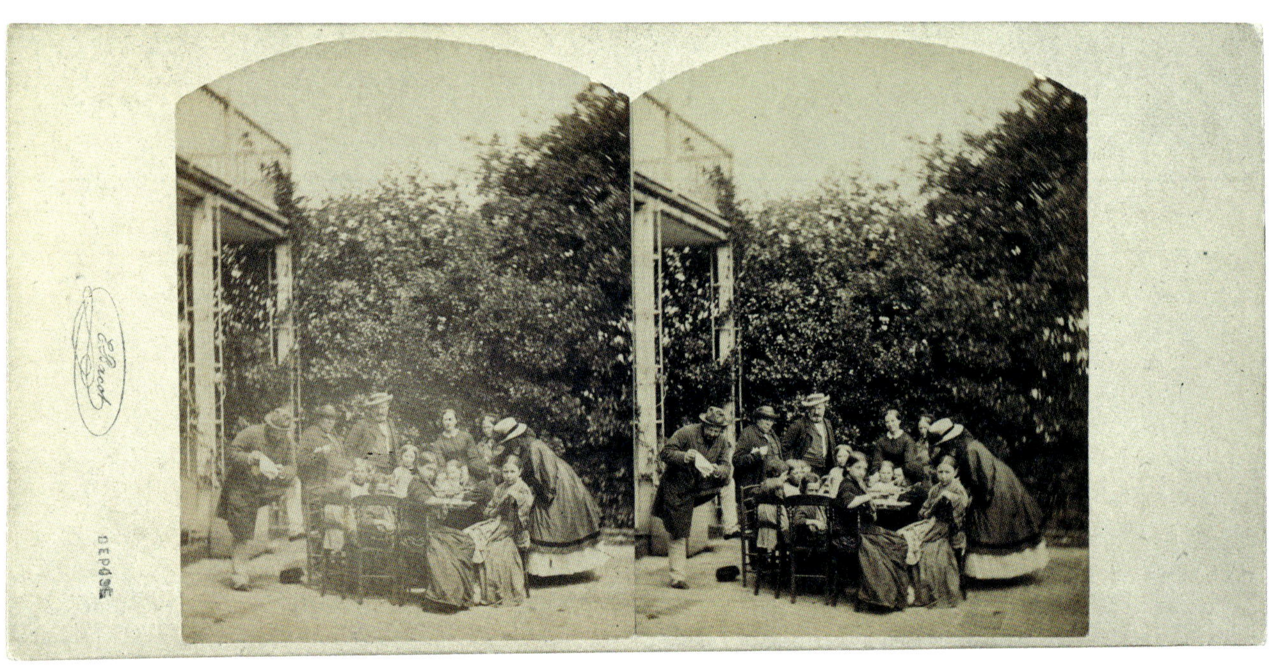

1869

Publication of the novel *L'Homme qui rit*. Also published under the title *By Order of the King*, the story is set in England and depicts the lives of English royals and aristocrats during the 1700s.

1870

19 JULY   France declares war on Prussia.
2 SEPTEMBER   The French army is defeated at the Battle of Sedan and Napoléon III is captured by Prussian forces. After the fall of Napoléon III and the proclamation of the Third Republic, Hugo returns to France for the first time in nineteen years, arriving at the Gare du Nord in Paris to cries of 'Vive Victor Hugo!'.[4]
23 SEPTEMBER   Prussian forces besiege Paris, and Hugo and his family remain there until the siege is lifted on 20 January 1871.

1871

Hugo is elected Deputy for Paris in the National Assembly but resigns a month later. His son Charles dies suddenly aged 44. Hugo travels to Brussels during the Paris Commune but is expelled for offering asylum to Communards.

1872

Finding Paris too much of a distraction, Hugo returns to Guernsey for a year to write *Quatrevingt-treize*, his last novel. His daughter Adèle is admitted to an asylum outside Paris, where she lives until her death in 1915. Hugo publishes a series of poems entitled *L'Année terrible*, which recounts the siege and Commune of Paris.

1873

Hugo's son François-Victor dies of tuberculosis. Having outlived all his sons, Hugo notes 'the clock that has struck for the sons will perhaps one day soon strike for the father'.[5]

1874

Publication of Hugo's last novel *Quatrevingt-treize*, which is set in 1793, during the French Revolution.

1875

Publication of *Actes et Paroles*, Hugo's first collection of political speeches and articles. The engraver Fortuné-Louis Méaulle produces two monumental engravings of drawings by Hugo: *The Castle with the Cross* (cat. 46) and *Lighthouse with Bell* (*c.* 1886; Maisons de Victor Hugo, Paris / Guernsey, inv. no. 2017.0.4041).

1877

Publication of a book of poems entitled *L'Art d'être grand-père* and the essay *Histoire d'un crime*, an account of Napoléon III's coup.

1878

Hugo suffers a stroke and gradually stops writing and drawing. His family returns to Guernsey with him so that he can convalesce (fig. 27), but they move back to Paris in the winter. Publication of the poem *Le Pape*.

1879

Publication of the long poem *La Pitié suprême*.

1880

Publication of the long poems *Religions et Religion* and *L'Ane*.

1881

Publication of the collection of poems *Les Quatre Vents de l'esprit*.

1882

Having first been published in 1869 with illustrations by François Chifflart, the novel *The Toilers of the Sea* is republished with Hugo's own drawings, copied by the engraver Fortuné-Louis Méaulle. Publication of the play *Torquemada*.

1883

After a long battle with cancer, Juliette Drouet dies in Paris, aged 77. Hugo is too grief-stricken to attend the funeral. He meets Auguste Rodin, who plans to create a bust of him. Publication of his tribute to the Channel Islands, *L'Archipel de la Manche*, Hugo's last book to be published during his lifetime.

1885

22 MAY   Death of Hugo from pneumonia in Paris, aged 83.
1 JUNE   His state funeral is reportedly attended by more than two million people. He is buried in the Panthéon and later shares a crypt with Emile Zola (from 1908) and Alexandre Dumas (from 2002). Hugo's lifelong friend Paul Meurice becomes his literary executor. Hugo bequeathes his manuscripts and many drawings to the Bibliothèque nationale de France.

1888

Meurice organises an exhibition in Paris of Hugo's drawings and manuscripts, the first public showing of his drawings.

1903

Following a proposal from Meurice, the City of Paris establishes a museum in Hugo's honour.
30 JUNE   The Maison de Victor Hugo opens at 6, Place des Vosges, where Hugo had lived from 1832 to 1848. Meurice and his family generously donate to the museum their collection of Hugo's works, as well as Juliette Drouet's collection, which Meurice had acquired from her nephew, Louis Koch.

Fig. 34

André, *Victor Hugo in the 'Lookout'*, 1878. Photograph. Maisons de Victor Hugo, Paris / Guernsey, inv. no. 2014.0.82

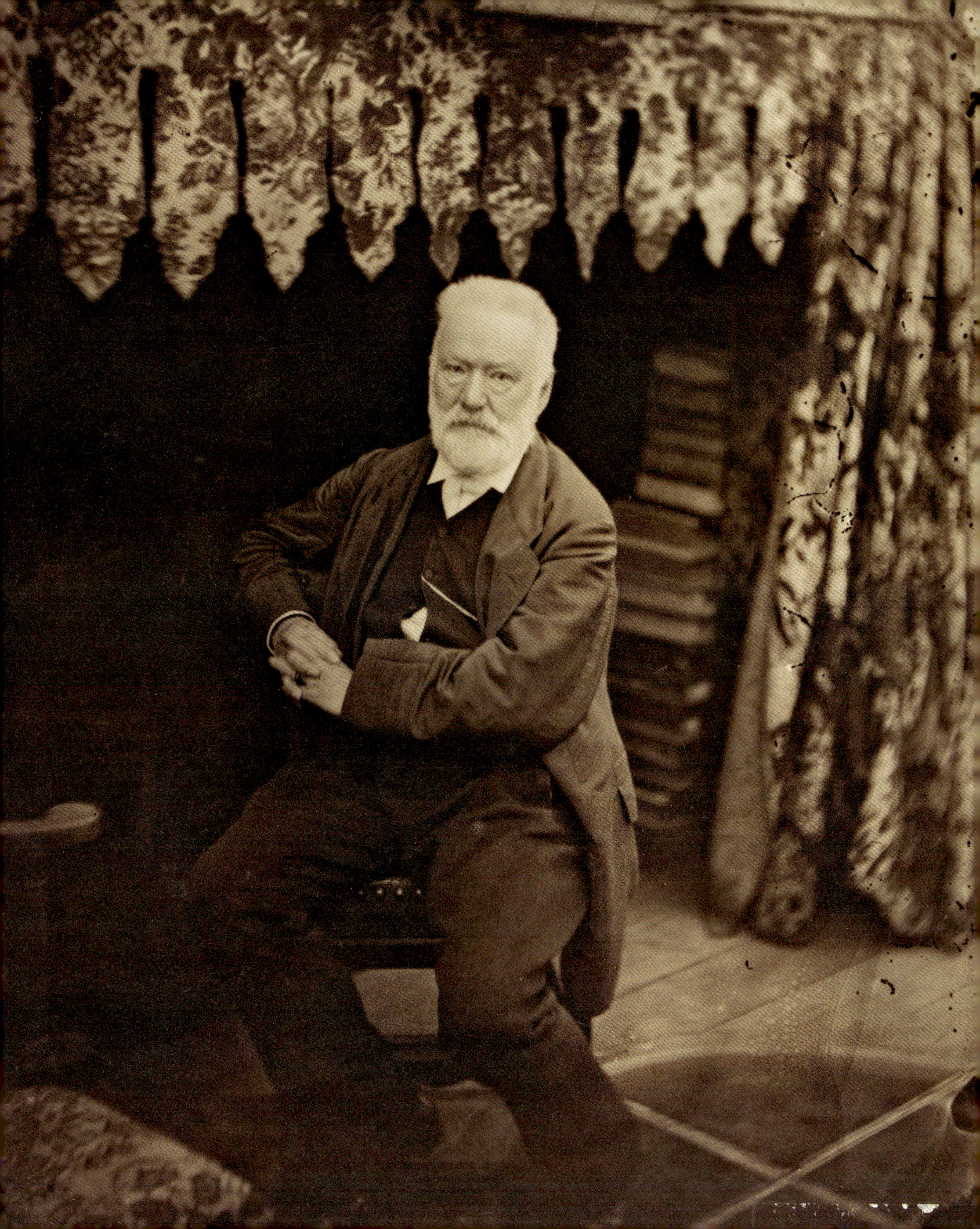

Notes

Double Vision: Victor Hugo's Mind's Eye

SARAH LEA

1   Léon Bloy, quoted by Robb 1998, p. 533. For Paul Lafargue's comments, see Robb 1998, pp. 513, 533.

2   Victor Hugo, quoted by Barbou 1882, p. 265. Digitised from an original at Harvard University, 14 May 2008: https://books.googleco.uk/books?id=VsAaAAAAYAAJ&source=gbs_navlinks_s (accessed 29 July 2024). This English translation of a contemporary report on Hugo's views conflates ideas from several of Hugo's speeches. For precedents and the geopolitical contexts of Hugo's developing concepts of historical progress and republicanism, see Metzidakis 1994, pp. 72–84, especially p. 77 for a quotation from the preface to *Les Burgraves* (1843): 'avoir pour patrie le monde et pour nation l'humanité'. The idea of 'la République universelle' is mentioned in Hugo's speech on the occasion of the planting of the 'Tree of Liberty' in Place des Vosges in 1848 during his one-week tenure as mayor of the arrondissement (*Actes et Paroles* I, Avant l'exil 1841–1852, quoted in Beecher 2021, p. 175).

3   For a discussion of print reproductions of Hugo's art, see Burlingham 2018, pp. 31–45.

4   For helpful evaluations of Hugo's relationship to artistic traditions and movements, see Georgel 1998, pp. 13–20; Rodari 1998B, pp. 21–8.

5   Hugo does not mention Michel, this is an observation of the author: although executed in different mediums, compare, for example, the brooding atmosphere and use of stark tonal contrast in Michel's *Mills at Montmartre* (undated; Musée Carnavalet, Paris) with Hugo's *Flemish Mansion at Dusk* (1837; Maisons de Victor Hugo, Paris / Guernsey, inv. no. 44) in which Hugo has spliced a section of paper into the sheet to introduce the upper, angled swathe of light.

6   Michel's historiography in Alfred Sensier's 1873 biography has been discussed in Taws 2021, pp. 221–46, 222. Although Constable's work was heralded at the Paris Salon of 1824, it was not being warmly received in England at the time that Michel was working.

7   Sante 1998, p. 8.

8   Robb 1998, pp. 71–2, 84.

9   See Robb 1998, p. 114, on the Restoration's recognition of the propaganda potential of Romanticism.

10 Hugo quoted in Robb 1998, p. 112.

11 They were to marry in 1822.

12 Robb 1998, p. 24.

13 Stephens 2019, p. 22.

14 Hugo's *Les Misérables* quoted in Robb 1998, p. 45.

15 For the context in which *Bug-Jargal* sits, see Yee 2021, pp. 344–61.

16 See Chris Bongie's introduction to the 2004 English edition of this contentious text, which he presents in both versions alongside an important set of contextual appendices: Hugo 2004, pp. 9–47. On possible biographical links between Hugo and the former French colony of Saint-Domingue, see p. 32.

17 Robb 1998, pp. 123, 132–3. On the use of initials and lettering in Hugo's drawings, see Rodari 1998A, pp. 172–8. See also Audinet 2020, pp. 170–91.

18 Yee 2008, p. 51.

19 Hugo 2004, p. 38.

20 See Bongie in Hugo 2004, pp. 28–9. On the introduction of doubt via supposedly factual explicatory footnotes in *Bug-Jargal*, see pp. 35–6.

21 Léopoldine (1824–1843), Charles (1826–1871), François-Victor (1828–1873) and Adèle II (1830–1915).

22 Cazentre 2023, p. 16.

23 'To Albrecht Dürer', *Interior Voices* (1837), in Hugo 2001.

24 Nanteuil's illustration for the 1832 edition of *Bug-Jargal* has tones of the irrationality of Goya's *Los Caprichos*.

25 Like Adèle (whose affair with the critic C.-A. Saint-Beuve, Hugo's close colleague and friend, he discovered around 1831), Juliette tolerated the many other sexual partners Hugo recorded in secret codes in his diaries and suffered later rivals for his true affection. Hugo's passionate affair with Léonie d'Aunet was hushed up, but whereas he was immune as a recently appointed peer, Léonie was punishable by law and was imprisoned then sent to a convent.

26 *Idole chinoise devant un temple à pavillons bulbeux*, 1837; Maisons de Victor Hugo, Paris / Guernsey, inv. no. 900.

27 For a published visual record of Hugo's interior decoration, see the photographs by Jean-Baptiste Hugo reproduced in Hugo, Hugo and Hugo 2016.

28 Audinet 2020, p. 52.

29 Hugo's poem quoted in Robb 1998, p. 69.

30 The note is currently framed with the drawing.

31 By the age of 25 Hugo had buried both his parents. His brother Eugène died aged 36 in 1837, having never recovered from his unrequited love for Adèle (he had lived in an asylum since 1823, the year that Adèle and Victor lost their firstborn baby, Léopold, at three months old). In the footsteps of her uncle, Adèle II was committed to an asylum in 1872. Hugo's sons Charles and François-Victor died in 1871 and 1873 respectively.

32 For a detailed account of Hugo's activity in this complex political climate, see Beecher 2021, especially pp. 167–202. For Hugo's experience of the June Days, see Robb 1998, pp. 268–80.

33 'Gallia', 1850; Maisons de Victor Hugo, Paris / Guernsey, inv. no. 176.

34 *Dolmen and Menhirs*, 1850; Maisons de Victor Hugo, Paris / Guernsey, inv. no. 130.

35 Audinet 2020, p. 128; Audinet quotes Hugo in 1851, p. 118.

36 With the exception of the steamship, the *Durande*, engulfed by the ocean

(see Rose Thompson, p. 131 and cat. 71). For an exploration of images of telegraphy in this period, see Taws 2016, pp. 400–21.

37   Hugo quoted in Quandt 2017, p. 64.

38   The inscription reads: 'It was nap time. / it was midday, the sun in full / triumph was shining! the plain / immense and bare / had the breath of an oven mouth. he was looking for / a tree in the shade of which he could sleep and rest. he / met a manchineel.' ('C'était l'heure de la sieste. / il était midi, le soleil en plein / triomphe resplendissait! la plaine / immense et nue / avait l'haleine d'une bouche de four. il cherchait / un arbre à l'ombre duquel il / pût dormir et se reposer. Il / rencontra un mancenilier.')

39   Alexander Cozens, *The Shape, Skeleton and Foliage of Thirty-Two Species of Trees*, 1771 (reprinted c. 1785), British Museum, London, pressmark for album: 167*.c.50; *Series of Skies*, part of *A New Method of Assisting the Invention in Drawing Original Compositions of of Landscape*, c. 1785, Tate, London, T11464–T11483. For John Constable's copies see, for example, Courtauld Art Gallery, London, D.1932.LF.31.

40   Chambers 2008, pp. 26–7.

41   See Robb 1998, pp. 339–41, and Chambers 2008, p. 77, on Hugo's religious beliefs. In a surprising circularity, Victor Hugo is held as a key figure in the faith of Cao Dai, which has approximately two million followers in Vietnam; see Robb 1998, pp. 539–40, and Chambers 2008, pp. 1–3.

42   Pesenti 2018, pp. 46–67.

43   Robb 1998, p. 228.

44   'Où se heurtent sanglants les peuples furieux; – / Et que tout cela fasse un astre dans les cieux!'. ('?', *Les Contemplations*, III).

45   For discussions of Hugo's ideas about a United States of Europe, see Ousselin 2005, pp. 32–43; Metzidakis 1994, pp. 72–84. See also Robb 1998, pp. 403–4.

46   *Discourse on Africa* (1879). *Actes et Paroles* IV, Depuis l'exil 1876–1885.

47   Brahamcha-Marin 2023.

48   Robb 1998, p. 513.

49   London 1974, no. 71 (unpaginated).

50   Stephens 2019, pp. 14–18.

51   For a photograph of the fountain, see André, *View of Fort George and the garden from the roof of Hauteville House*, c. 1870–75; Maisons de Victor Hugo, Paris / Guernsey, inv. no. 2014.0.97. For a discussion of the inscription and related diaries, letters and poems, see object catalogue: https://www.parismuseescollections.paris.fr/fr/maison-de-victor-hugo/oeuvres/miroir-aux-oiseaux#infos secondaires-detail (accessed 22 July 2024).

52   *Les Contemplations*, XXIX, 'La Nature'.

53   Robb 1998, pp. 393, 425; Baudelaire, quoted in Benjamin 1977, p. 61.

54   Benjamin 1977, p. 61.

55   Ibid., pp. 60–6.

56   Quandt 2017, pp. 64, 71.

57   Hugo, quoted by Théophile Gautier in the preface to *Dessins de Victor Hugo, gravés par Paul Chenay*, Paris, 1863, quoted in Salatino 2019, p. 533.

58   Hugo, quoted by Robb 1998, p. 492 (*Choses Vues*, February 1874).

How a Poet Becomes a Painter
GÉRARD AUDINET

1   Nothing apparently dates from the journey in the autumn of 1847. But the Revolution in February 1848 distracted Hugo from his drawing as well as from his work on *Les Misérables.*

2   'En attendant que ce moment fortuné arrive, je regarde passer les jolis dessins que vous faites chez moi et j'ouvre ma GEULE toute grande et mes yeux comme la porte Saint-Denis.' Letter from Juliette Drouet to Victor Hugo, 7.45 am, Friday 23 July 1847.

3   Maisons de Victor Hugo, Paris / Guernsey, inv. no. 893.

4   The Mäuseturm stands on an island near Bingen am Rhein.

5   'Ce matin en m'éveillant mon premier soin a été de regarder ton ravissant dessin. Je regrette de n'être pas assez riche pour l'acheter. Je m'en rapporte à ta générosité pour me le donner quand le graveur l'aura copié.' Letter from Juliette Drouet to Victor Hugo, 7.30 am, Tuesday 21 July 1846.

6   'Du reste tout cela n'est qu'une feinte pour me subtiliser mon dessin et le donner à la place du vôtre et en votre nom au graveur.' Letter from Juliette Drouet to Victor Hugo, 3 pm, Tuesday 21 July [1846].

7   Maisons de Victor Hugo, Paris / Guernsey, inv. nos 620.1–2, 621.1–2, 622.1–2 and 623.1–2.

8   1840; Maisons de Victor Hugo, Paris / Guernsey, inv. no. 942.

9   'Vous avez raison de priser bien haut Marvy; C'était pour moi en particulier un admirable traducteur.' Letter from Victor Hugo to Philippe Burty, 27 January 1863, published in Georgel 1973, p. 39.

10   1847; Maisons de Victor Hugo, Paris / Guernsey, inv. no. 51.

11   1850; Maisons de Victor Hugo, Paris / Guernsey, inv. no. 40. This work, Hugo's largest drawing, was placed in a frame the artist painted himself in 1871.

12   'Le crépuscule blêmissait son beau front et couvrait ses yeux de ténèbres.' *Les Misérables*, IV, 5, 6. This was the appearance of Jean Valjean to Cosette, near the fountain.

13   If we exclude the collection *Les Chants du crépuscule*, published in 1835, in which 'crépuscule' is used symbolically.

14   'J'ai toujours aimé ces voyages à l'heure crépusculaire. C'est le moment où la nature se déforme et devient fantastique.' Letter from Victor Hugo to Adèle Hugo, 8 September 1837.

15   'Mon âme était en deuil; c'était l'heure de l'ombre.' Dated 1 January 1846, published in *Toute la Lyre*, V, XIV, Paris, 1935.

16   These were to be published in the posthumous collection, *Toute la Lyre*.

17   The collection is divided into two parts: 'Autrefois' (Yesterday), 1830–43, and 'Aujourd'hui' (Today), 1843–55. It was published in April 1856.

18   'Qu'est-ce que les *Contemplations*? C'est ce qu'on pourrait appeler, si le mot n'avait quelque prétention, *les Mémoires d'une âme* … Ce sont, en effet, toutes les impressions, tous les souvenirs, toutes les réalités, tous les fantômes vagues, riants ou funèbres, que peut contenir une conscience, revenus et rappelés, rayon à rayon, soupir à soupir, et mêlés dans la même nuée sombre.' *Les Contemplations*, Preface.

Architecture in the Drawings of Victor Hugo
THOMAS CAZENTRE

1   According to Jean Mallion (see note 4 below), everything that Hugo describes about England in *L'Homme qui rit* (1869) is taken from books, in particular from James Beeverell's *Les Délices de la Grande-Bretagne et de l'Irlande* (1707).

2   *Les Feuilles d'automne* (1831), XXVII; Hugo finally visited Rouen some years later.

3   'La Pente de la rêverie' (1830), in ibid., XXIX.

4   On Hugo's familiarity with architecture, the main reference work is Mallion 1962.

5   Audinet 2020, p. 51.

6   1847; Maisons de Victor Hugo, Paris / Guernsey, inv. no. 51.

7   This is the title under which this group of drawings appears in the inventory of the graphic work of Hugo: see Hugo 1967–70, vol. 18 (1969).

8   1866; Maisons de Victor Hugo, Paris / Guernsey, inv. no. 181; see Mallion 1962, p. 340.

9   *The Toilers of the Sea*, Part I, Book VI, Chapter I, 'Les rochers Douvres', p. 186.

10 This German word was already in general use during Hugo's lifetime, although he seldom used it.

11 *Notre-Dame de Paris*, Book V, Chapter II, p. 170.

12 Georgel 2007, p. 46. The Greek word *ananké*, engraved in a wall of Notre-Dame (*Notre-Dame de Paris*, Book VII, Chapter IV, pp. 254–67), means 'fatal destiny'.

13 *Notre-Dame de Paris*, Book III, Chapter II, pp. 111–34.

Catalogue plates
with section introductions by
ROSE THOMPSON

1   'nous restons jusqu'à minuit dans le cabinet de Victor causant, devisant … Victor dessinant aussi, faisant les petites caricatures … qu'ils trouvent en s'éveillant, le matin, à leur grande joie', Audinet 2020, p. 13.

2   From *History of the Museum*, https://www.maisonsvictorhugo. paris.fr/en/paris/museum/history-museum (accessed 27 June 2024): 'In 1901, in anticipation of Victor Hugo's centenary, and in agreement with the poet's grandchildren (Georges and Jeanne) and their mother (Alice Lockroy), Paul Meurice made a proposal to the City of Paris to create a "Maison de Victor Hugo", similar to the houses of Dante, Shakespeare or Goethe. The location that was chosen was the Hôtel de Rohan Guéménée, at 6, Place des Vosges, where the poet lived from 1832 to 1848, and which was owned by the City of Paris.'

3   'DESSINÉ / SUR LE SOMMET / DU RIGI / Le 11 7bre 1839 / au coucher du soleil / 5676 pieds au-dessus du niveau de la mer. VICTOR HUGO.'

4   Artwork details for *Le Mythen* are available on the *Paris Musées* online collection records. See https://www. parismuseescollections.paris.fr/fr/ maison-de-victor-hugo/oeuvres/ le-mythen#infos-secondaires-detail (accessed 27 June 2024), where it states the following: 'Hugo s'inspire du dessin de son carnet de voyage de 1839, "Sommet du Pilate, Weggis – 12 7bre 9h du matin" BnF, Ms. NAF 13347 f° 12, soit correction d'une erreur, soit volonté de changer un nom pour un autre plus évocateur, le Pilate devient le Mythen. Il s'agit en fait de deux sommets le Grand et le Petit Mythen, dans les Alpes suisses.'

5   See Robb 1998, p. 3, but also Stephens 2019, p. 22.

6   As above, artwork details for *Le Mythen* are available on the *Paris Musées* online collection records: https://www.parismuseescollections. paris.fr/fr/maison-de-victor-hugo/ oeuvres/le-mythen#infos secondaires-detail (accessed 27 June 2024).

7   Artwork details for *Vianden Seen Through a Spider's Web* are available on the *Paris Musées* online collection records. See https://www. parismuseescollections.paris.fr/fr/ maison-de-victor-hugo/oeuvres/ vianden-a-travers-une-toile-d-araignee#infossecondaires-detail (accessed 27 June 2024): '13 août 1871. J'ai dessiné sur mon livre de voyage la grande toile d'araignée à travers laquelle on aperçoit la ruine de Vianden comme un spectre.'

8   It is thought that this drawing is based on Chartres Cathedral but that it is not an entirely accurate representation. See Thomas Cazentre's essay in this book, p. 42.

9   Robb 1998, p. 391.

10 Letter dated 29 April 1860: 'J'ai fini par y mêler du crayon, du fusain, de la sépia, du charbon, de la suie, toutes sortes de mixtures bizarres qui arrivent à rendre à peu près ce que j'ai dans l'œil et surtout dans l'esprit.' See https://collections. louvre.fr/en/ark:/53355/cl020567992 (accessed 27 June 2024).

11 See references in Chambers 2008; Paris 2012.

12 Sueur-Hermel 2002, pp. 32–45.

13 *Letters on American Slavery from Victor Hugo, de Tocqueville, Emile de Girardin, Carnot, Passy, Mazzini, Humboldt, O. Lafayette - &c.*, published by the American Anti-slavery Society, Boston, in 1860. See https://tile.loc.gov/storage-services/ service/rbc/lcrbmrp/t1302/t1302.pdf (accessed 27 June 2024).

14 For more information on this series of works, see Burlingham 2018, p. 31.

15 See Hugo, Hugo and Hugo 2016, p. 15. From French: 'Mon mari est très content et complètement plongé dans sa maison. Ce sera un poème que ce logis. Mon mari grave des inscriptions, met son âme sur les murs de sa maison, il prend le rabot lui-même et lui donne sa sueur. Enfin ce sera un monument élevé par le grand exilé.'

16 'Quand vous viendrez à Guernesey, vous verrez que j'ai manqué ma vocation et que j'étais fait pour être décorateur!'; from Claretie [1902], p. 73.

17 Victor Hugo to Edmond Bacot, 10 February 1853. Letter details are available on the *Paris Musées* online collection records: https://www. parismuseescollections.paris.fr/fr/ maison-de-victor-hugo/oeuvres/ lettre-de-victor-hugo-a-edmond-bacot#infos-principales (accessed 25 July 2024).

18 19 November 1846. See Hugo 2001, p. 572.

19 See Stephens 2019, p. 15.

20 See Hugo, Hugo and Hugo 2016, p. 104. 'Et cependant, pensif, j'écris à ma fenêtre, je regarde le flot naître, expirer, renaître, et les goélands fendre l'air. Les navires au vent ouvrent leurs envergures, et

ressemblent au loin à des grandes figures qui se promènent sur la mer.' Reference from Hugo 1961.

21   Robb 1998, p. 399.

22   The first illustrated edition of *The Toilers of the Sea* was published in 1869 with illustrations by François Chifflart. In 1882 *The Toilers of the Sea* was published with Hugo's drawings, which were copied by the engraver Fortuné-Louis Méaulle, along with pictures by other artists.

23   Hugo 1928.

24   In the early 1980s, in preparation of the centennial exhibition 'Soleil d'encre' (1985), it was decided to remove the drawings permanently and restore them: they were by then damaged and could not be shown separately when bound into the volumes.

Chronology

ROSE THOMPSON

1   Stephens 2019, p. 100.

2   Ibid., p. 134.

3   Robb 1998, p. 399.

4   Stephens 2019, p. 160.

5   Ibid., p. 168.

Selected Bibliography

AUDINET 2020
Gérard Audinet, *Victor Hugo, Dessins*, Paris, 2020

AUDINET, BLANCHETTE, DULUC AND BAIL 2019
Gérard Audinet, Odile Blanchette, Stéphanie Duluc and Cédric Bail, *Hauteville House*, Maisons de Victor Hugo, Paris / Guernsey, Paris Musées, Paris, 2019

BARBOU 1882
Alfred Barbou, *Victor Hugo and His Time*, trans. Ellen Elizabeth Frewer, New York, 1882. Digitised from an original at Harvard University, 14 May 2008: https://books.google.co.uk/books?id=VsAaAAAAYAAJ&source=gbs_navlinks_s (accessed 29 July 2024)

BEECHER 2021
Jonathan Beecher, *Writers and Revolution: Intellectuals and the French Revolution of 1848*, Cambridge, 2021

BENJAMIN 1977
Walter Benjamin, *Charles Baudelaire, A Lyric Poet in the Era of High Capitalism*, trans. Harry Zohn, London, 1977

BRAHAMCHA-MARIN 2023
Jordi Brahamcha-Marin, 'Victor Hugo raciste?', *Revue Alarmer*, 2023, https://revue.alarmer.org/victor-hugo-raciste-a-propos-du-discours-sur-lafrique-et-de-quelques-autres-textes/ (accessed 18 July 2024)

BURLINGHAM 2018
Cynthia Burlingham, '"Nothing but Shadow and Light", Hugo's Drawings in Print', in *Stones to Stains: The Drawings of Victor Hugo*, Cynthia Burlingham, Allegra Pesenti and Florian Rodari, exh. cat., Hammer Museum, Los Angeles, 2018, pp. 31–45

CAZENTRE 2023
Thomas Cazentre, *Têtes, 100 Dessins de Victor Hugo*, Paris, 2023

CHAMBERS 2008
John Chambers, *Victor Hugo's Conversations with the Spirit World, A Literary Genius's Hidden Life* (1998), London, 2008

CLARETIE [1902]
Jules Claretie, *Victor Hugo. Souvenirs intimes*, Paris, [1902]

GAUTIER 1863
Dessins de Victor Hugo, gravés par Paul Chenay, preface by Théophile Gautier, Paris, 1863

GEORGEL 1973
Pierre Georgel, 'Romanticism of the 1860s. Correspondence Victor Hugo–Philippe Burty', *Revue de l'art*, 20, 1973, pp. 8–64

GEORGEL 1985
Pierre Georgel, *Les Dessins de Victor Hugo pour Les Travailleurs de la mer*, Paris, 1985

GEORGEL 1998
Pierre Georgel, 'The Artist in Spite of Himself', in *Shadows of a Hand: The Drawings of Victor Hugo*, Florian Rodari, Pierre Georgel, Luc Sante and Marie-Laure Prévost, exh. cat., The Drawing Center, New York, 1998, pp. 13–20

GEORGEL 2007
Pierre Georgel, *1850, Le Burg à la croix*, Paris Musées, Paris, 2007

HUGO 1864
Victor Hugo, *William Shakespeare*, trans. A. Baillot, Boston, Mass., 1864, https://www.gutenberg.org/files/53490/53490-h/53490-h.htm, Chapter 2 (accessed 28 July 2024)

HUGO 1928
Victor Hugo, *Hugo's Toilers of the Sea*, ed. Ernest Rhys, trans. W. Moy Thomas, London and New York, 1928, https://www.gutenberg.org/files/32338/32338-h/32338-h.htm, Preface (accessed 28 July 2024)

HUGO 1961
Victor Hugo, 'Océan, Tas de pierres', *Oeuvres poétiques complètes*, Paris, 1961

HUGO 1967–70
Victor Hugo, *Oeuvres complètes*, ed. Jean Massin, 18 vols, Paris, 1967–70

HUGO 2001
Victor Hugo, *Selected Poems of Victor Hugo: A Bilingual Edition*, trans. E. H. and A. M. Blackmore, Chicago and London, 2001

HUGO 2002
Victor Hugo, *The Toilers of the Sea*, trans. James Hogarth, New York, 2002

HUGO 2004
Victor Hugo, *Bug-Jargal*, trans. and ed. Chris Bongie, Peterborough, Ontario, 2004

HUGO 2018
Victor Hugo, *Notre-Dame de Paris*, trans. John Sturrock, Harmondsworth, 2018

HUGO, HUGO AND HUGO 2016
Jean-Baptiste, Laura and Marie Hugo, *Hauteville House, Victor Hugo décorateur*, Paris Musées, Paris, 2016

LONDON 1974
Drawings by Victor Hugo, Pierre Georgel, exh. cat., Victoria and Albert Museum, London, 1974

MAILLION 1962
Jean Mallion, *Victor Hugo et l'art architectural*, Paris, 1962

METZIDAKIS 1994
Angelo Metzidakis, 'Victor Hugo and the Idea of the United States of Europe', *Nineteenth-Century French Studies*, 23, 1/2, 1994, pp. 72–84, JSTOR, http://www.jstor.org/stable/23537320 (accessed 10 July 2024)

MEURICE 1896
Paul Meurice (ed.), *The Letters of Victor Hugo*, Boston, New York and Cambridge, MA, 1896

MOLINARI 2010
Danielle Molinari, *Victor Hugo: Visions Graphiques*, Paris Musées / Les collections de la Ville de Paris, Paris, 2010

OUSSELIN 2005
Edward Ousselin, 'Victor Hugo's European Utopia', *Nineteenth-Century French Studies*, 34, 1/2, 2005, pp. 32–43, *JSTOR*, http://www.jstor.org/stable/23537726 (accessed 10 July 2024)

PARIS 1985
Soleil d'encre. Manuscrits et dessins de Victor Hugo, Judith Petit, Roger Pierrot and Marie-Laure Prévost, exh. cat., Petit-Palais, Paris, 1985

PARIS 2002
Victor Hugo, l'homme océan, Marie-Laure Prévost, exh. cat., Bibliothèque nationale de France, Paris, 2002

PARIS 2005
'Cet immense rêve de l'océan'. Paysages de mer et autres sujets marins par Victor Hugo, Pierre Georgel, Maison de Victor Hugo, Paris, 2005

PARIS 2012
Entrée des médiums: Spiritisme et art d'Hugo à Breton, Gérard Audinet, Jérôme Godeau, Alexandra Viau, Renaud Evrard and Bertrand Méheust, exh. cat., Maison de Victor Hugo, Paris, 2012

PESENTI 2018
Allegra Pesenti, 'The Promontory of Dream: Cosmic Landscapes and Infinite Visions of Night in the Drawings of Victor Hugo', in *Stones to Stains: The Drawings of Victor Hugo*, Cynthia Burlingham, Allegra Pesenti and Florian Rodari, exh. cat., Hammer Museum, Los Angeles, 2018, pp. 46–67

PICON, FOCILLON, PICON AND BARGIEL 1985
Gaëtan Picon, Henri Focillon, Geneviève Picon and Réjane Bargiel, *Victor Hugo. Dessins*, Paris, 1985

QUANDT 2017
Karen Quandt, 'Victor Hugo and the Politics of Ecopoetics', in *French Ecocriticism: From the Early Modern Period to the Twenty-First Century*, Daniel Finch-Race and Stephanie Posthumus (eds), New York, 2017, pp. 61–81

ROBB 1998
Graham Robb, *Victor Hugo*, London, 1998

RODARI 1998A
Florian Rodari, 'Un espace chiffré', in *En collaboration en soleil, Victor Hugo photographies de l'exil*, Françoise Heilbrun and Danielle Molinari (eds), exh. cat., Paris Musées, Paris, 1998, pp. 172–8

RODARI 1998B
Florian Rodari 'Victor Hugo, a Precursor a posteriori', in *Shadows of a Hand: The Drawings of Victor Hugo*, Florian Rodari, Pierre Georgel, Luc Sante and Marie-Laure Prévost, exh. cat., The Drawing Center, New York, 1998, pp. 21–8

SALATINO 2019
Kevin Salatino, 'Review: Ego Hugo', *Master Drawings*, 57, 4, Winter 2019, pp. 533–52

SANTE 1998
Luc Sante, 'The Octopus Bearing the Initials V.H.', in *Shadows of a Hand: The Drawings of Victor Hugo*, Florian Rodari, Pierre Georgel, Luc Sante and Marie-Laure Prévost, exh. cat., The Drawing Center, New York, pp. 8–12

STEPHENS 2019
Bradley Stephens, *Critical Lives: Victor Hugo*, London, 2019

SUEUR-HERMEL 2002
Valérie Sueur-Hermel, 'Fortuné Méaulle interprète de Victor Hugo, ou la gravure sur bois au service du "choc des rayons et des ombres"', *Nouvelles de l'estampe*, 185–6, 2002, pp. 32–45

SUND 1992
Judy Sund, *True to Temperament. Van Gogh and French Naturalist Literature*, Cambridge, 1992

TAWS 2016
Richard Taws, 'Telegraphic Images in Post-Revolutionary France', *Art History*, 39, 2, April 2016, pp. 400–21

TAWS 2021
Richard Taws, 'A Storm Is Coming: Georges Michel in the Wind', in *Time, Media and Visuality in Post-Revolutionary France*, Richard Taws and Iris Moon (eds), London, 2021, pp. 221–46

YEE 2008
Jennifer Yee, 'Victor Hugo and the Divided Self in Bug-Jargal', in *Exotic Subversions in Nineteenth-Century French Fiction*, Jennifer Yee, Oxford, 2008, pp. 45–62

YEE 2021
Jennifer Yee, 'Colonial Encounters in the Nineteenth-Century Novel', in *The Cambridge History of the Novel in French*, Adam Watt (ed.), Cambridge, 2021, pp. 344–61

Index